Ben Hartley

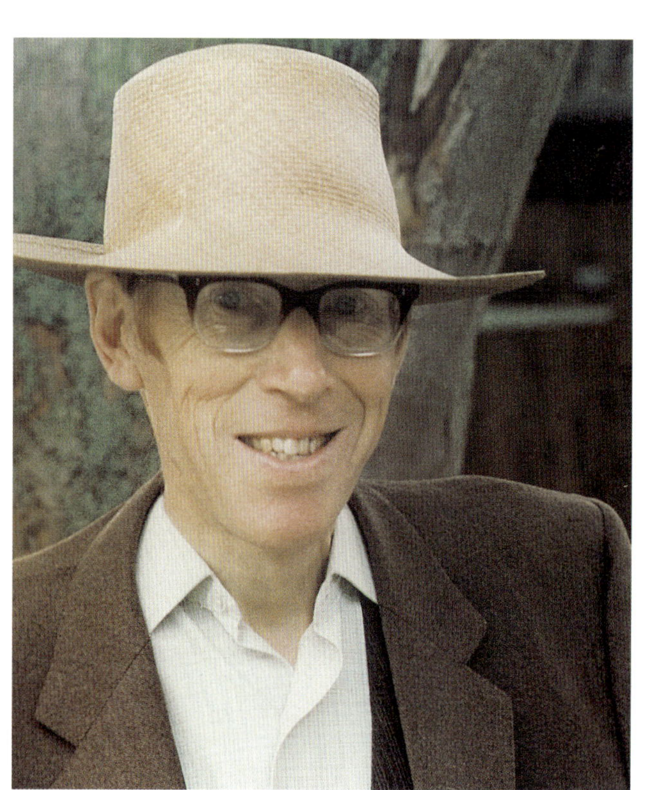

Bernard Samuels

Ben Hartley

Sansom and Company

First published in 2001 by
SANSOM & COMPANY LTD
81g Pembroke Road, Bristol BS8 3EA

Tele: 0117 973 7207

ISBN 1 900178 73 7

British Library Cataloguing in Publication Data
A catalogue record for this book is available from The British Library

Designed by Peter Campbell
and printed by Hackman Print, Tonypandy, Rhondda

FOR MARY

Contents

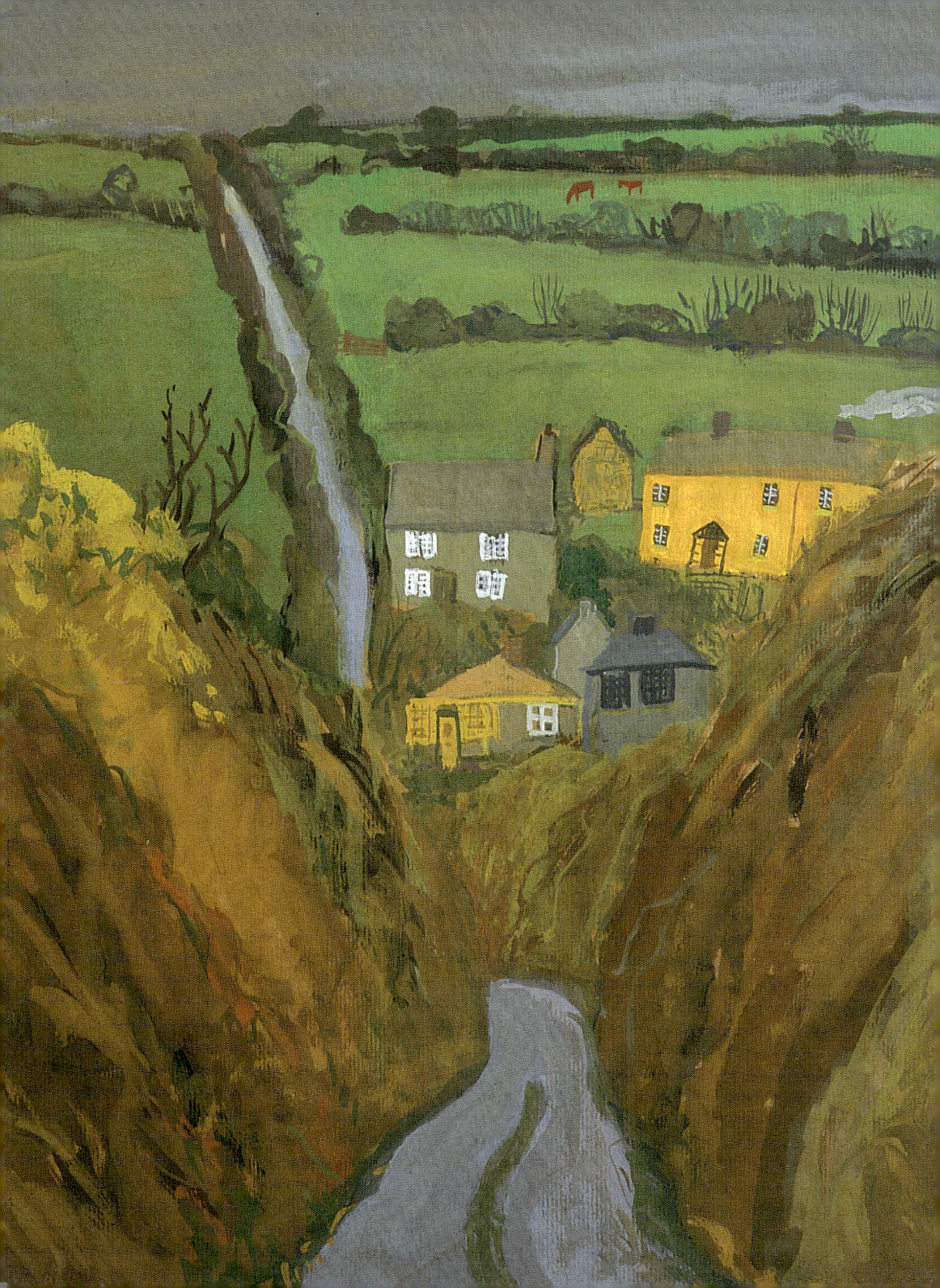

Preface

In March 1996, not long before I was due to retire, I received a letter from a solicitor in Wales informing me that Ben Hartley, an artist I had known and worked with for many years, had died and left me all his work. I hadn't heard from Ben for several months. The week before I had sent off a cheque for some paintings I had sold on his behalf. Naturally, I was greatly saddened by the news. I had known Ben for twenty years, during which time I had been more or less constantly active in promoting his work. I had always been aware of his lifelong struggle with a congenital chest problem. I was also very aware of his frugal way of life and the toll it could take on his frail constitution. His death at the early age of sixty-two did not entirely come as a surprise. Ben was never destined for ripe old age.

The moment I received the news of the bequest I knew immediately what I wanted to do. Though I had worked consistently on Ben's behalf for so long, right up until the very end, so it turned out, I had always gone out of my way to spare him the pressure that can be brought to bear on an artist, particularly one whose work had such enormous appeal. Though he acquired a considerable following in the south-west, I was always sure his reputation could have spread much further afield. This might have brought him more money. On the other hand it is extremely difficult to promote the work of an unknown artist to the full without subjecting him or her to the gaze of publicity. It could be difficult enough persuading him to go through the hoops I set up for him in the region, let alone looking for some kind of national recognition. Consequently my mission as the recipient of his gift was clear from the outset. I was about to retire: I would set out to achieve for Ben the kind of reputation and widespread appreciation I and many others had always thought he deserved.

This book constitutes an important step towards fulfilling that mission. It brings together, for the first time, within the covers of a single publication, a comprehensive selection of images which is fully representative of the lifetime's work of Ben Hartley. It is a tribute to Ben. It is a token of thanks to the many people who have helped me over the years in promoting his art, the galleries who have shown Ben's work, collectors who have bought the work, friends, colleagues and former students who have shared their recollections of Ben and their enthusiasm for his work. I have also to thank Ben's two sisters, Monica Bate and Mary Towle most sincerely. Without their help it would have been impossible to achieve whatever degree of insight I have gained towards understanding Ben's early life

I have dedicated my book to Mary Thomson who played such an important part in the long years of my association with Ben and his work, right up until her death in July 1999. The spirit of poetry resided in them both and lives on in their memory.

B.S.

Detail, *Devon Lane, Westlake*, plate 6

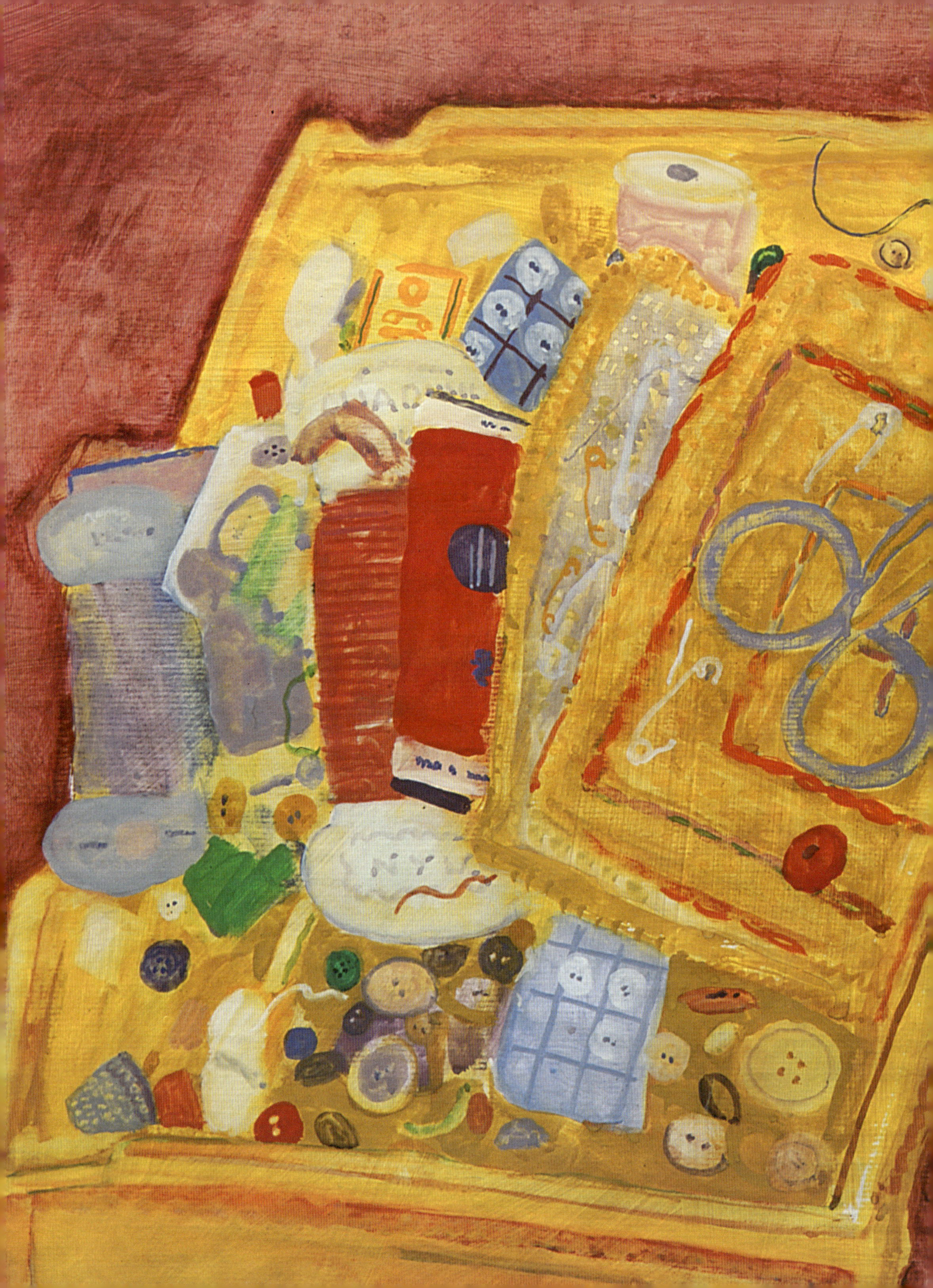

Introduction

Celui qui chante n'est pas toujours heureux
Pierre Bonnard, 1944

The first time I heard of Ben was in 1976. Brian Bottomley, a friend and colleague of his at Plymouth College of Art, came up to me one evening at an exhibition opening at Plymouth Arts Centre, where I had been director since 1971, and said I ought to go and see the work of an artist by the name of Ben Hartley. Though I knew a large number of the artists in the area, the name was completely unknown to me. Earlier that year I had persuaded the *Sunday Times* to publish in its colour supplement a full-length article, complete with a full-colour illustration and headline on the front cover, about an exhibition I had mounted at the Centre of the work of a local, self-taught artist by the name of Beryl Cook. Brian had been very impressed by this achievement and the resulting success that came to Mrs. Cook, more or less overnight. He was hoping I might be able to do something to help Ben who had come to Plymouth in 1960 to become a part-time lecturer at the College of Art. His principal role was as a tutor for the adult education classes run by the College. From the conversations I have had with his fellow lecturers over the years, it is clear that they were well aware of his exceptional qualities as an artist. At the same time they were also conscious of his physical frailty and his somewhat eccentric approach to feeding himself.

I wrote to Ben and he agreed to let me come and see his work at his house in Ermington. Ermington is a quiet village, twelve miles outside Plymouth, just off the B3210 to Totnes, not far inland from the sea, close to the mouth of the river Erme. The whole area between Ermington and the coast, embracing the Flete estate, Holbeton and the beach at Mothecombe, is one of the most magical places in the South Hams, a particularly beautiful part of Devon. The church is noted for its crooked spire. Hence the name of the village pub, the Crooked Spire. Ben had lived in this quiet village since 1961. The house was in a dull-looking terrace with some parking space and a large telegraph post in front on the other side of the road. Inside was almost completely bare. I noticed a bicycle in the lobby. The house was built against a hillside with the living space upstairs. I had been warned in advance that Ben was extremely shy and retiring, living alone, rarely receiving visitors. Conversation, as I expected, was not easy. I explained a little about the work of the Arts Centre. I had the impression I was telling him little that he did not already know. My next move paid off handsomely. The sole decoration in the living room consisted of a few postcards and the odd poster: reproductions of Fauve paintings, Matisse, Bonnard, Derain, Dufy and so on. I ventured the

Detail, *Pins and Doodles*, plate 13

comment that Bonnard was my favourite painter. Ben nodded in agreement. 'Food and drink,' he said most fervently, 'food and drink.' I had passed a test. I was accepted; little more need be said.

After a cup of tea I asked to see some work and was shown into the room opposite. Ben disappeared before I had time to take anything in. Again the room was utterly spartan. There were some books, a small figure of the Virgin Mary on the fireplace and a few paintings in poor frames, standing on the floor, propped up against the skirting board. Also stacked up against the wall was a fairly neat pile of paintings, unframed works on paper. I started looking through them and was instantly taken by the colour, the energy, the vitality, the sometimes extraordinary juxtapositions of people, animals and objects. The overall impression was of a creative adventurousness and an exuberance totally belied by the manner of the person I had come to see. All the work was in gouache, painted on pieces of brown wrapping paper, some of it the remains of made-up parcels with bits stuck together here and there. Many were on irregular-shaped pieces of paper with bits missing from the edges. In no time an exhibition was offered and agreed. The exhibition took place the following year and was a great success. Thus began the most intensive, uninterrupted working relationship I had with any artist in my twenty-five years as director of Plymouth Arts Centre.

Though I saw Ben very frequently indeed, he was such a private person I scarcely ever pressed him to tell me about himself or his work. In fact for all the many hours we must have spent in one another's company, I find it very difficult to remember anything of the conversations that passed between us. There was always some business to be arranged regarding an exhibition either at the Arts Centre or as part of a tour somewhere, usually in the region, or a selling show at another gallery. Ben was obviously such a private person, it was difficult to pass beyond his somewhat anxious, apprehensive exterior. Had I been a fellow artist or a country person with a true knowledge of the countryside, it might have been easier. I did on one occasion manage to persuade him, out of sheer necessity, to commit to paper a statement about the thinking that lay behind his work. This was in 1979, when he revealed that the subject of the appealing, brightly coloured work I had begun to show was memory and the reason why the work was so appealing to so many people, including many fellow artists, was his ability, his deliberate wish, to capture the feeling of the freshness of childhood experience. As for questions on matters such as the evolution of his style, what he had done as an artist in the past before I got to know him, all such questions were allowed to go unanswered. The work in the bequest answered all such questions and more about his work, revealing in full the entire span of his life as a painter.

The quantity of work in the bequest was enormous: probably everything Ben had ever painted, aside from the two hundred or so paintings I estimate were sold in his lifetime. The overall total came to some nine hundred paintings plus various prints and a few drawings and small paintings from his student days. He never dated anything and would never think of keeping his work in any kind of order. The business of going through this vast amount of work took some considerable time. Nevertheless it rapidly became apparent that there were major surprises in store. As I examined the paintings I soon realized that Ben had bestowed on me a most enormous gift, such was the quality of so many of the works I now had in my possession. What was most exciting of all was the discovery that there was a clear process of evolution to be discerned of which I had previously had really very little idea. It emerged that there had been three clear and distinct phases. The work that I had seen and exhibited had come more or less exclusively from the 1970s, ten years after his arrival in Plymouth. From the look of the work alone – the paper, the brushwork, the way the gouache was used – it was possible to see that there had been a whole phase of work which predated the work I had come to know so well, and another phase of work which came from the period following on from his departure to settle in Wales. As if all this were not excitement enough, I found that there came with the bequest a collection of three hundred and eighteen notebooks, of the existence of which I had known nothing, aside from two he had given to a friend who some years previously had passed them on to me.

The notebooks form a truly memorable record of an artist of great sensitivity with a rare gift of draughtsmanship and a poetic turn of mind and phrase. They are bereft of vanity, completely without self-regard. At the same time I cannot imagine a documentary collection more revealing of a civilized man, in love with nature, profoundly religious and steeped in the reading that made him the person he had become when I met him.

The first notebook is dated September 1953. Though quite a number thereafter are not dated, it is clear he maintained the practice of keeping notebooks through to the end of his life. With the help of the notebooks I am now able not only to outline the life and work of Ben Hartley but also to provide an account of the mind and spirit behind the work that has given me and so many other people I know so much pleasure.

Ben Hartley was born in November 1933 in Mellor, a village on the edge of the Peak District, at that time in Derbyshire, now in Cheshire. It has changed little since Ben was a child and remains dominated by a landscape of rugged hills, moorland and drystone walls, with remnants here and there of mines and factories. Ben's childhood landscape gave him a kind of dual nationality. Mellor is in fact not many miles from Stockport and Manchester. Ben's father was a tailor whose business took him daily into Ancoats, at that time the grimmest district in grimmest Manchester. In contrast, his mother's parents had a farm which was just down the road from where the family lived.

Ben was the youngest of three, himself and two sisters. Because of health problems his childhood was spent very largely indoors, reading and drawing. The only outdoor childhood activity he ever spoke of was going down the road to his grandparents' farm to watch the round of farming life, the harvest, the bringing in of the cows and the caring needed for all the other animals.

Ben was an able boy academically. At eleven he entered Manchester Grammar School, one of the leading schools of its kind in the country. Unfortunately his health did not cope with the physical strain and he had to be kept off school for a whole year. It was also clear that Ben's only real wish in life was to paint and draw. Consequently at sixteen he left to go to art school in Stockport. Two years later he went to the Regional Art School in Manchester; from there to the Royal College of Art where he was a student in the printmaking department from 1954 to 1957.

He had made a strong impression in Manchester. Norman Jaques taught Ben and remembers him to this day as the best student he ever saw: 'There were other good students but none to match him for the poetry of his vision.' Like everyone I have spoken to who taught him, Norman Jaques also remembers him as the most reticent of students, extremely difficult to draw out.

During his time at the Royal College he had lodgings at the home of Carel Weight, that most kindly of artists, who became professor of painting at the College. I managed to speak to him several times after Ben died: not long before he died himself in 1997. He reminisced about Ben's need to take care of his health and mentioned the fact, as though it could be taken for granted, that Ben took a first in his degree. Summarizing his thoughts about Ben, he said on one occasion 'Ben was of the soil', a wonderful expression that for me encapsulates virtually everything one could say about Ben, even at the very deepest level.

After his degree, when he finished at the Royal College, there was talk of a Prix de Rome, which came to nothing, perhaps not surprisingly, given his love of his native countryside and his recent struggle to survive in London. But he did receive a travelling scholarship. I don't think he used that right away. He simply returned to Mellor to take up some part-time teaching at his old art school in Manchester. He remained there for three years before obtaining his part-time post in Plymouth. During that time Monica, his older sister, and her family moved to live in Herefordshire, at a place called Shobdon where her husband was to work on an estate which, at one time, belonged to Lord Bateman. It is an extremely beautiful part of the world. The nearest town is Presteigne, just six miles away, literally on the border, on the Welsh side. Ben immediately became a frequent and regular visitor to the area from 1958 until 1983 when he left to settle permanently in Presteigne.

I have no precise explanation as to why Ben chose to move to Plymouth.

I can only assume he thought it would be good for his health and was attracted by the thought of Devon. Again Ben found himself living in a large town, but at least a town within easy reach of the countryside. He also had the comfort of finding he had a colleague whose wife was Jane Micklewright, a fellow student at the Royal College a year ahead of him. The couple had a young family for whom Ben made beautiful objects, such as cut-out folding cards and an alphabet book, now family treasures (see Plate 47). People I have spoken to who went to his classes remember him as quiet and courteous, with a sly sense of humour. Undemonstrative though he was, the general impression seems to be that he rather enjoyed his teaching.

When he arrived in Plymouth he immediately continued with his practice of keeping notebooks. From the bequest it is also apparent he began painting now more than he had ever done in the past, when he had mainly drawn and made prints; though from paintings found in a large notebook dated 1953 it is clear he had been a master of watercolour and gouache from early on. So there is ample evidence that Ben had no difficulty working. A year after he came to Plymouth he bought a house in Ermington, an environment which suited him perfectly, and fell in love with the surrounding countryside, painting and drawing, walking and cycling day in day out. However, from the notebooks it is clear that he became increasingly preoccupied with matters of faith and Christian doctrine. He had grown up in a conventionally Christian household. The ensuing years in Plymouth were to be a time of utmost importance in the development of his spiritual life, culminating in his conversion to Catholicism in 1968.

Though he was always quiet and unassuming and revealed very little of his intellectual life when you were with him, from the range of reading found in the notebooks of the 1960s, with page upon page of extracts from the writings of great religious thinkers, Augustine, Aquinas, Kierkegaard, Simone Weil, Karl Barth, the poetry of Donne and Traherne, it is clear he was possessed of a searching intellect as well as real gifts as a linguist.

The general tenor of his inner life is not difficult to gauge. In autumn 1965 there was a rather curious episode when he left his job at Plymouth College of Art to join a project in Norfolk called the Church Art Community. It was based at the rectory of the parish of North Repps near Cromer. The project was the idea of David Ainsworth, an Anglican priest and former art student. As with Ben's teachers, David Ainsworth remembers Ben vividly but has no recollection of exactly how it came about that Ben joined the project or what he was hoping to achieve. The charming notebook that derives from this stay in Norfolk is no more informative on such matters either. He remained at North Repps until Christmas, spent the holiday period with his parents in Mellor and then simply walked back into his job at Plymouth College of Art.

By 1966–67 with the stay in Norfolk behind him, it is clear he is moving from being a practising Anglican towards some High Church form of worship. In his notebooks for the following year, having recorded various meetings with Catholic clerics and visits to places of worship, he then announces, quite dramatically, that on 26th September 1968 he was received into the Catholic church.

Obviously this was a decision of massive importance in his life. Prior to his coming to Plymouth, the notebooks contain only drawings. Naturally these tell us a great deal about the kind of person he was, what he was interested in depicting. From the time of his settling in Devon, they remain full of drawings, but side by side with the drawings we begin to find little comments about the weather, the look of the countryside, the remarks he might hear whilst on his walks, an occasional brief recording of what he had done, but we almost never find any comment or even a mention of his work. He had a great fondness for playing with words, so the notebooks are very much tinged with the humour found in his paintings; all of which works as a kind of barometer of his moods and feelings, his inner state of being. Certainly his conversion to Catholicism brought him in contact with new people. He became extremely friendly with the members of the Augustinian order at the Priory at nearby Cadleigh. This gave something of a new dimension to his life and he records in some detail his frequent visits to the Priory, vignettes of encounters with the friars and their love of banter in their moments of relaxation, as well as accounts of the menial tasks he undertook as a member of the congregation.

Ben produced a large number of paintings throughout the 1960s. They are much darker than the work I saw when I first went to see him in 1976. However the work changed, either through change of circumstance or the progression of his unending reflection on the nature of painting, the subject matter remained the same subject matter that formed the inspiration for the whole of his life, namely country life and the world of the farmyard. Putting his work of this period, with its dark browns and greens, in the context of British art of that time, it had very much the look of the English Neo-Romantics whose work came to prominence around the time of the Second World War. It would appear from studying the notebooks that a major change began to take place in his work very soon after his conversion. It is as though this was a release, as though the intellectual and emotional stress he had experienced was now behind him and he could find new energy and apply the same intensity to shape the future direction of his painting.

In the 1970s the content of his reading as recorded in his notebooks changes and focuses on art rather than philosophy and religion. His prime preoccupation becomes the ideas behind the work of Matisse and Bonnard and their fellow artists of the modern French school, Picasso, Braque, Dufy, Derain, Miró, Chagall, elements of whose work, especially Bonnard,

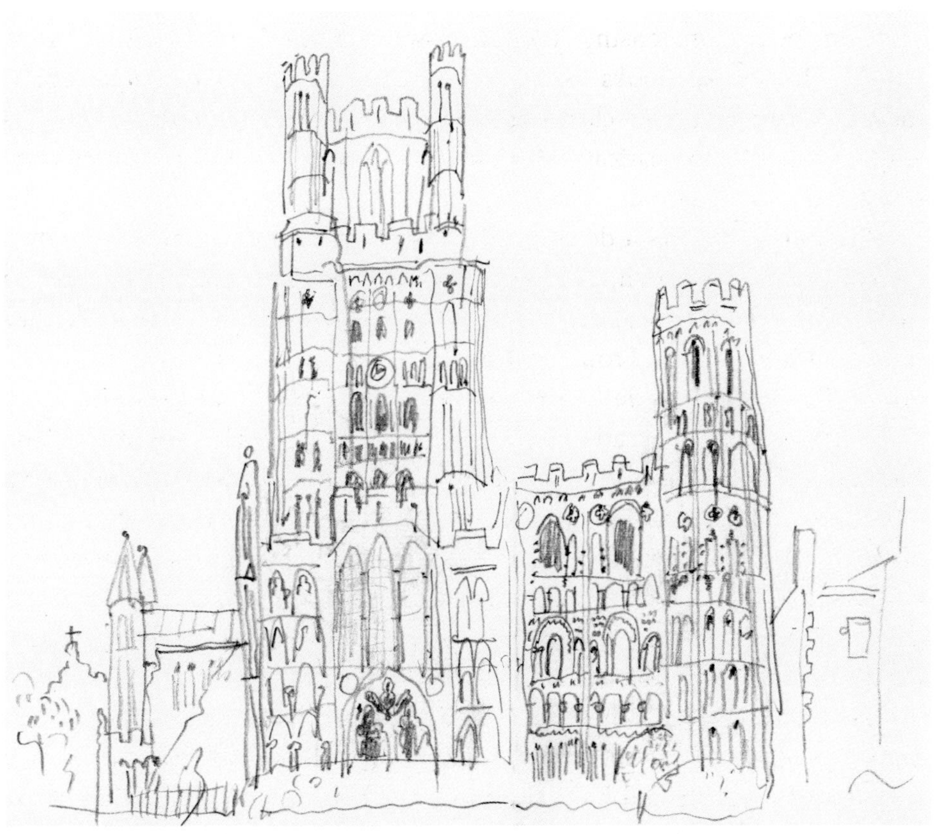

Drawing, *Ely Cathedral*, notebook 1961

Matisse, Chagall and Miró, could be detected when I first went to see him in 1976.

There is no doubt that Ben's years from the time he came to Plymouth were a time of great inner richness. I am sure he found his solitary existence and the constant struggle to cope with his chest problems a great burden. But in terms of his spiritual life, I am equally sure these were rich and important times. The notebooks reveal that in 1975, the year before I met Ben, he reached a kind of fusion of his religious and artistic beliefs. This is encapsulated in a painting which grew out of the drawings he made during visits to a house called Rose Cottage in the hamlet of Langbrook, not far from his own house. I will discuss this work in some detail when I look at specific paintings (see Plate 20).

One aspect of Ben's life I have yet to mention is the fact that in spite of his health he did a great deal of travelling. The first notebook in the bequest, dated 1953, begins with numerous drawings about a visit to a remote area of Scotland. In 1958 he became very fond of touring in the border country, the Welsh hills and the Wye Valley. There are two excellent notebooks about a journey to Belgium and Holland. Unfortunately they are not dated but they look as though they come from the late 1950s, when perhaps he was using the money from his travel scholarship from the Royal College. In 1961 he visited Ely Cathedral. In 1963 he paid the first of four visits to Ireland. In 1964 he made a tour of Yorkshire including York and Beverley. The visits to Ireland were especially fruitful, yielding many of the finest paintings of the early period.

Ben visited France many times; how many is difficult to say. Fifty of the three hundred and eighteen notebooks are taken up with drawings about visits to France. Few of them have dates in them. Sometimes there is internal evidence as to the year, going by references to the careers of various presidents or events such as the centenary Chardin exhibition at the Grand Palais in 1979. In spite of their lack of exact dates, anyone with a love of France would find these notebooks a sheer delight.

As regards the impact on Ben of our meeting and everything that flowed on from that, it is extremely difficult to comment. Ben was a person for whom the life of the mind and the imagination was all. He had spent the first twenty years after graduating from the Royal College constantly making work but without exhibiting, aside from putting the occasional painting into the exhibitions of the local Society of Artists. He now found he had exhibitions of his own most years, some years several. He became a frequent visitor to my flat in Plymouth Arts Centre where he could enjoy the hospitality of my good friend Mary Thomson and the pleasure of seeing Miró, our well-fed, golden-eyed black cat.

Nothing of any of these new developments warrants a mention in his notebooks. All the same I do have valued memories of the fact that this painfully shy person came to find it very easy to climb the stairs to my flat, as he later reminisced in one of his letters to me and Mary from Wales. Ben realized that we both loved and admired his work. However whereas my demonstrations of enthusiasm might be accompanied by some proposal for an initiative to promote his work, Mary could communicate hers simply by the way she received him. Somehow there was always delicious food ready to appear on the table whenever he arrived and he would quite happily join us. Mary would put him at his ease, relieving him of the burden of making conversation by recounting her memories of country life going back many years, the coastal beauty of Northumberland, wild ducks on Holy Island, childhood visits to her grandmother in a remote part of Scotland, as well as her recollections from her younger days in the north-east when she came to know the work of Winifred Nicholson, that most lyrical of British painters, then later on, in the Lake District, the sight of Beatrix Potter in her final years, by then not so much the celebrated writer of children's books, rather more the stern old lady, seriously involved in the business of farming.

In 1979 Ben's teaching hours, which had been dwindling for some time, went down to three hours a week; at which point this was no longer viable. He carried on living in Ermington. I had no idea how he survived or what he lived on. I never asked. The response to the first exhibitions had created considerable demand for more exhibitions in the region. John Lane, a painter and writer and at that time a trustee of Dartington Hall, took a great interest in Ben, buying pictures for himself and the Trust. In 1983 I introduced his work to the Beaux Arts Gallery in Bath and from then on until 1991 they put on a show every two years.

In the summer of 1983 his physical condition deteriorated to the point where he was barely able to walk. The cause was simply lack of food. Friends rallied round when they saw what was happening. I, like many others, was going out to Ermington with old-fashioned nourishment like beef broth to build up his strength. This had the desired effect. Then to the astonishment of us all, he suddenly announced in the autumn that he had sold his house and was moving to Presteigne. I have the impression that his decline had given him a shock and he decided he needed to be somewhere less remote than Ermington; so he opted for Presteigne, where he would be near his sister and brother-in-law, both of whom he was very fond of, where he lived in the main street with shops, a doctor and a Carmelite monastery adorned by carvings by the artist David Jones, all within easy walking distance.

Ben's lifestyle changed not at all. He lived alone. He spent his days drawing, painting and walking. Tall and thin with a long-legged gait, he became a distinctive, familiar figure in the town. At the same time he managed to keep all knowledge of the fact that he was a painter from people in the town who knew him, apart, that is, from his closest Catholic friends. He became a deeply committed member of the congregation at the monastery chapel, helping with many tasks, just as he had done at the Priory in Cadleigh.

He was extremely fond of Presteigne. His first letters from there were full of descriptions of life in this small country town, very like the scenes to be

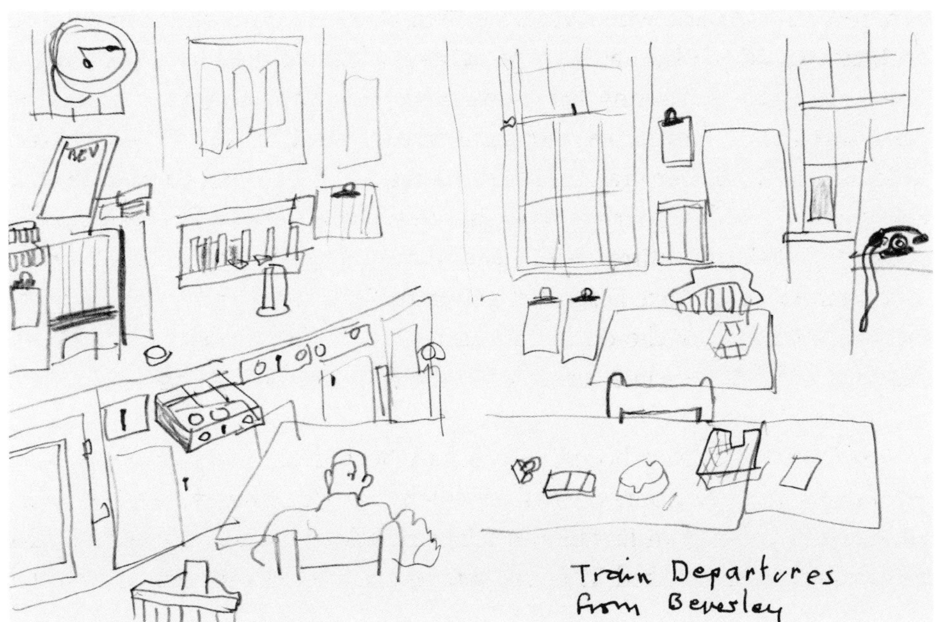

Drawing, *Beverley Station*, notebook 1964

Drawing, *A Ferry to Belgium*, notebook *circa* 1960

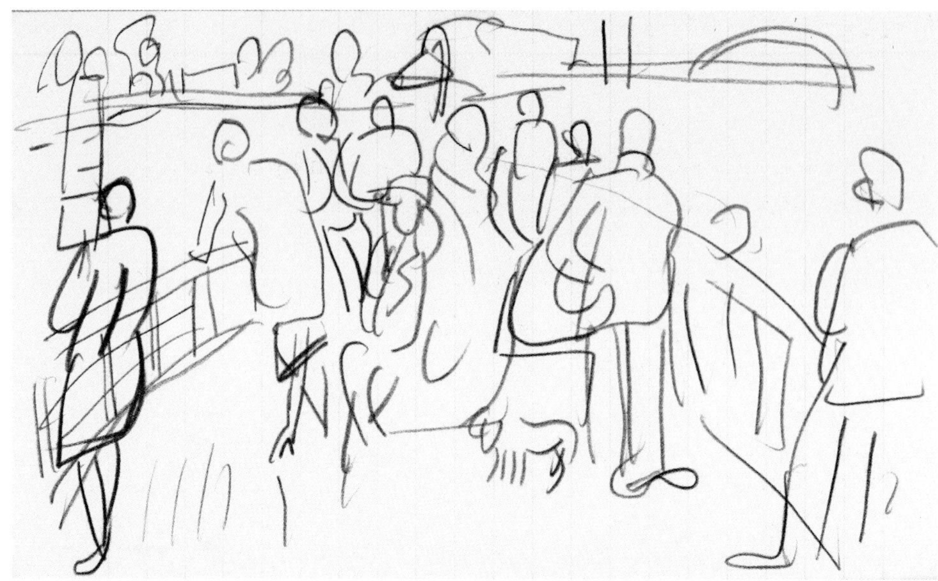

found in his paintings. I carried on promoting his work, setting up quite a number of exhibitions including a tour of several very good galleries in Wales. Mary Thomson and I visited him from time to time. The house was noticeably more comfortable but the way of life was the same: an air of bleakness and little sign of food, even though he had a vegetable patch of his own.

After a few years his letters, which in the past had always been a delight to receive, became full of complaint and talk of loss of inspiration. In the winter of 1996, after he had had problems with the heating system in his house, which was vital for keeping his chest problems at bay, his general condition declined to the point where in January his doctor took him into the cottage hospital. He came out after a few weeks but by March he was in hospital again, this time in the County Hospital in Hereford, and did not survive.

Ben's final years were indeed particularly sad. It is therefore worth taking note that in spite of the many letters to me and others of his friends bewailing the feeling that his inspiration was failing, he still managed to produce the best part of one hundred and fifty paintings after leaving Plymouth. The years in Presteigne were not only productive, they were the years in which he painted some of his most moving pictures. He mined, more deeply than ever, the vein of his memories of country people. These paintings form a great gallery of farming folk, all, to use Carel Weight's expression, of the soil. They are old. Sometimes there is a touch of caricature in the way they are depicted. They are certainly never mournful, often a touch comic. Together they make a unique and poignant coda to Ben's creative years. In colour they are often close to the work of the early years, giving a feeling of completeness to the life of a man whose life had been dedicated to his art and his beliefs.

THE WORK

An asterisk beside a title indicates that it was given by the author. All other titles are Ben Hartley's own.

All sizes shown height first

Materials : all works gouache on paper, mostly brown parcel paper

Early prints and notebooks

If the salient features of the life and personality of Ben Hartley were reticence and self-effacement, he was liberal in the generosity of his bequest. Not only does it contain a vast quantity of work, it also richly reveals the inner content of his creative life. For this we have to thank Ben for having kept his notebooks together. In all probability the three hundred and eighteen notebooks that came with the bequest constitute all but a handful of the entire output of Ben's drawing spanning forty years of his working life as an artist.

The relationship between the notebooks and the paintings is very close indeed. In fact it is fundamental to Ben's working method. He scarcely ever made preparatory drawings; on the other hand virtually every painting relies on its motifs coming from somewhere in one of the notebooks, sometimes several different notebooks. They serve as a kind of treasure chest of imagery which Ben drew on at will, a memory bank from which to conjure up and piece together his evocative paintings.

There is little sign of things Ben did in childhood. Of the work he did in his student days, a great deal is seen in the notebooks, starting in September 1953, his second year as a student at Manchester Regional School of Art. This first notebook is entirely taken up with notes and drawings made during a visit to Scotland. Thereafter, for the next few years, they are exclusively about Manchester and the immediate environs of Mellor, his birthplace, and the Peak District. Most of the drawings are observations of people, showing a minimum of detail, mainly working-class people in the post-war years, housewives in headscarves and pinafores, workmen simply designated by their occupations, such as railwayman or policeman.

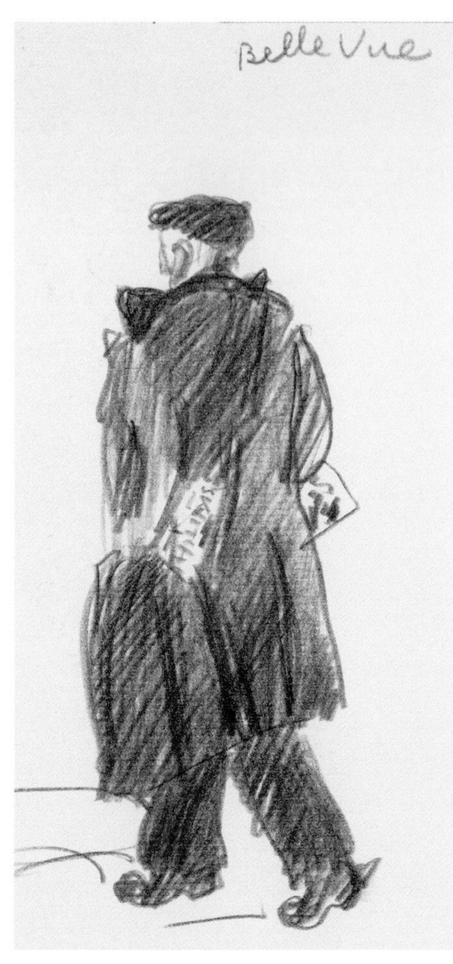

Drawing, coloured pencil, *Belle Vue, Manchester*, notebook 1957

The notebooks are nearly all pocket-size and mostly home-made. Fewer than a dozen are larger bought-in ready-made items. One of the most extraordinary is the notebook begun in December 1953. Foolscap in size, it is the largest and full from start to finish of draughtsmanship of a high order, showing the poetry of vision spoken of by Norman Jaques, one of his teachers at that time. The first half reflects the art school syllabus, with a significant assignment in lettering, as well as numerous scenes of farm buildings, sheds and greenhouses, the facades of shops and rear views of terraced old properties. A great deal of the book is taken up with drawings of people, mostly elderly men, seated, wearing hats and heavy overcoats. A reference to St. Pancras suggests this work was done in 1954, during the first year of study at the Royal College.

The whole book shows great maturity and the figures are deeply moving with a kind of weight and seriousness which never surfaced again.

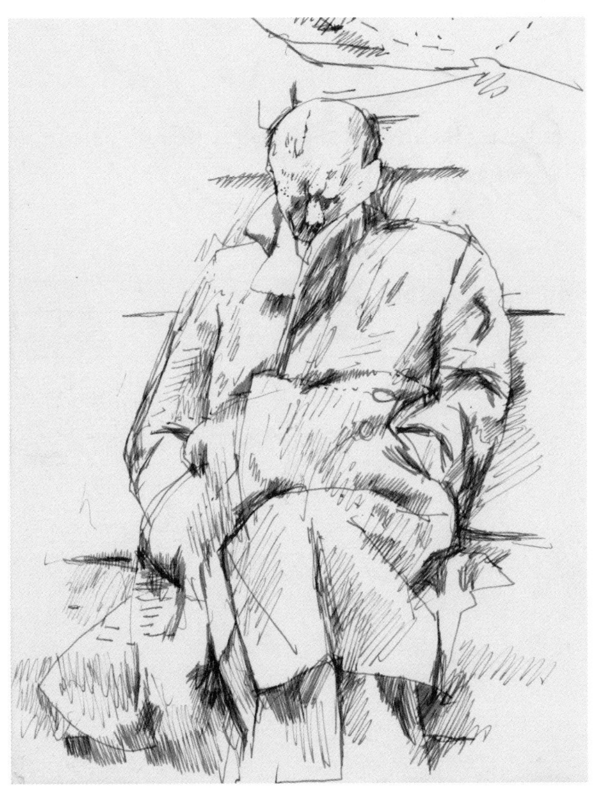

Drawing, ink, notebook December 1953

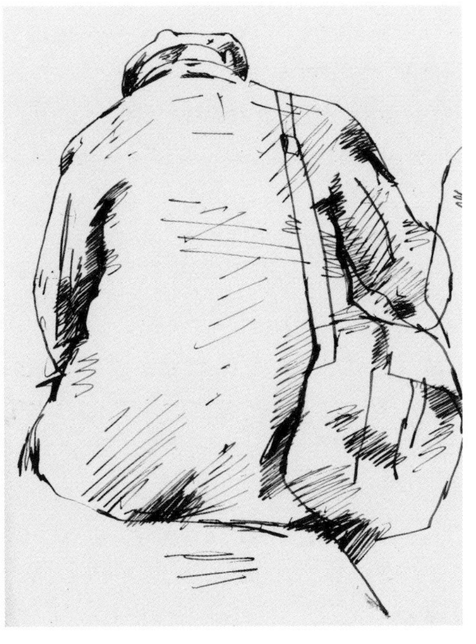

Drawing, ink, notebook December 1953

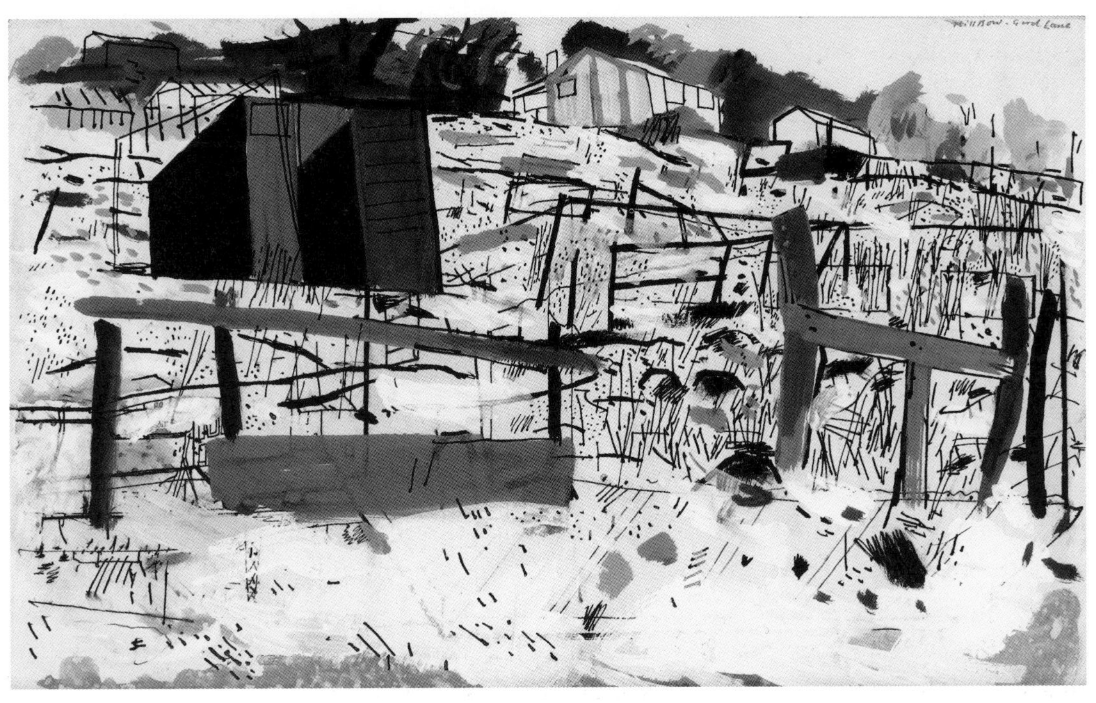

Drawing, gouache and ink, notebook December 1953

A small collection of loose drawings and prints, found in a folder that came with the bequest, includes some excellent items: a drawing of railway wagons in pencil, charcoal and gouache, a delicately coloured etching somewhat in the manner of Ben Nicholson, another of a fruit and vegetable stall, incorporating a motif of hanging grapes that appears several times in the notebooks. There are several lithographs, including a print called *Pullets*, one of the loveliest items in the whole bequest. The composition is worked out in beautifully simple black outlines, showing typical Ben Hartley farm jumble, set off in the foreground by dozens of pullets, tinted in with watercolour. There is no sign of this lithograph ever having been editioned.

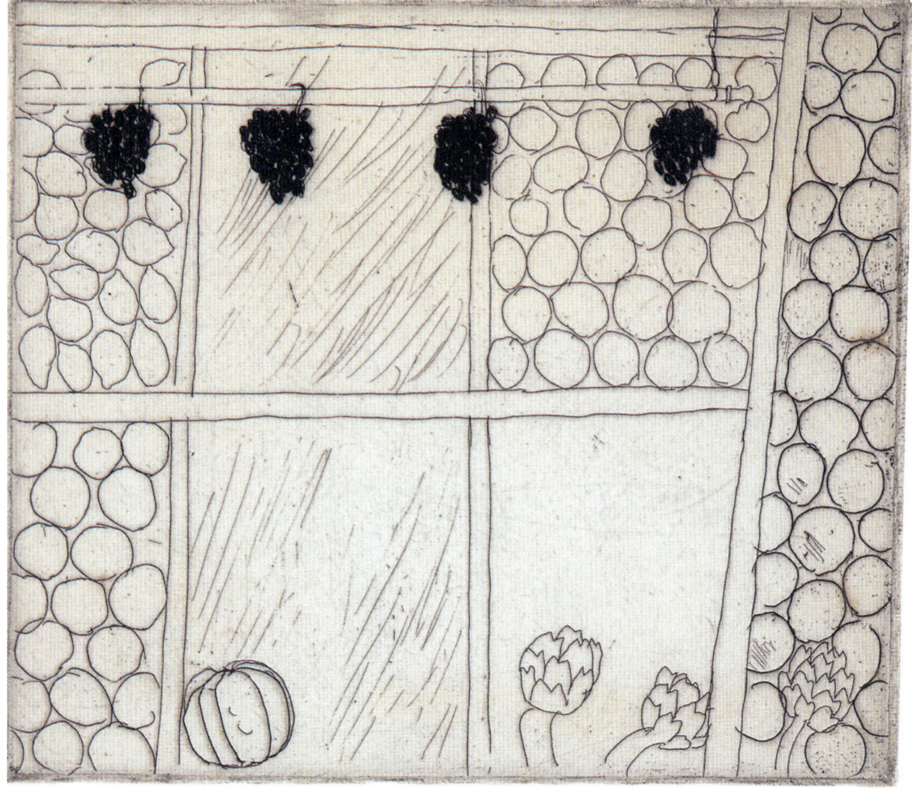

*Fruit and Veg** Etching, 12.5 × 15.5 cm

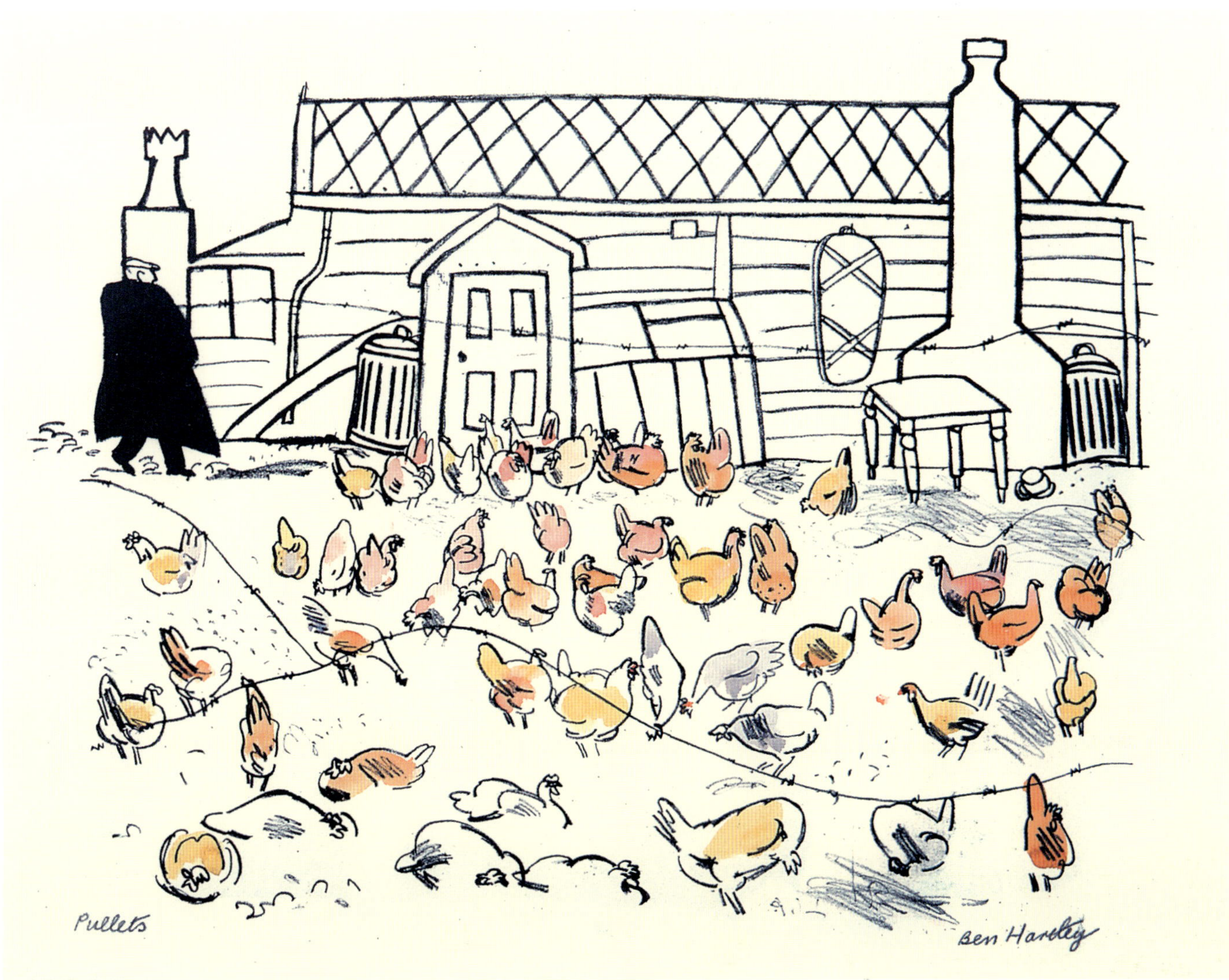

Pullets, lithograph with watercolour 37 × 45 cm

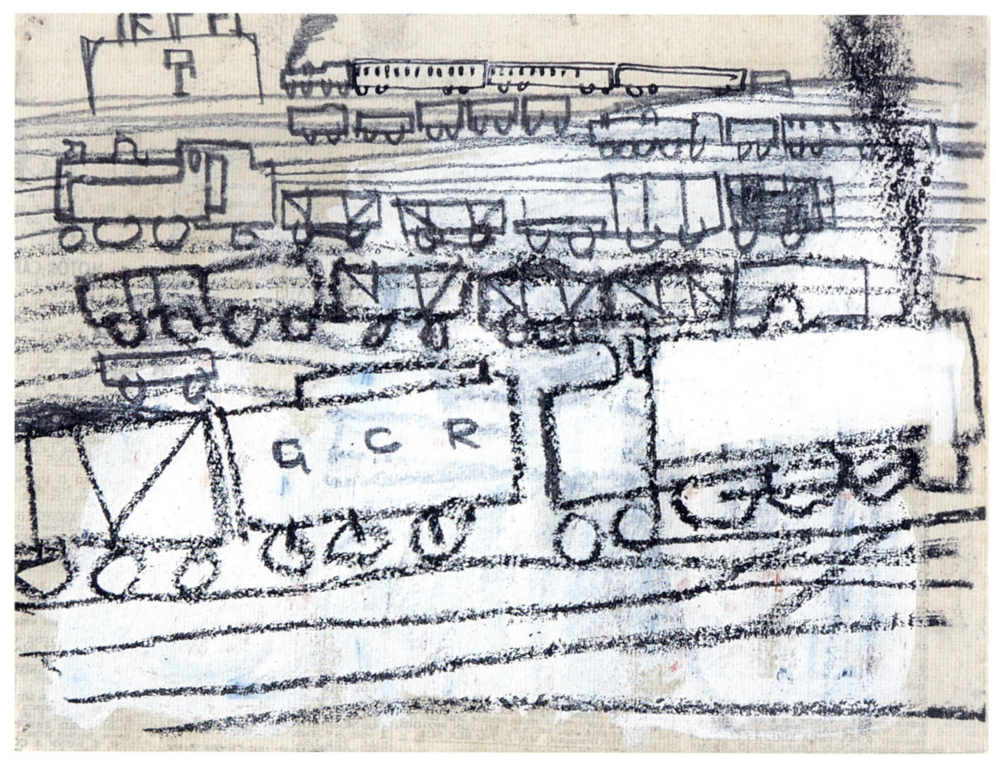

*Goods Wagons** Pencil, charcoal and gouache, 14 × 19 cm

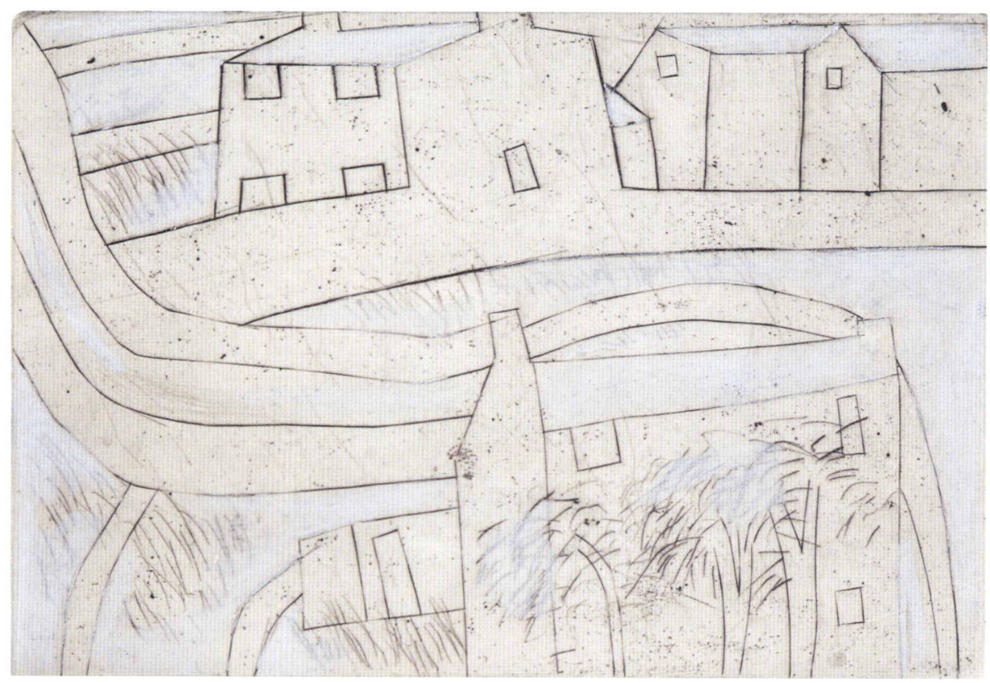

*Townscape** Tinted etching, 10 × 15 cm

Early paintings, places and travels

'Early paintings' means essentially work done in the 1960s. The large notebook of 1953–54 contains fine examples of landscapes in watercolour and gouache, but there is little sign of individual paintings datable from before 1960. The subject matter is very much the world of the farm, a mixture of observation and a burgeoning fantasy. There are many straightforwardly beautiful paintings, landscapes of a more or less topographical nature. Among the less straightforward images are *Farm Scene** and *Two Buckets**. They have their origins in motifs found in two of the larger format notebooks of the first half of the 1960s.

An important distinguishing feature of the early paintings is the fact that the gouache is applied direct to the brown paper which was his standard material. Later on, in the 1970s, when brightness of colour becomes so important, a white ground is applied as an undercoat to the gouache.

1. Farm Scene*

58 × 49 cm
Bequest Collection

In *Farm Scene* we find a heterogeneous collection of motifs, divorced from perspective; looming large in the middle a farmer, his scruffy coat tied at the waist; there are various birds barely noticeable amid the foliage and undergrowth; we find two white ducks and a gate, the most common motif in Ben Hartley. The image, in rich greens and browns, is dominated by a magnificent tree. The urge to reorder reality is well illustrated in the comparison between the painting and this closely related drawing.

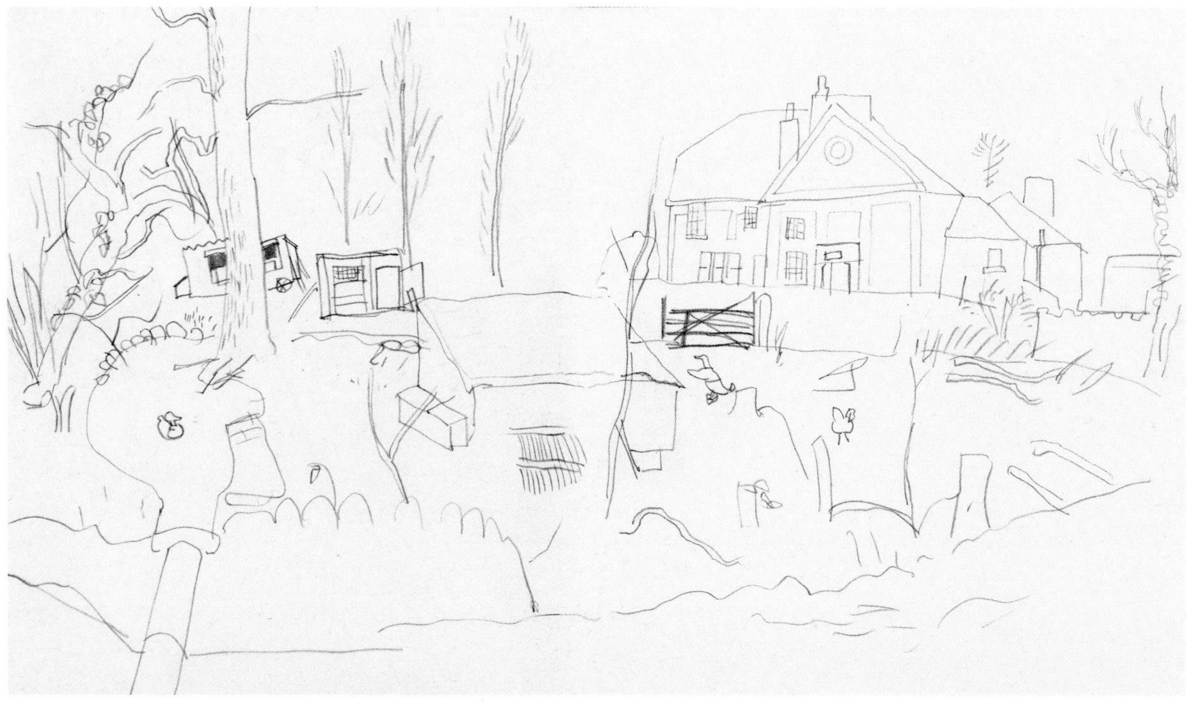

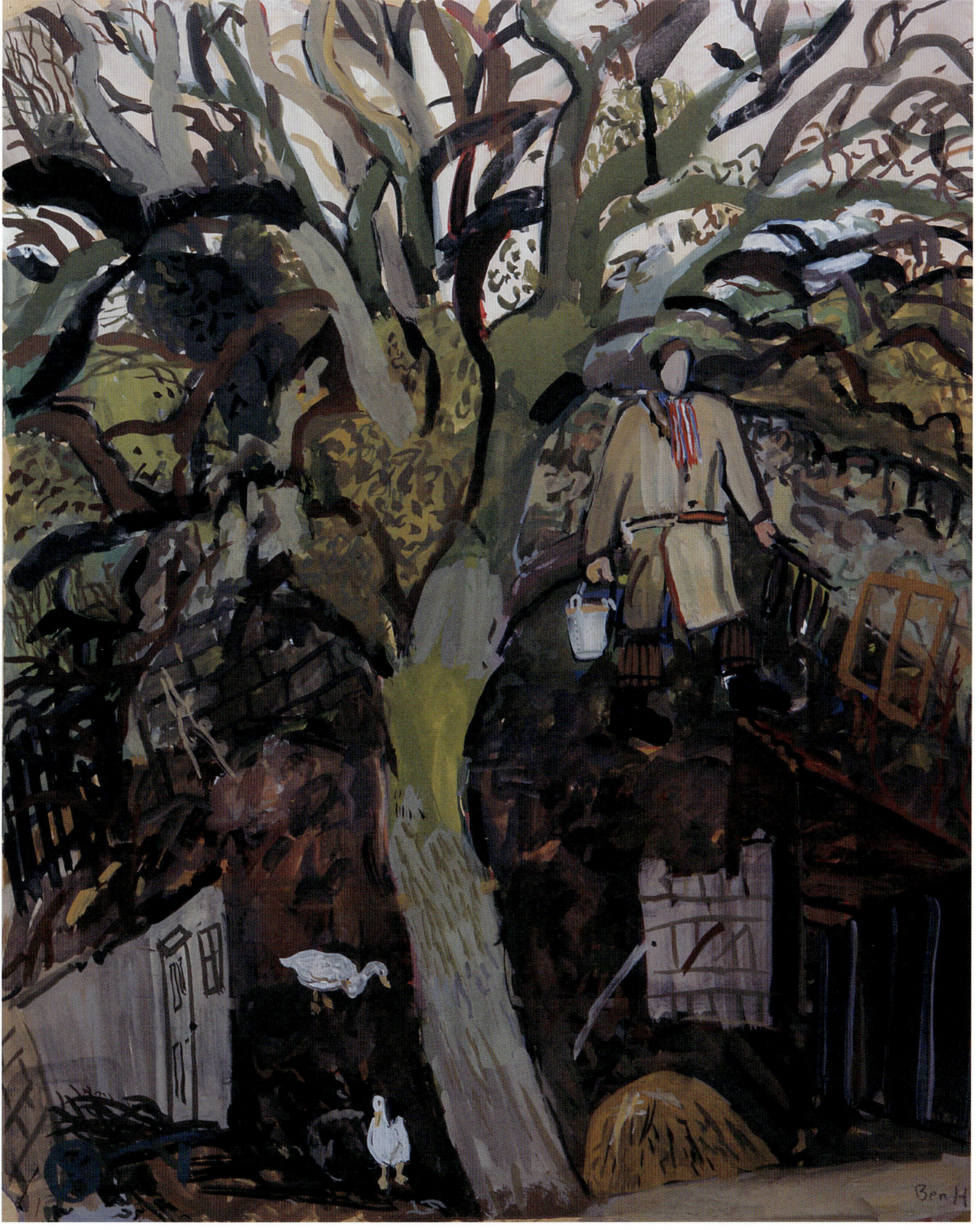
Ben H

2. Two Buckets*

54 × 73 cm
Bequest Collection

Two Buckets is a particularly interesting and unusual image. Agricultural instruments, tools and machinery abound in the notebooks and paintings. This is the only instance where two isolated objects, a pair of battered old buckets, become the central subject matter, filling virtually the entire picture space. The painting is a faithful translation of a drawing Ben made quite near his house in Ermington. There are notes on the drawing referring to bits of broken pottery or roof tile and spots of meal – golden-coloured in the painting. These items, seemingly of little significance, come together in the painting to create the poetic setting of the picture and become symbols of the farmyard at its most humble level.

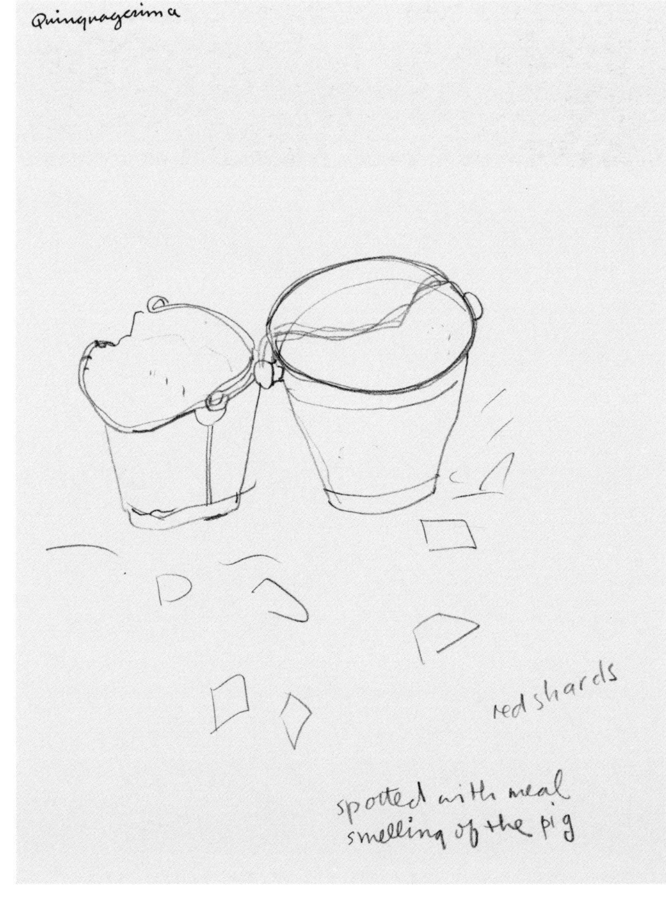

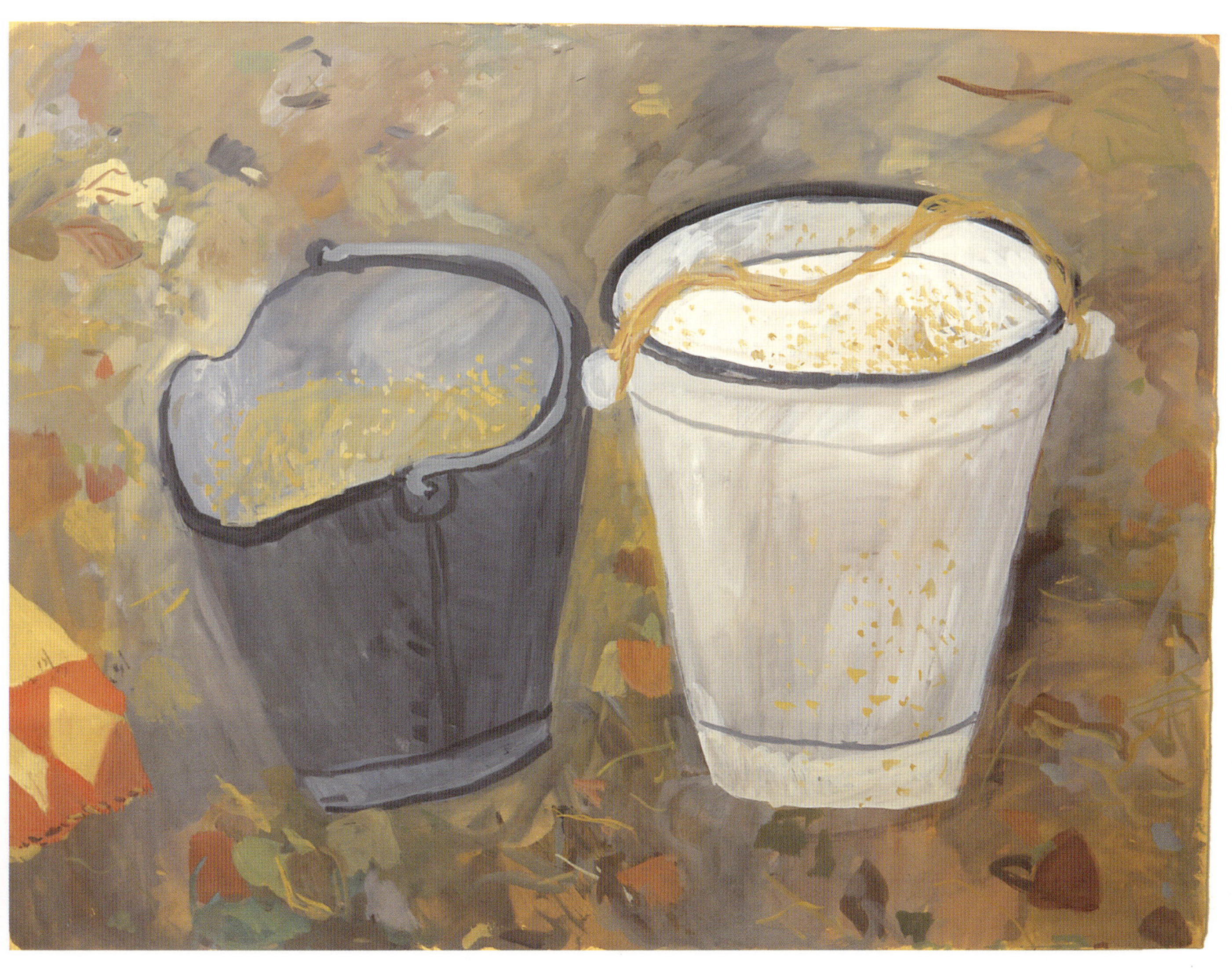

3. Weobley Knight*

58 × 77.5 cm
Bequest Collection

There is much that is straightforwardly topographical in the work of this period. Two very striking paintings come from the time spent with his sister and her family at Shobdon from 1958 onwards. *Weobley Knight* comes directly from the notebook of 1958 recording visits to churches along the Golden Valley in Herefordshire, as far down as Abbey Dore. In *Weobley Knight* the sepulchral subject is transformed by the colour and the vase of flowers into a joyous painting.

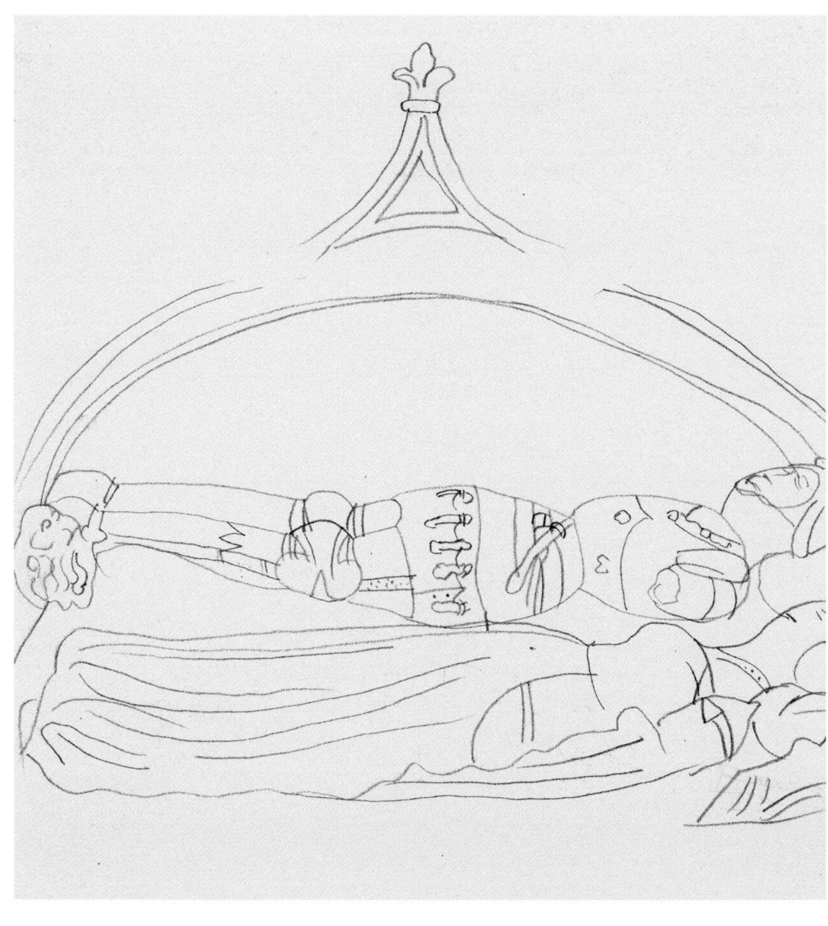

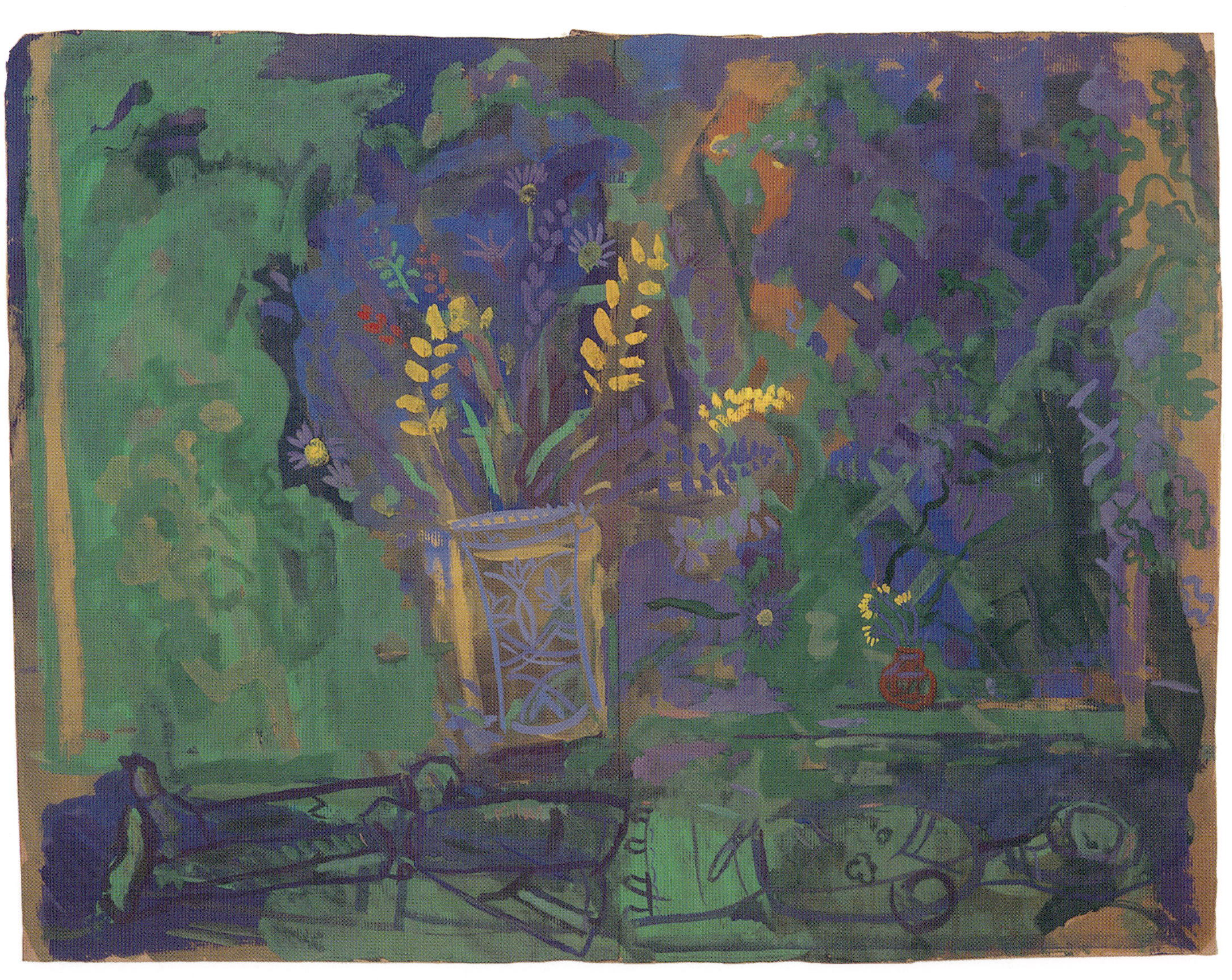

4. Dovecot and Sugar Loaf

57.5 × 76 cm
Bequest Collection

The beautiful pink brick dovecot, built by Lord Bateman on his estate at Shobdon, was drawn on many occasions. The painting represents the view from the back of the house lived in by Ben's sister and her family. The dovecot is not many yards away but is not actually visible from the house. On the distant horizon there is a small protrusion called Skirrid, a celebrated landmark referred to by many local people as the Sugar Loaf, seen here with a blueness recalling Housman's 'remembered hills'.

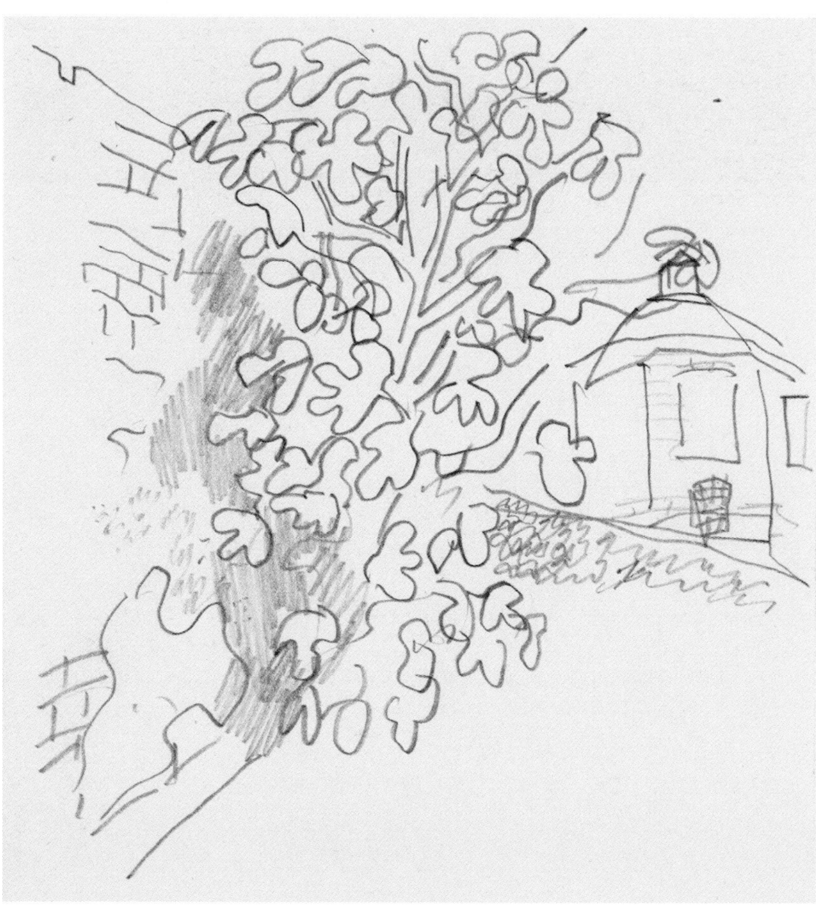

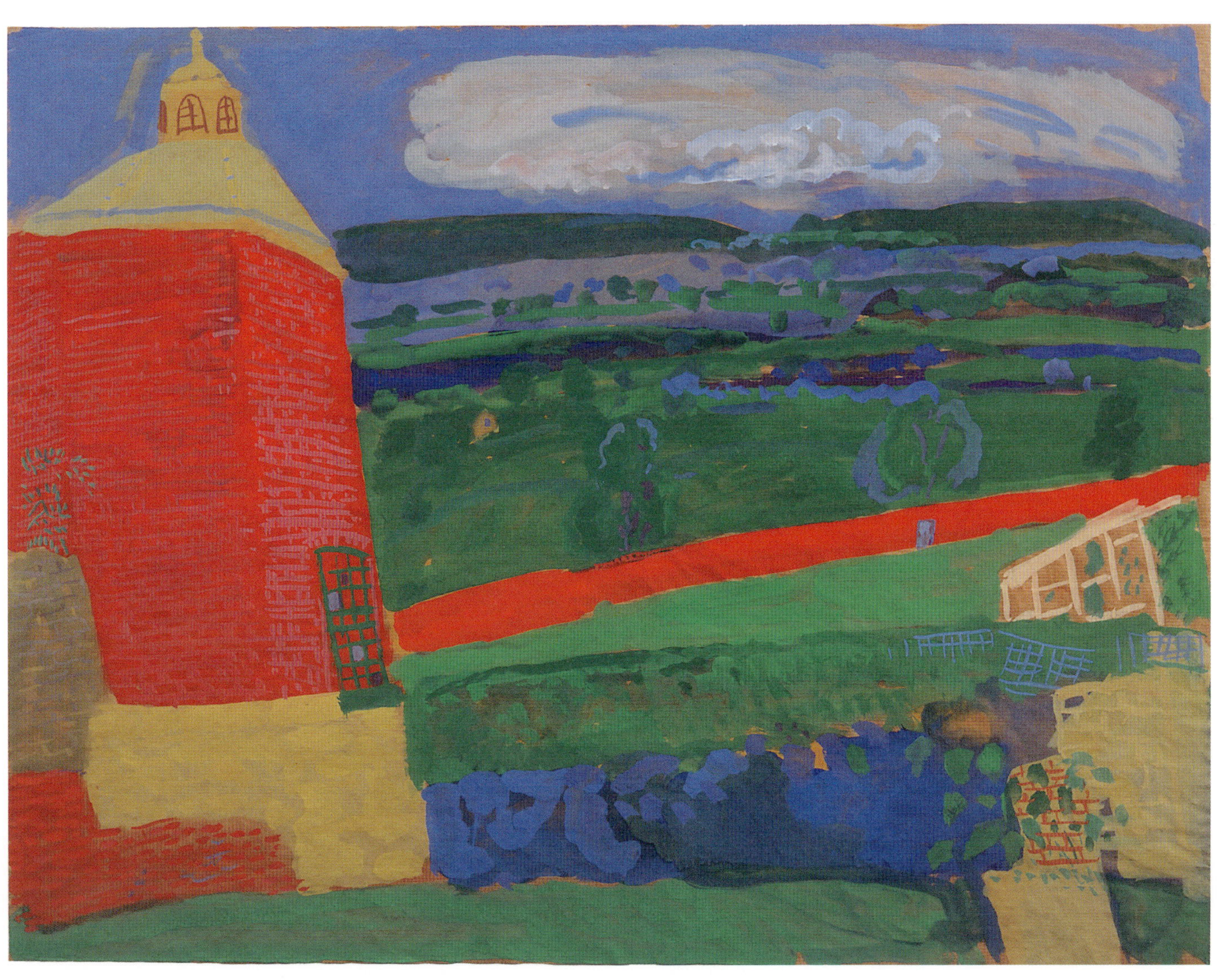

5. Winter Scene: Farm under Snow*

53 × 43 cm
Bequest Collection

The notebooks of Ben Hartley's first years in Plymouth and Ermington have a distinct buoyancy of feeling. *Winter Scene: Farm under Snow* comes from a notebook going from the late summer of 1961 through to the winter of 1962. It is a fusion of two drawings made around the time of New Year. It is difficult to make out the exact location; possibly Derbyshire, possibly Devon; probably Derbyshire. Whichever, the brushwork in this picture is some of the finest to be found in any of the paintings.

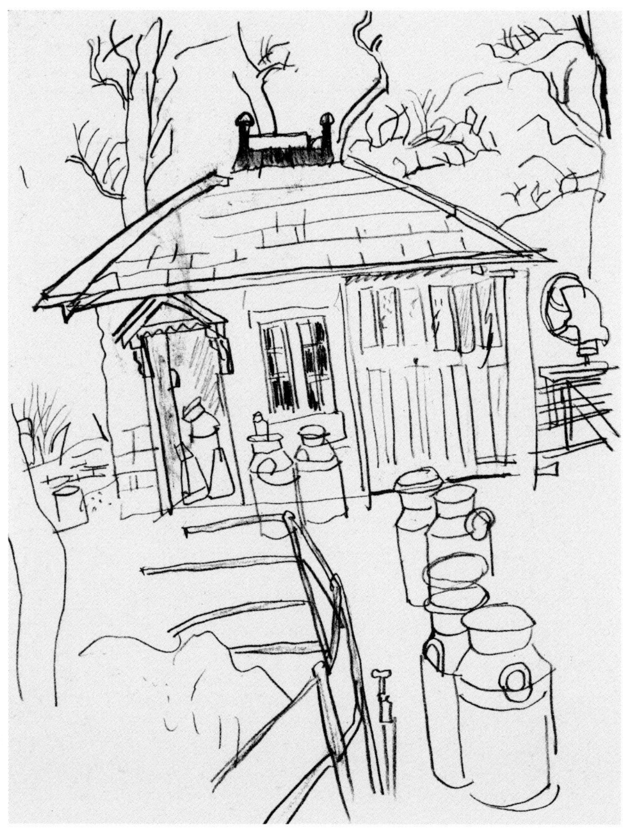

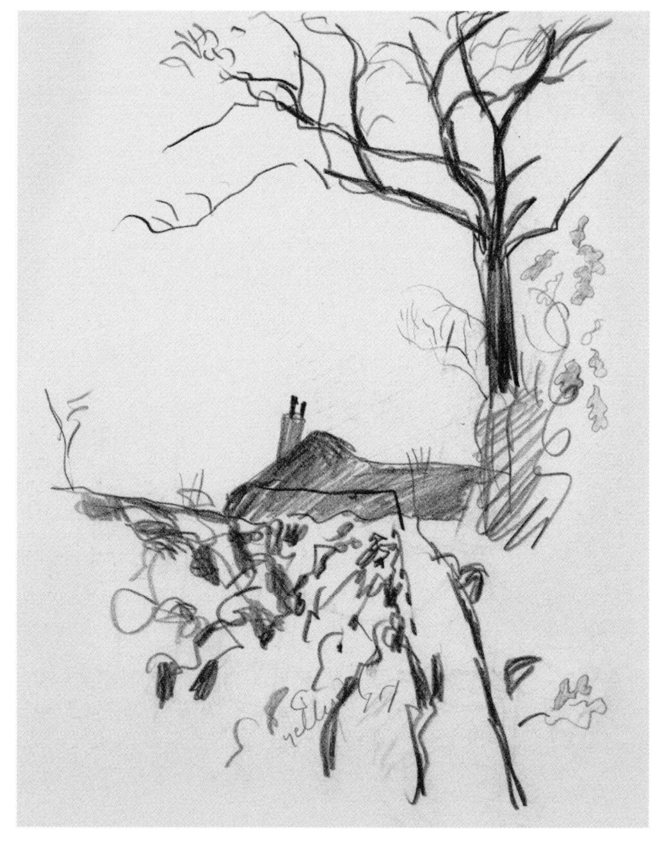

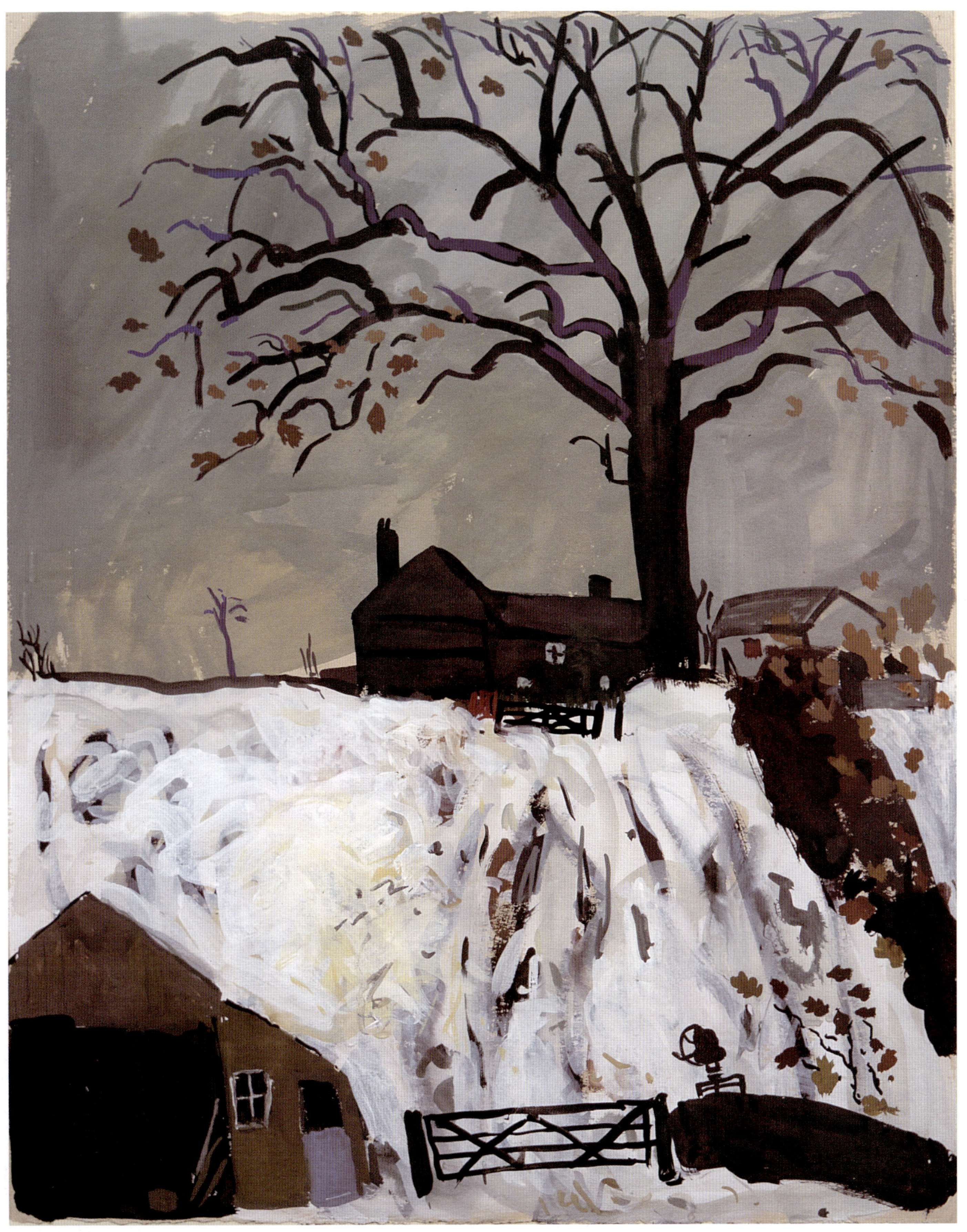

6. Devon Lane, Westlake*

57 × 71 cm
Bequest Collection

Devon Lane, Westlake is a painting of the finest quality. The related drawing, from a notebook dated 1968, is a rare instance of a preparatory drawing. The painting is an exact depiction of this location. Little if anything has been invented: we can identify the exact spot from which the point of view was taken. At this early stage Ben Hartley reveals a capacity for creating powerful, atmospheric landscapes. There is an expressionist force in the grey line of the lane that ploughs through the centre of the picture up to the brooding dark grey of the sky. The working of the huge banks in the foreground has the vigour and the richness of colour of the great tradition of English Romantic landscape.

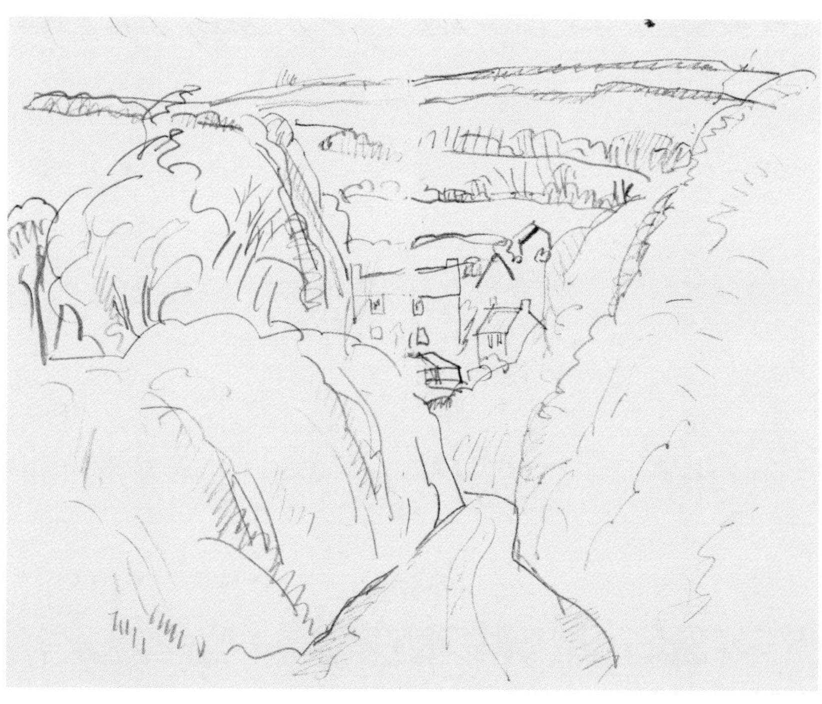

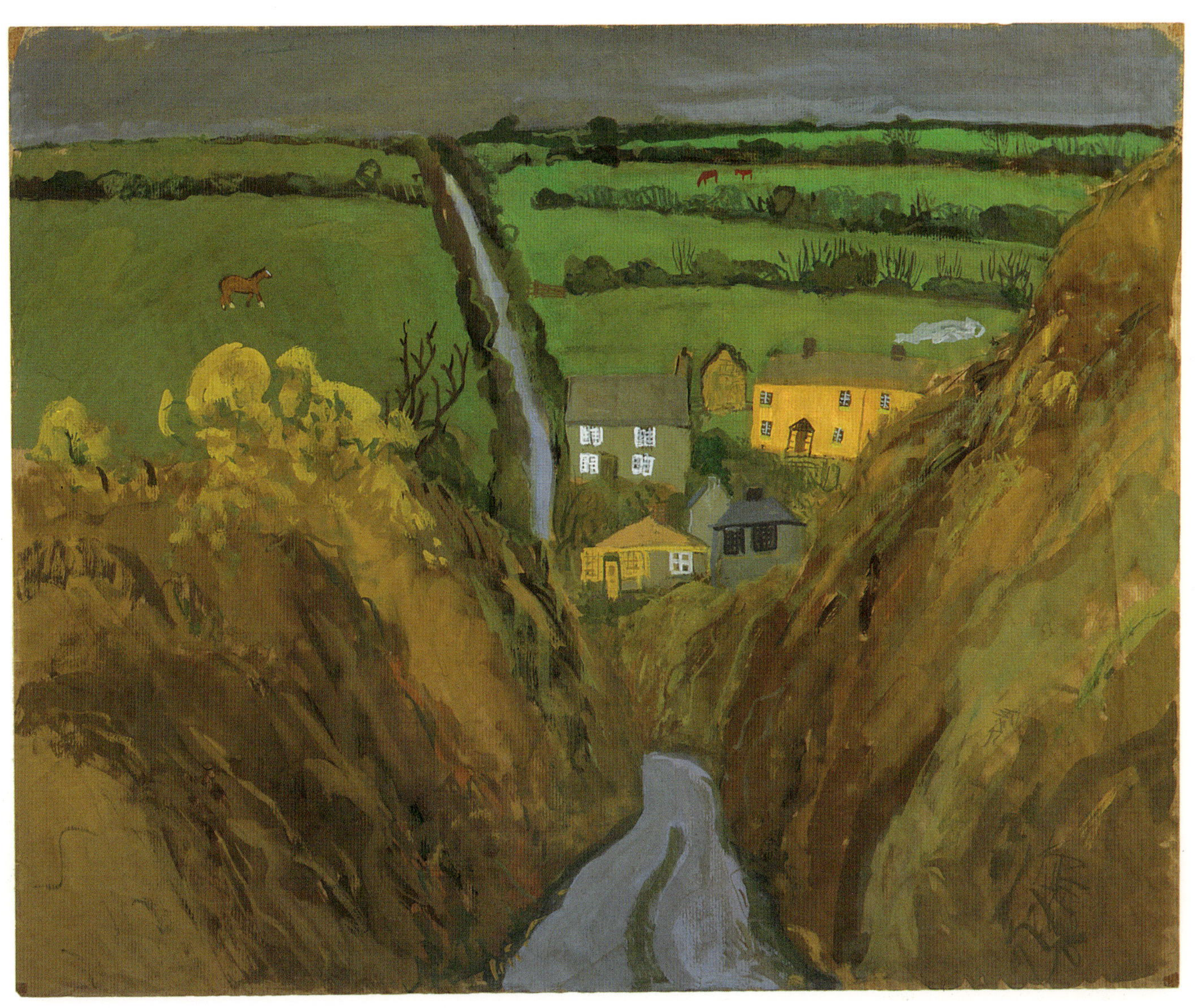

7. Fawns Autumn

58 × 76 cm
Bequest Collection

Fawns Autumn takes us into extraordinary territory. *Fawns* was the name of a large house, now an old people's home, just a few hundred yards from Ben's house, close to the main road to Kingsbridge. There is a fair amount of ground around it and a number of old farm buildings. From the notebooks, it would seem he went there quite often to draw. The drawings are all of an utterly unassuming nature, a dog crouching in front of the gate posts, the odd farm shed: nothing specifically about the place to give a hint of the flaming Van Gogh-like outburst which is *Fawns Autumn*.

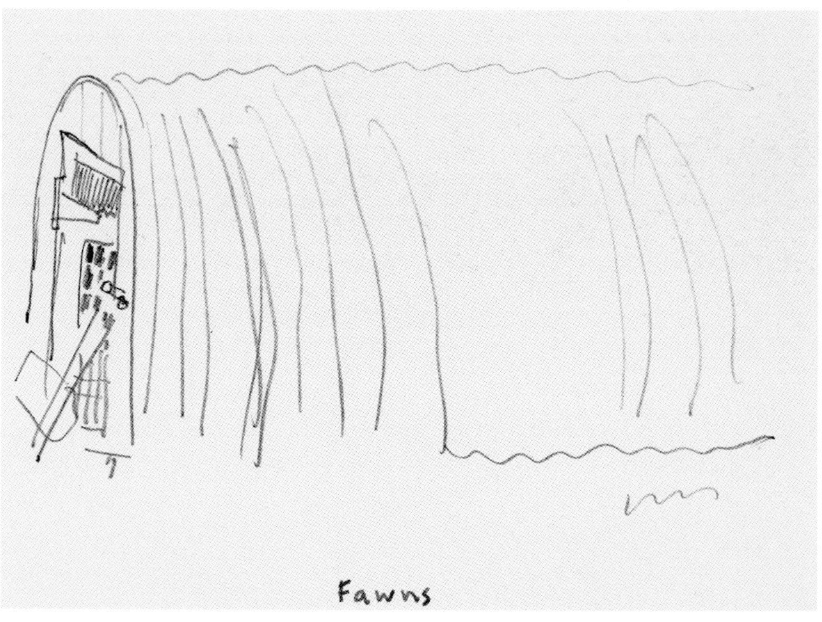

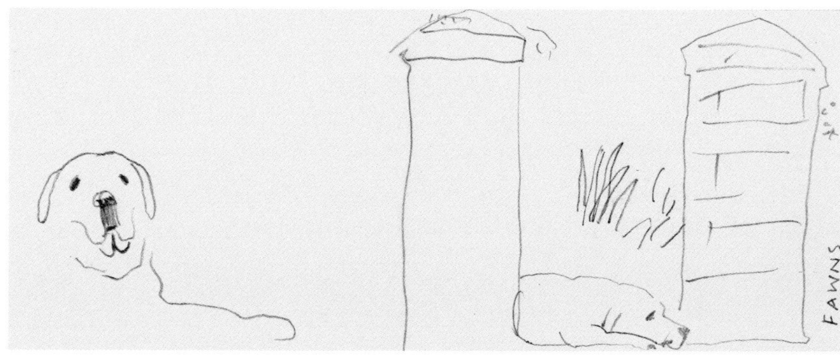

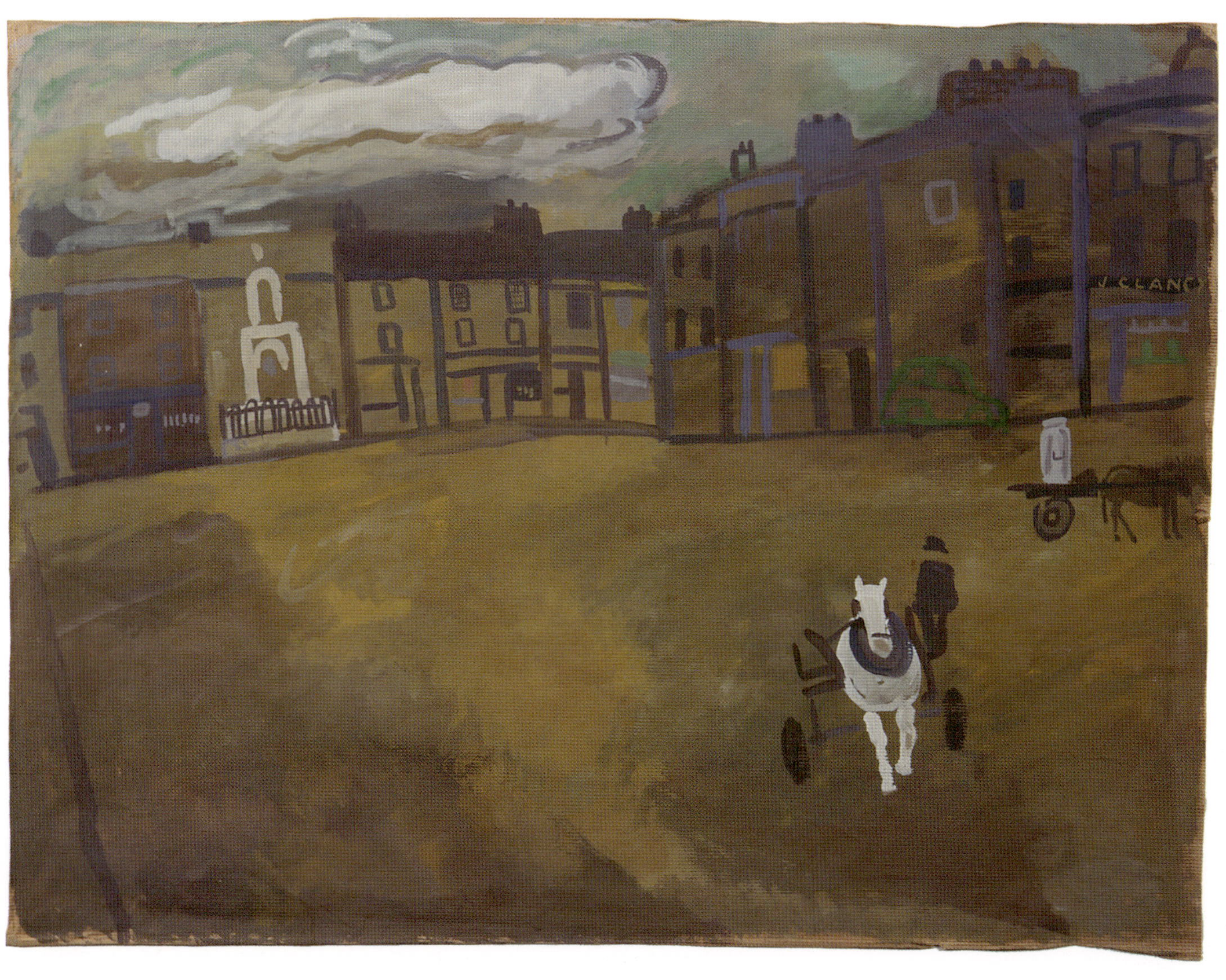

9. Wills Gold Cut Kilrush*

45 × 59 cm
Bequest Collection

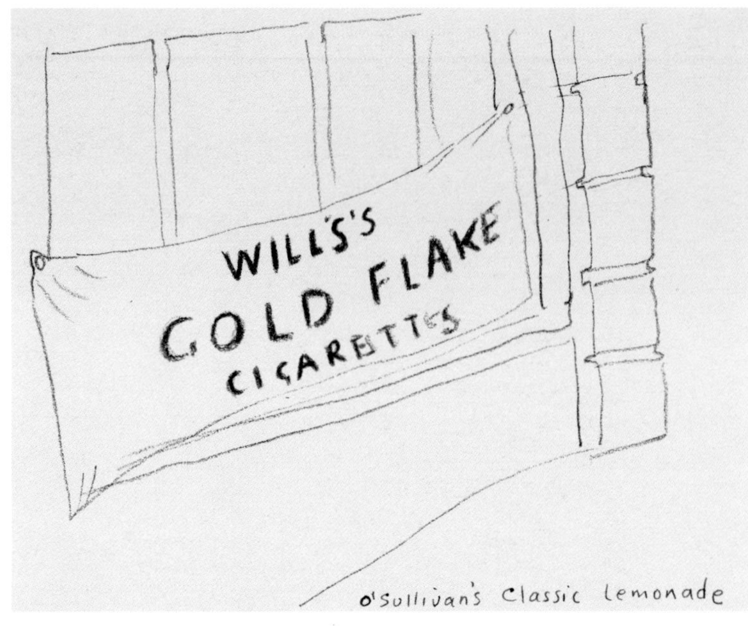

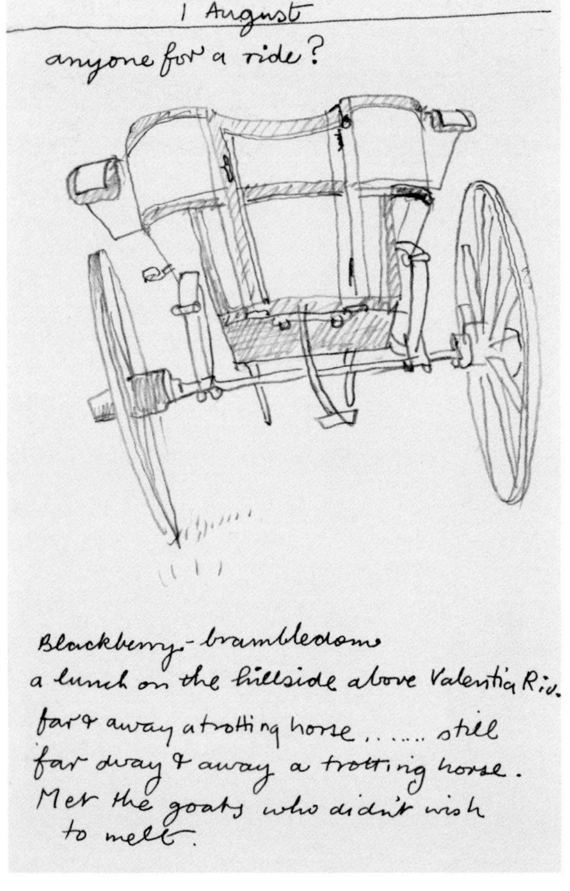

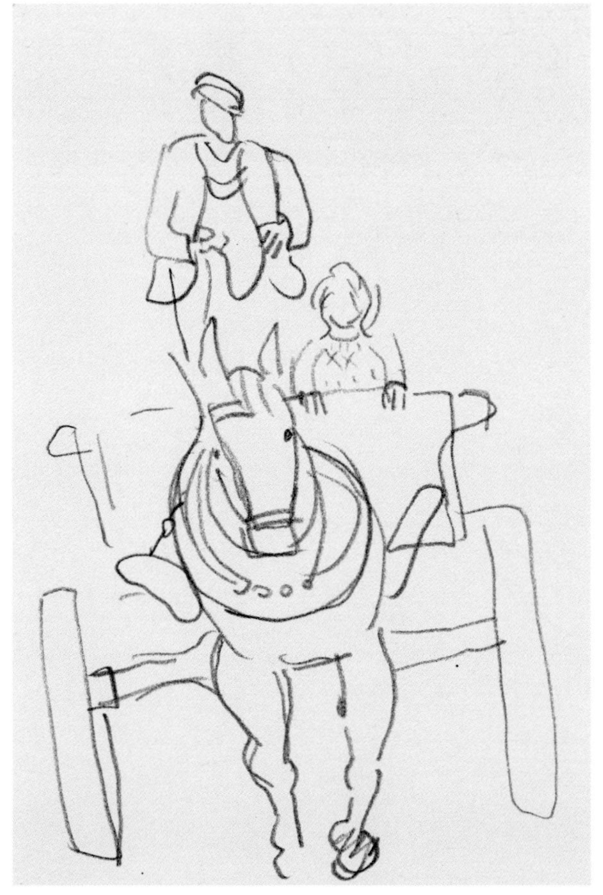

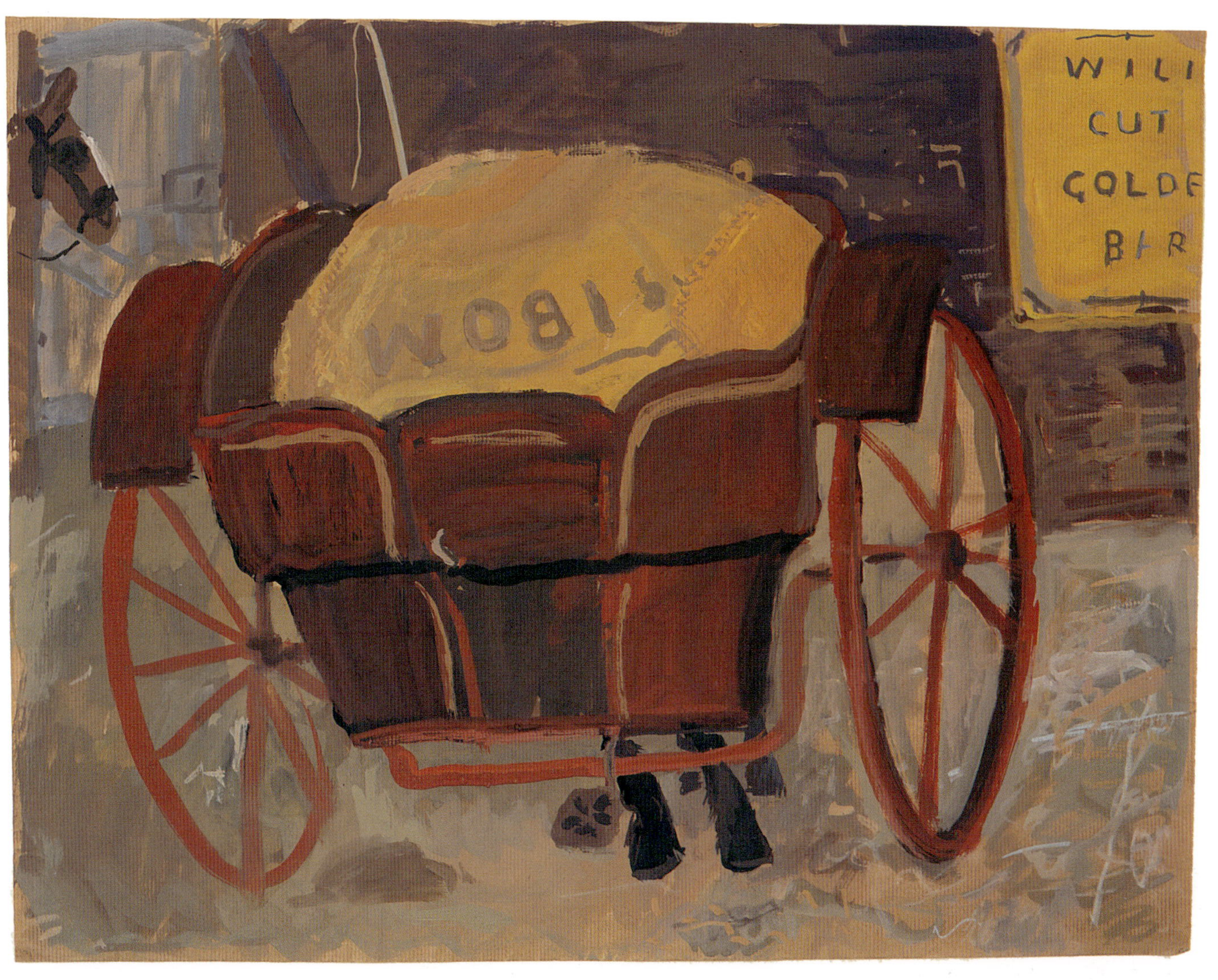
WILI
CUT
GOLDE
BAR

10. Cathedral at Sligo*

57 × 75.5 cm
Bequest Collection

A visit to Sligo in 1963 produced a powerfully atmospheric painting of the Roman Catholic Cathedral, a great louring building, charmingly set off by a bright tricolour. Patrick Gannon, a librarian in Sligo had this intriguing comment: 'The church in the drawing is the Roman Catholic Cathedral. In the painting he appears to have used the sketch to re-configure the elements of the building, enlarging some and getting rid of others entirely.'

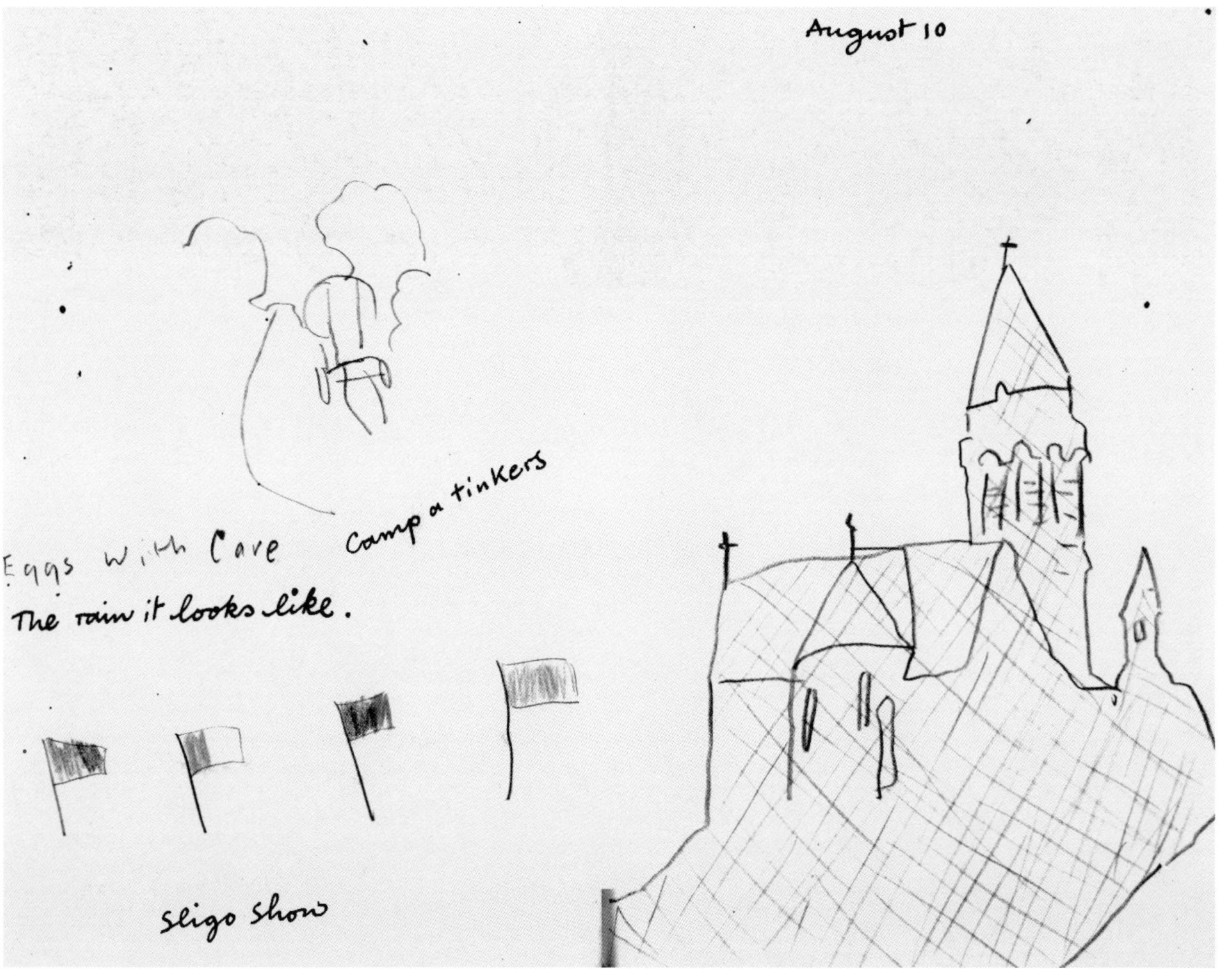

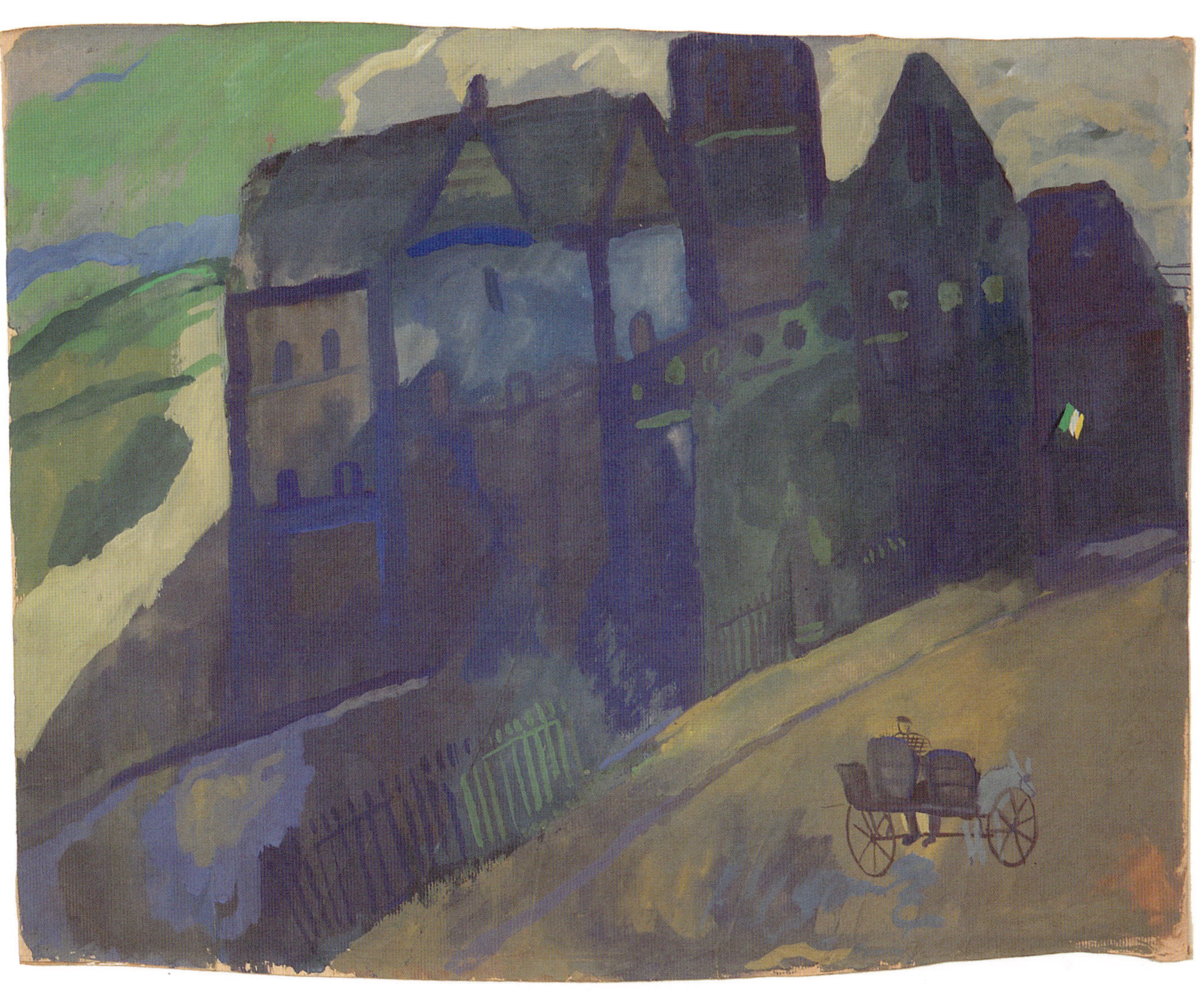

Humour

11. Ben Somewhen

102 ink drawings 18 × 14 cm

One of the most curious and appealing items in the bequest was a set of drawings entitled *Ben Somewhen*. The drawings were executed in thick black ink on small pieces of ivory coloured paper. They look as though they were done with a matchstick, a technique some people learn at primary school.

Though Ben's manner was always quiet and subdued and he was by no means given to telling jokes or funny stories, there is ample evidence that humour was extremely important to him and in many ways central to his work. This will become especially obvious when we look at the work of the middle period, where wit and humour are found in the imagery and Ben began giving his pictures titles which are extremely amusing and suggest a wish to emphasize a feeling of lightheartedness.

Ben's interest in humour embraced, on the one hand the highly sophisticated work of Saul Steinberg, the Romanian-born, Jewish artist who emigrated to America in 1940 and became celebrated for his covers on the *New Yorker* magazine, on the other the somewhat less elegant line of Peanuts cartoons, a vast number of which turned up in the bequest, cut out from newspapers and stuffed into a large envelope.

The drawings in *Ben Somewhen* are very much Ben Hartley at his most charming and original. There are one hundred and two drawings in the sequence. Many of the images are reworkings of earlier drawings or paintings. Captions are added which give a new slant to the prime source. The full title of the sequence is *Ben Somewhen Four Seasons and his Sundays*. Ben stuck the drawings down onto dark brown boards and, so it seems, exhibited them. Exactly when and where is unknown. There is a notice on one of the boards advertising offprints for sale at £3 3s 0d. The drawings are not laid out in any particular order, as the subtitle suggests they might be, but they do in fact touch on all the seasons of the year and include many allusions to churchgoing and the church calendar.

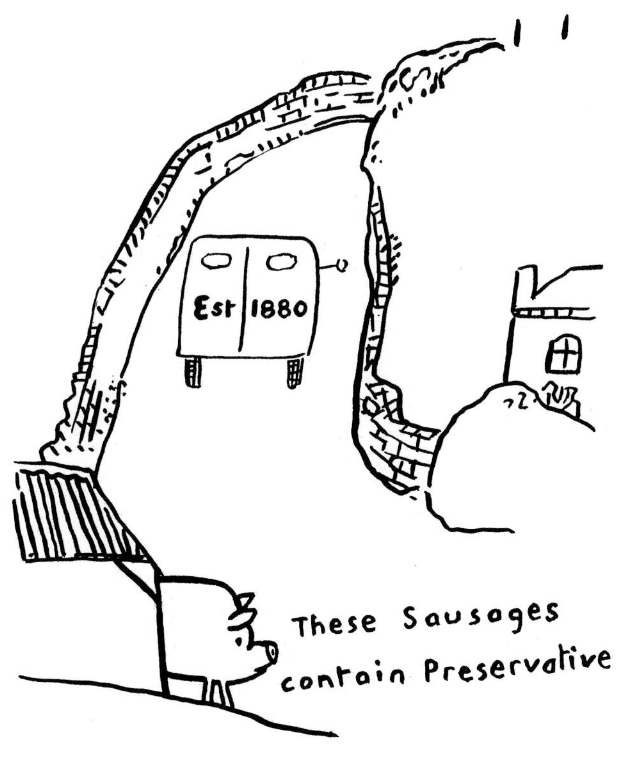
Est 1880
These Sausages
contain Preservative

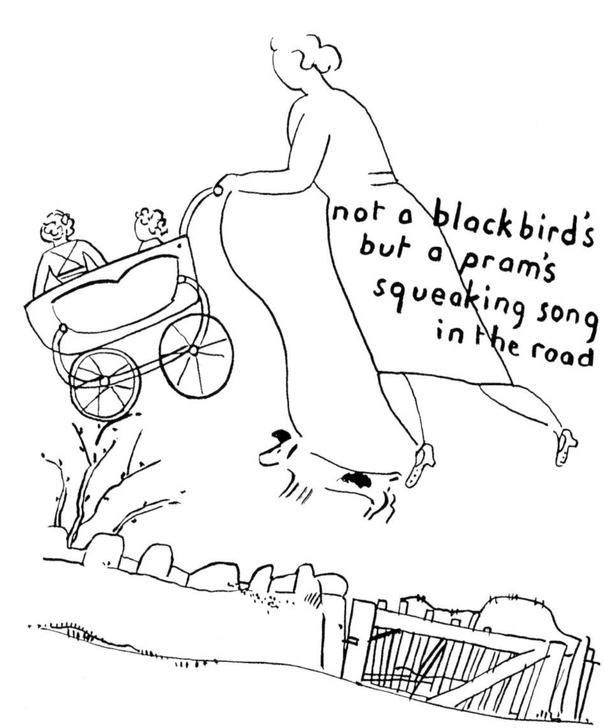
not a blackbird's
but a pram's
squeaking song
in the road

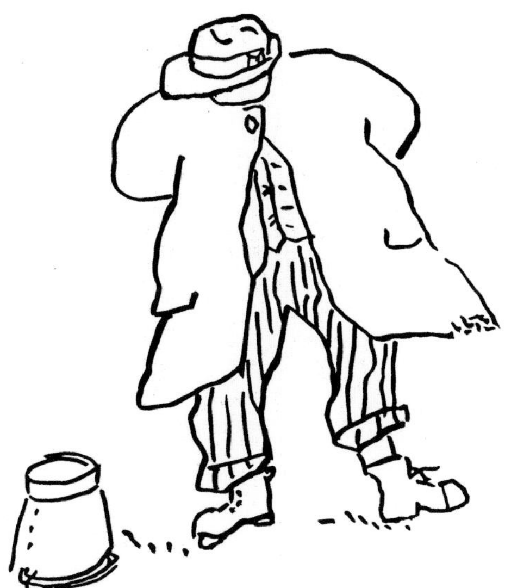
Robinson Scarecrow
Watching a slug go

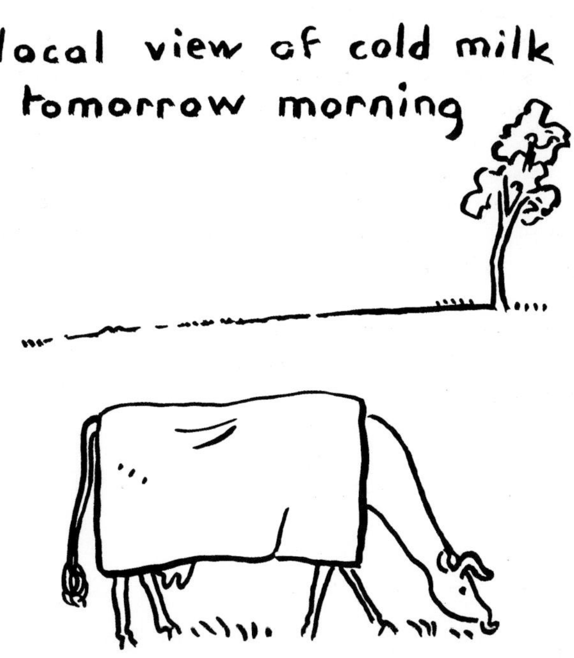
local view of cold milk
tomorrow morning

Middle Period

The work of this period is the work by which Ben Hartley first became known. It post-dates his conversion to Catholicism. The work that preceded was only discovered with the bequest. The appearance of lightheartedness and the overall mood of joyousness that it conveys greatly belies Ben Hartley's seriousness of mind and the range of his reading on art demonstrated in the numerous pages at the back of the notebooks, from the end of the 1960s through well on into the 1970s. They are filled with extracts from writing either by or about the work of the artists who most influenced him, Bonnard and Matisse especially. The new thinking these artists brought to painting was concerned above all with colour and the function of colour in determining space. Some extracts appear more than once, such as Matisse's famous dictum '*Plus c'est plat, plus c'est de l'art*', translated succinctly in the notebook for January/February 1976 as 'The more flat, the more art'. (Plate 12)

All the paintings, from now on through to the 1980s, proclaim Ben's adherence to the ideas propounded by these artists. He was powerfully influenced by the pronouncements of Matisse and Bonnard. However it was not only French artists who had such an effect on the developments which took place in this period. Leading French writers of that time also had an enormous and important effect on his thinking. This reading spans the period from Baudelaire and Rimbaud and on through to René Char among more recent poets. Among the novelists Proust and Colette came to be of central importance to him.

When in 1979 Ben agreed to put pen to paper himself to summarize the intellectual background to his work, he took as his starting point Baudelaire's celebrated remark '*le génie: l'enfance retrouvé à volonté*' (genius: childhood rediscovered at will). This profound insight was a source of inspiration for numerous artists from the early part of the last century, such as Picasso, Kandinsky and Klee, who became interested in child art. They began to collect it and even imitated or incorporated images found in children's work into their own work. Ben's approach was very different, something much more subjective; the intention being to give the viewer the feeling of the freshness of childhood experience, which in a sense has no necessary connection with the imagery of child art or its processes. His success in creating this feeling may well be the key to the delighted response his work so frequently evokes.

In Proust and Colette he found thoughts on the special nature of childhood experience. Where Proust evolved a theory of involuntary memory as a mechanism that brings back the experience of past sensations we believe are completely lost, Colette believed that in childhood we have direct access to sensation, whereas in adulthood, we have to 'recreate' sensation. Ben quotes her belief that children have a superior experience of the world, that they stand 'in immediate relation to colour and sensation', that they can 'present a universe directly felt and perceived', whereas all the adult artist can do is 'recreate the world', at one remove, as it were, from an earlier unverifiable experience. The quotation from Proust chosen by Ben for inclusion in his statement is especially illuminating: 'Every artist seems to have come from an unknown land which he has forgotten, a native land, different from that of any other artist.'

He also included in his statement another remarkably memorable comment, this time by Albert Camus: 'I know from my own experience that a man's life work is nothing but a long journey to find again by all the detours of art, the two or three powerful images upon which his whole being opened for the first time.' The idea can be made to apply to many artists. In Ben Hartley there is an apparent prodigal lavishness of imagery. Nevertheless, looking at the great mass of work he left, one becomes aware of his persistent return to certain subject matter. When he was interviewed by John Lane, author of the catalogue essay for a 1983 touring exhibition of his work, he told him that he found the process of painting absolute agony, which somehow suggests the notion of a constant mining of some deep seam of precious mineral that will never fully yield up its treasure. In short, for all his reticence, it is clear that Ben possessed a considerable degree of insight into his own creativity.

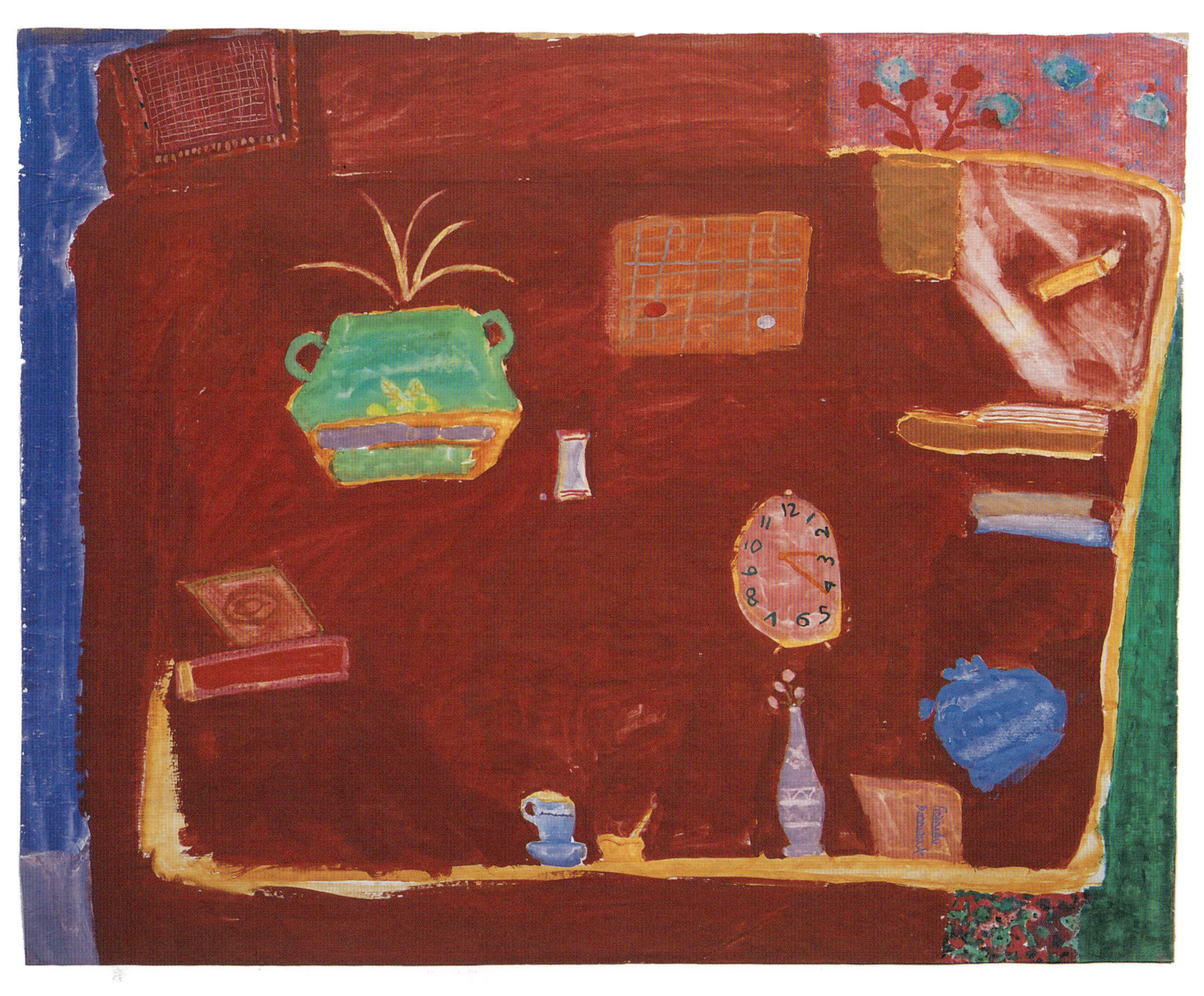

12. Plus c'est plat, plus c'est de l'art

57 × 76.5 cm
Bequest Collection

Memory and Domesticity

The role of memory comes through most potently when the paintings are concerned with interiors and the domestic world. If there is one key image, it is a picture called Pins and Doodles. We all remember a box of some kind or other from childhood days. Often the box, containing all kinds of small items, had experienced a change of use: here a cigar box which has been converted into a sewing box. The cigarmaker's name shown in the drawing has disappeared from the front of the box depicted, which is twice lifesize in the painting.

13. Pins and Doodles

57 × 74 cm
Bequest Collection

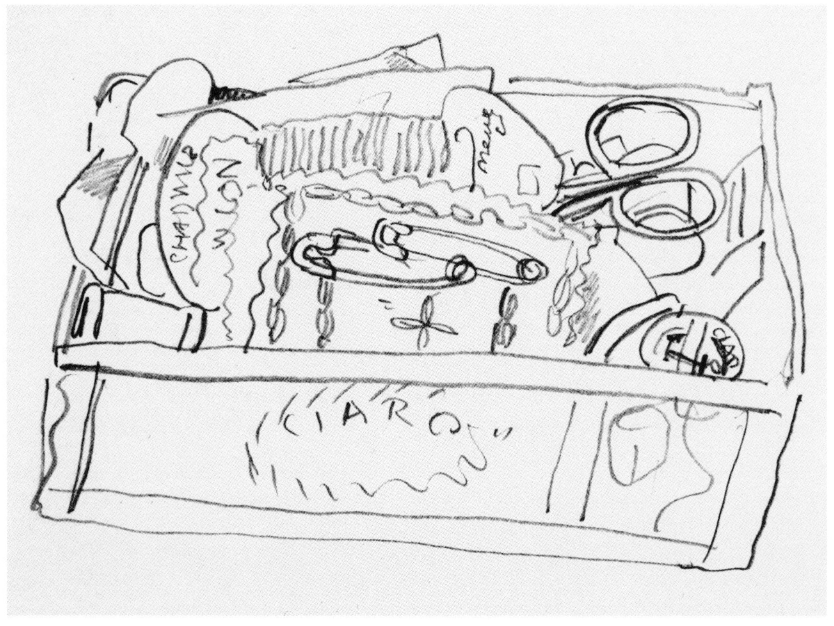

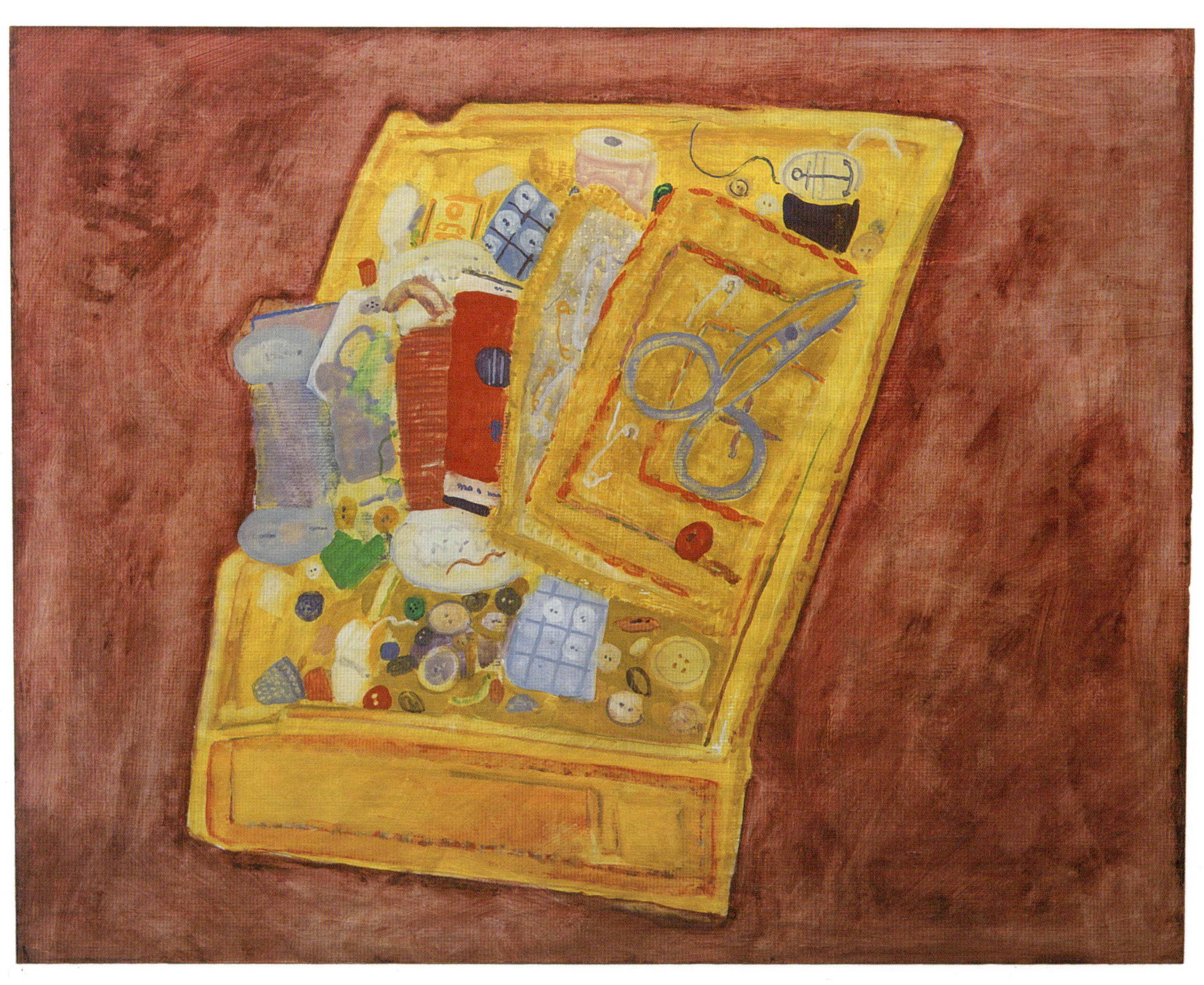

14. Home Economics

61 × 57 cm
Bequest Collection

Home Economics is an image where we feel the strong pull of domesticity. Though Ben's adult life was so marked by the loneliness of his bachelor existence, he was by no means a stranger to the feeling of family warmth, here conveyed by the multiplicity of motifs and the colour, the rich brown, orange and red, of this affecting work.

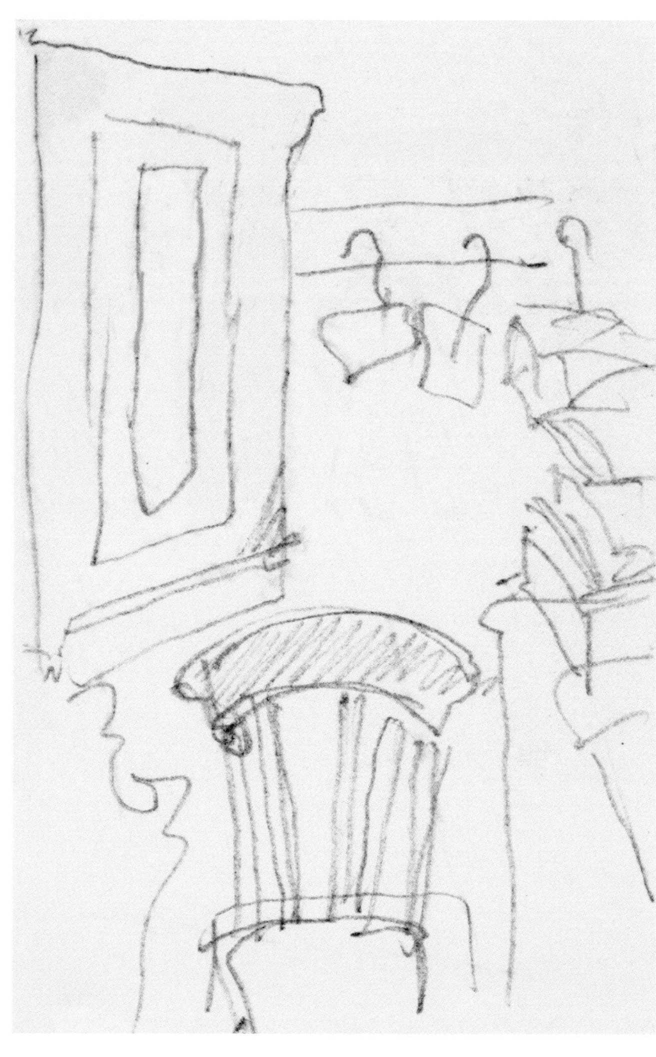

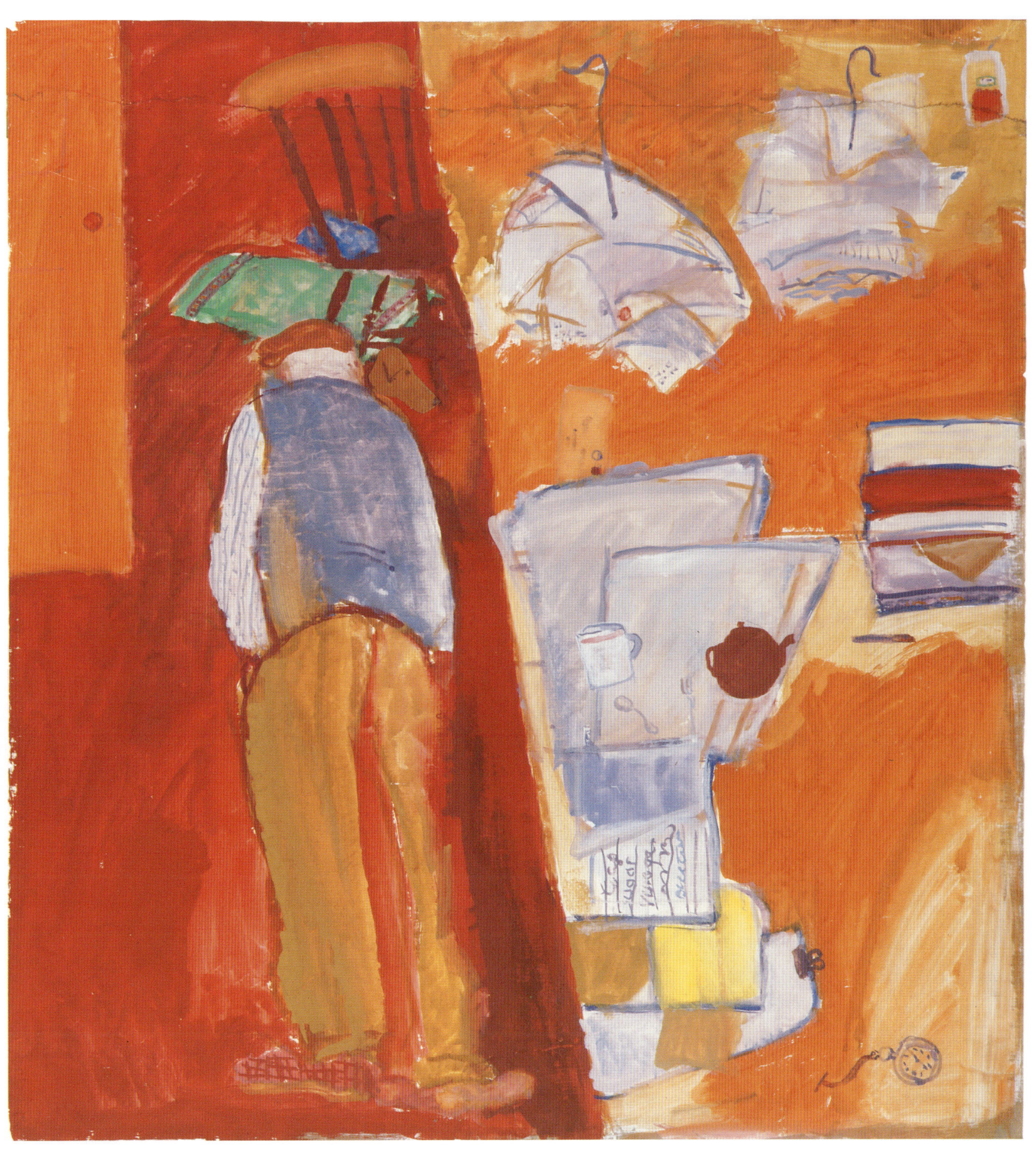
sugar
vinegar

15. Mrs. Ali Baba's Whist Drive Hat

74 × 57 cm
Private Collection

Mrs. Ali Baba's Whist Drive Hat began life as a drawing in a notebook appertaining to the three-month stay with the Church Art Community in 1965 at the lovely rectory of North Repps. The painting came some considerable time later. Whilst the comical dog remains in place, its black and white face sticking out from under the table, the drawing has been transformed from the very simple idea of 'Supper Coming?' to something more mysterious: the hat and note on the table suggestive of some private memory. It is one of the most Bonnard-like paintings in Ben Hartley. Though in Bonnard the dog is more likely to be somewhere towards the top of the table, the tilting of the table is very much a device found in his interiors.

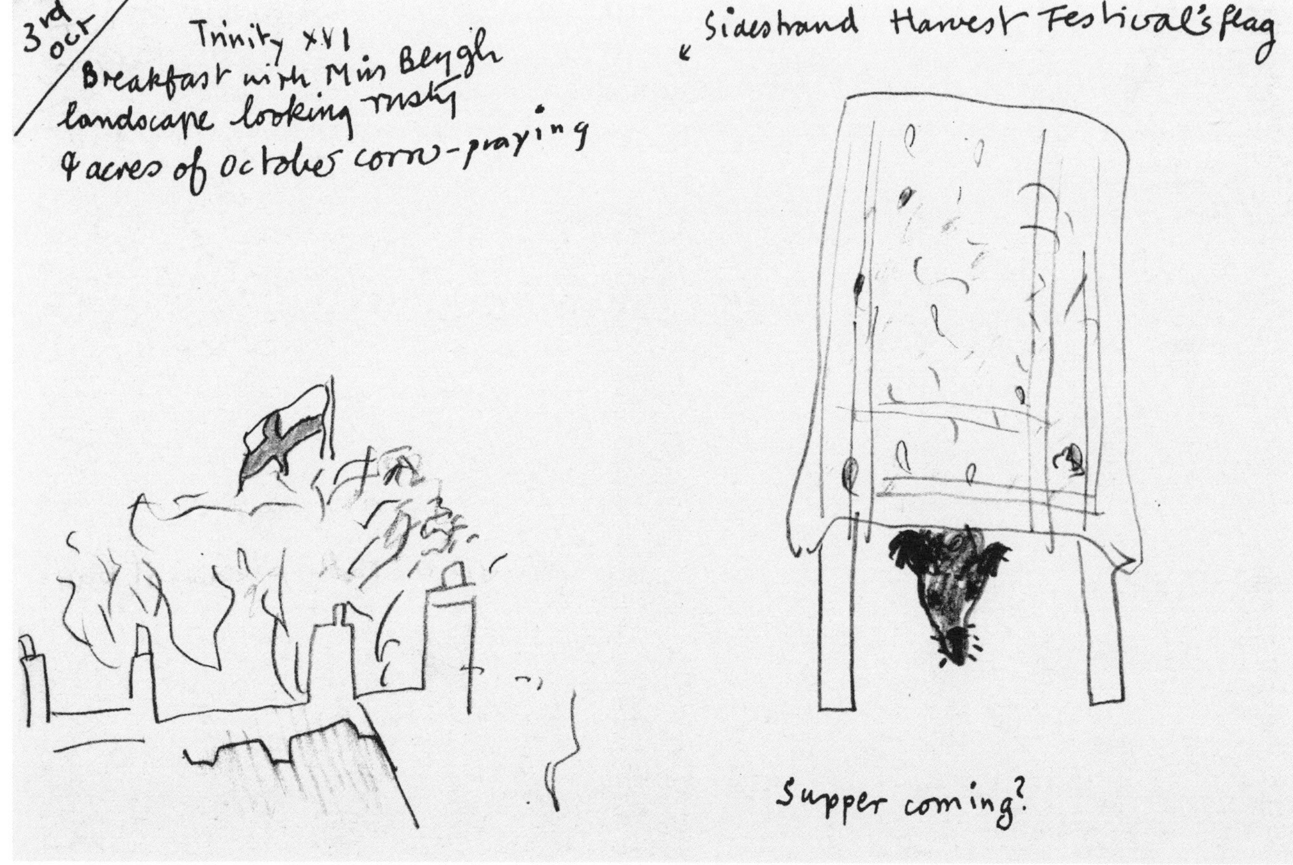

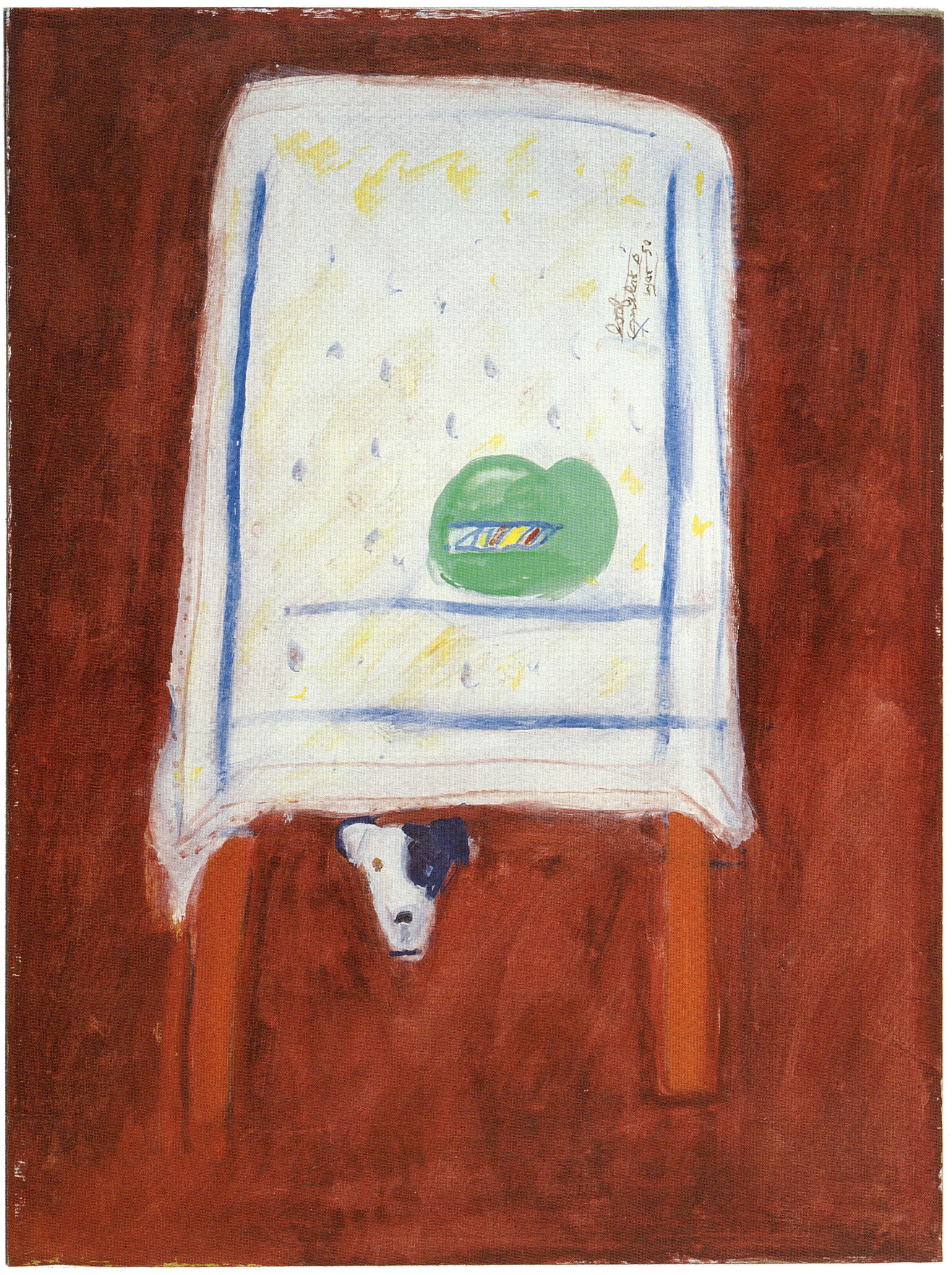

16. Mock Cream

45 × 63.5 cm
Reproduced by permission
of the Trustees, Dartington Hall

Mock Cream also recalls the two Norfolk notebooks of 1965, in particular a woman Ben entitled 'Lady Wymondham'. Again we are not far from Bonnard with a dachshund and a delicate teacup on the floor behind the armchair, the table suggested by just a few slashing marks. There are many drawings of cakes in the notebooks but not a drawing of a slice of sponge cake. We do however have a drawing of a sponge cake with a slice removed!

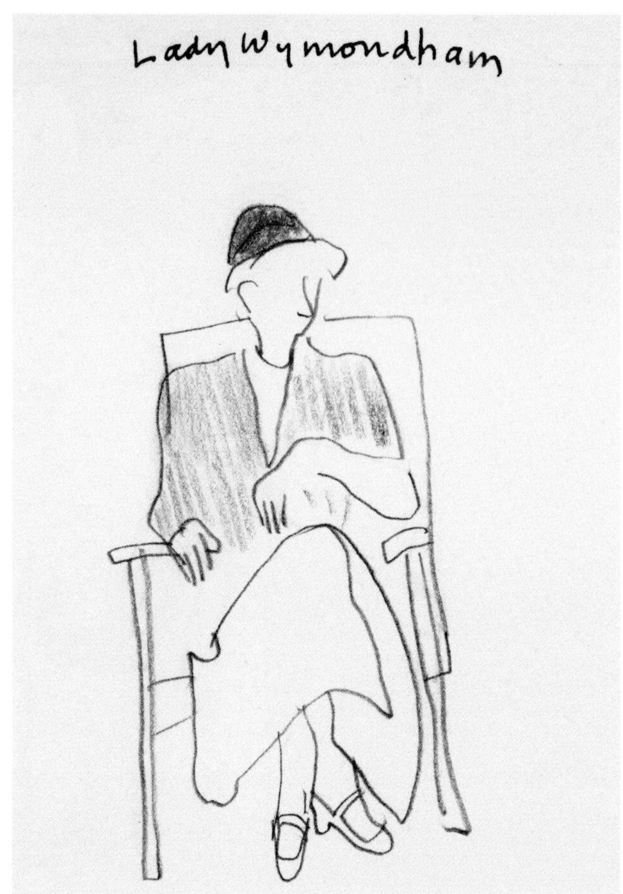

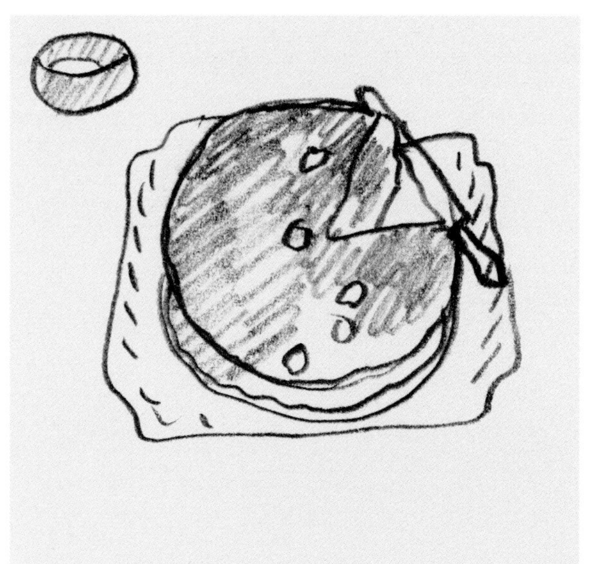

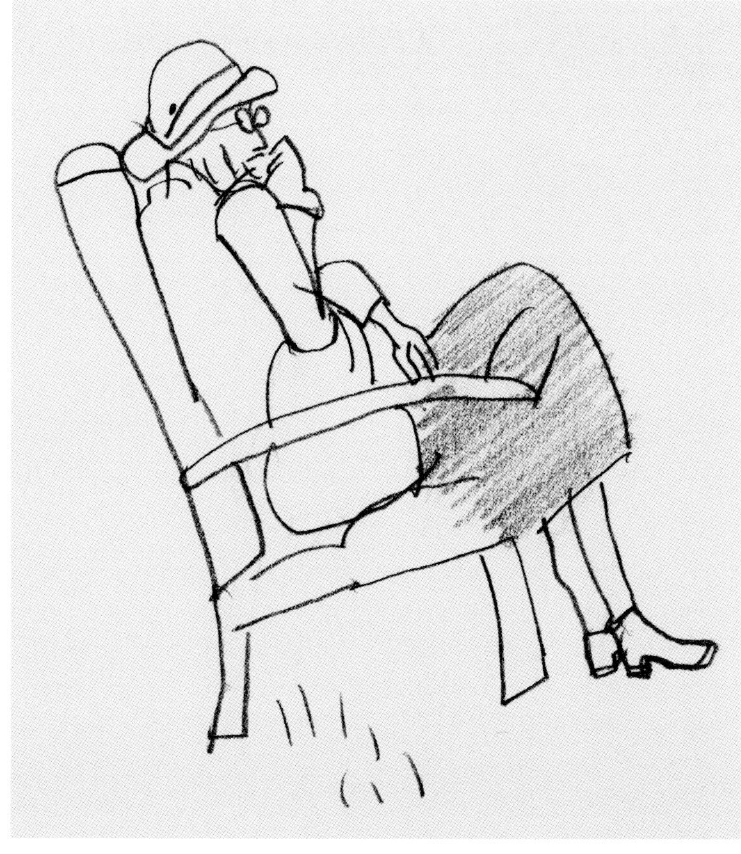

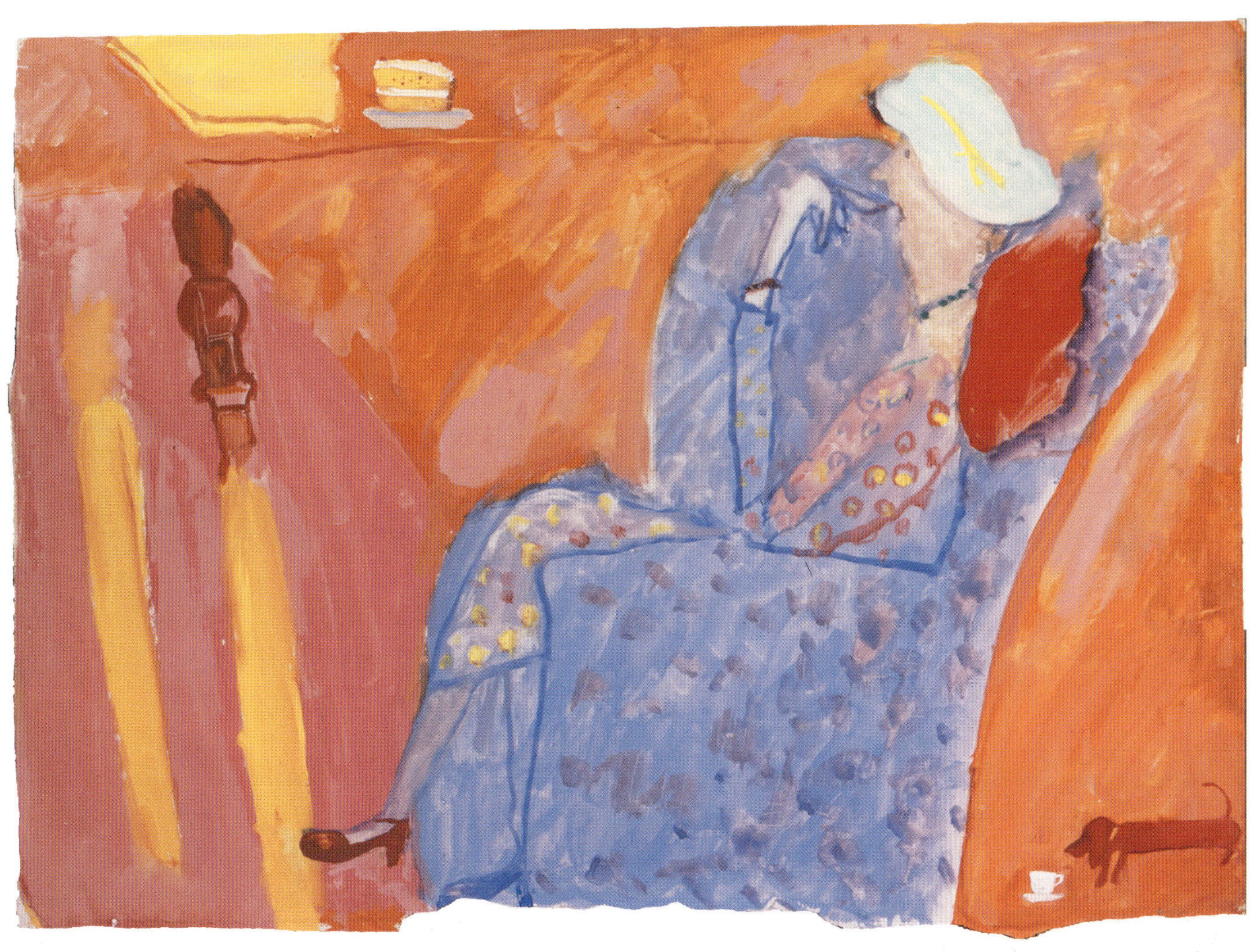

17. Kimono Cottage

Size and ownership not known

Though nearly all the motifs in this picture can be found somewhere in the notebooks, there is no hint as to who the old lady in an apron, wearing a hat, might be or where Kimono Cottage might be found. This picture was sold from the 1983 touring exhibition and its whereabouts are now unclear, maybe the United States. It was reproduced in 1990 as part of a series of greetings cards. With its combination of charm and exceptionally lovely colour (an instance of the way Ben could excel with the use of yellow), it rapidly sold out.

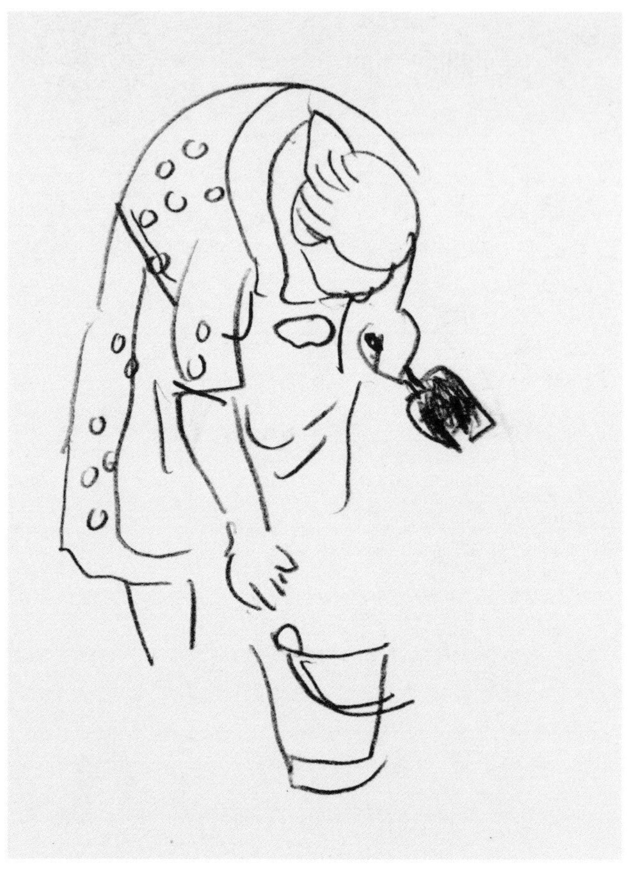

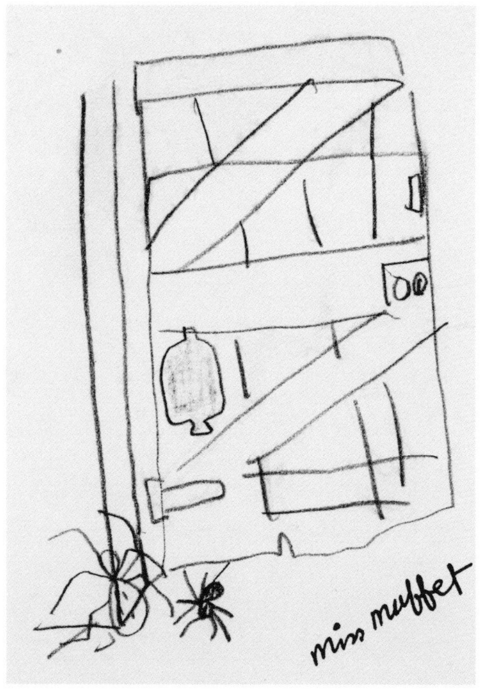

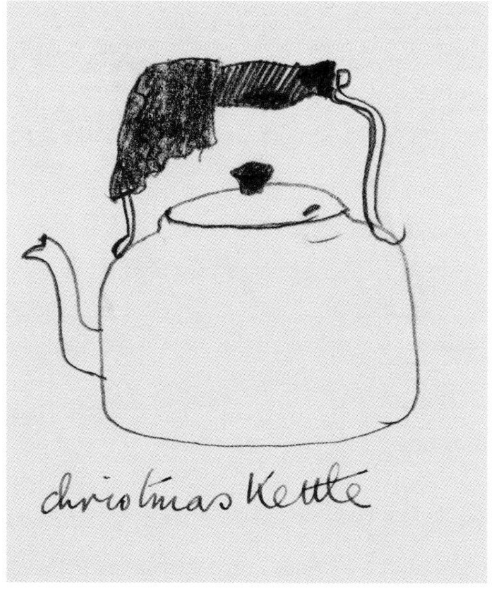

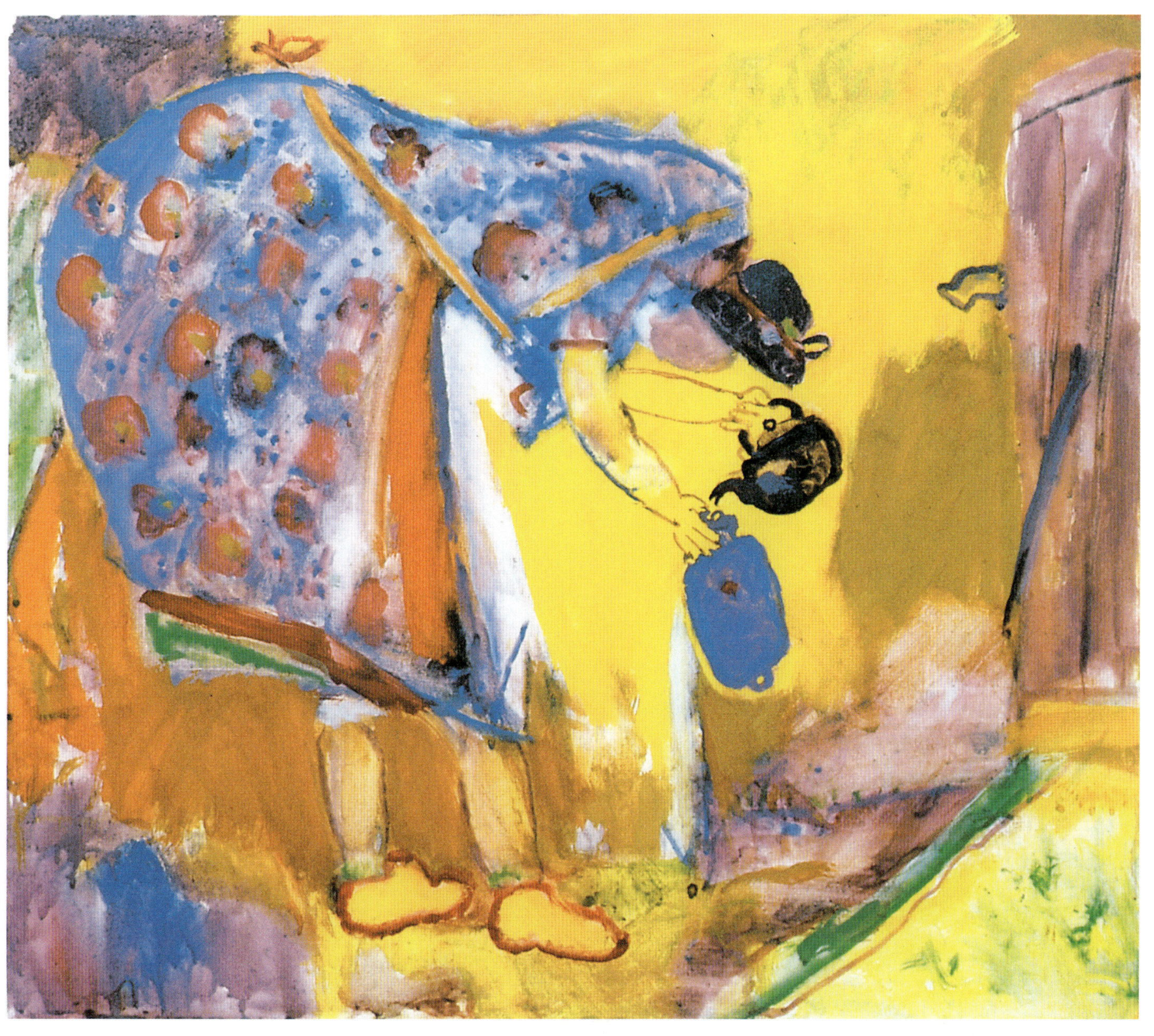

18. Cher Monsieur*

58 × 63 cm
Bequest Collection

Cher Monsieur has all the appearance of a domestic scene but is in fact a collection of motifs drawn from here and there in the notebooks. It is a particularly good example of the way Ben combined motifs, culling here and there from different notebooks. The 'principal player' in this exuberant painting is none other than the painter Monet, revealed by two motifs, the accompanying drawings of a pair of spectacles and a letter seen by Ben in a museum (unspecified).

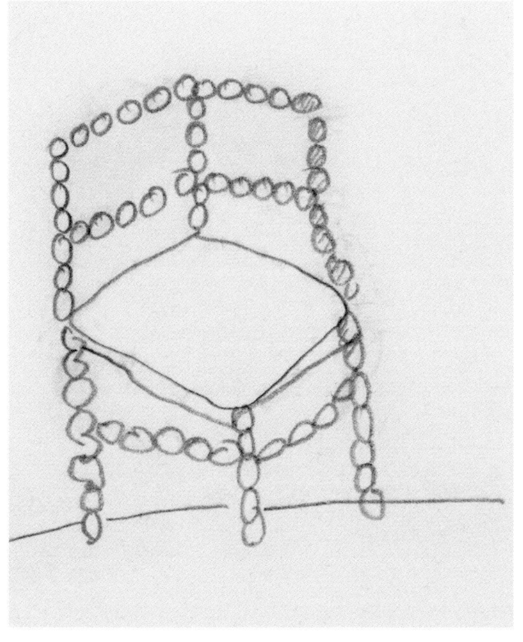

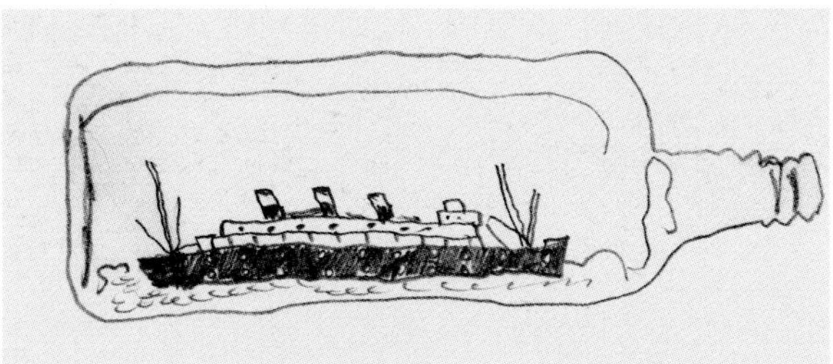

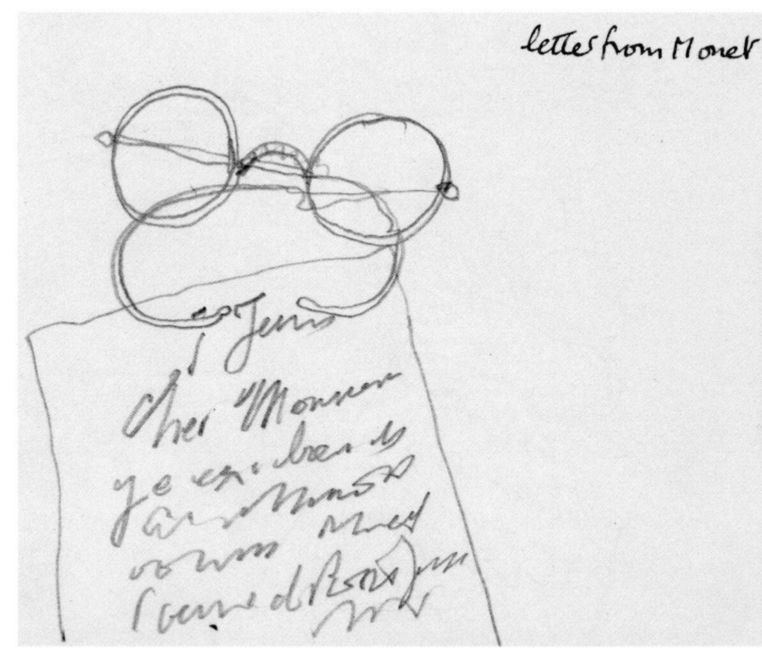

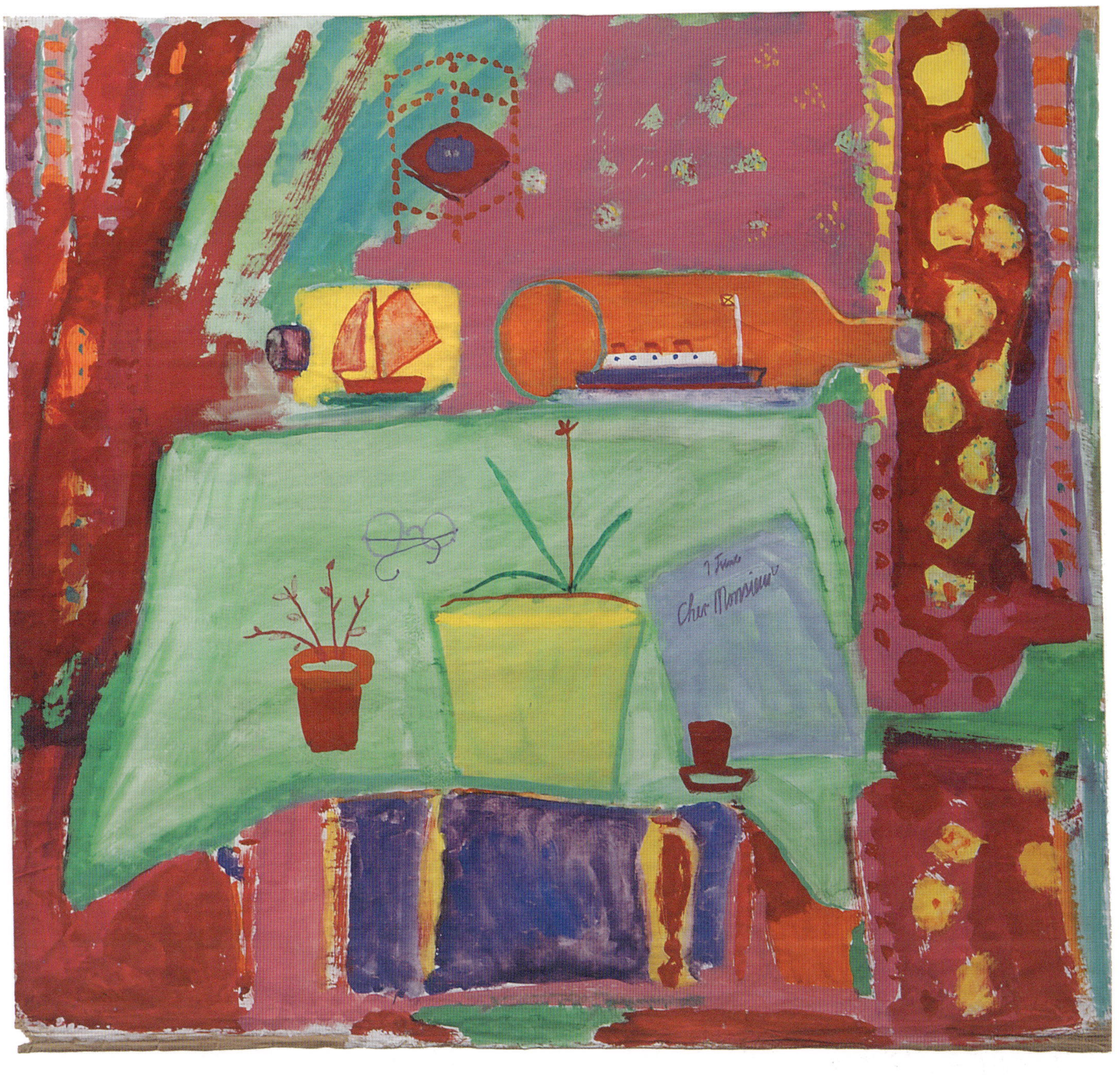
Cher Monsieur

19. Dickory Dock

61 × 51 cm
Bequest Collection

Timepieces appear quite frequently in the paintings. In *Home Economics* (plate 14) there is a pocket watch on a chain crawling along the bottom right hand corner like a tadpole. A feeling of the slow passing of time is something that comes through strongly in the notebooks, particularly so in the drawing of a clock in one of the Irish notebooks, immediately evoking the thought of Ben the lone traveller, watching time pass by in a pub. In the case of this particular picture we have a rare anecdote from Ben himself. It seems that he had a neighbour during his time at Ermington, a retired military gentleman, who kept an owl living in his house. This drawing is one of a sequence of drawings with the owl at various angles in relation to the clock. When Ben came to make the painting, he replaced the owl with the proverbial mouse that ran up the clock.

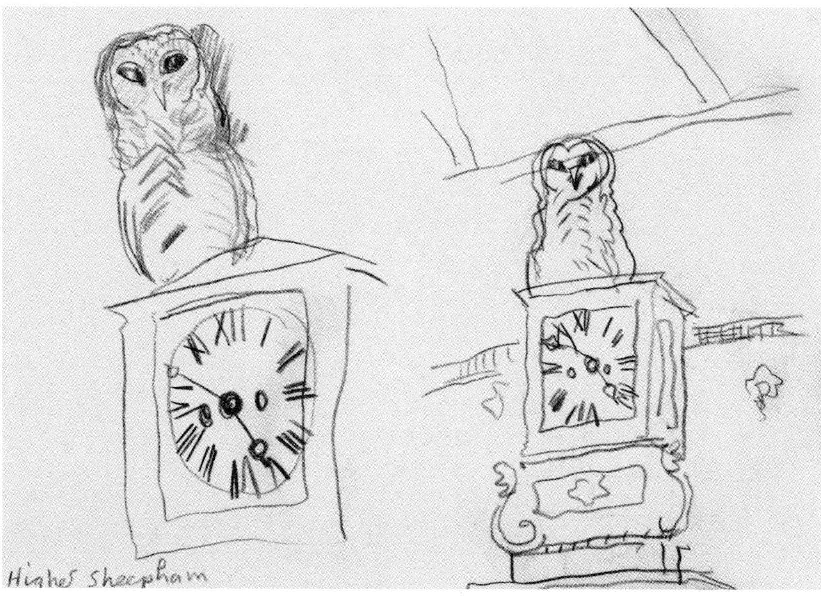

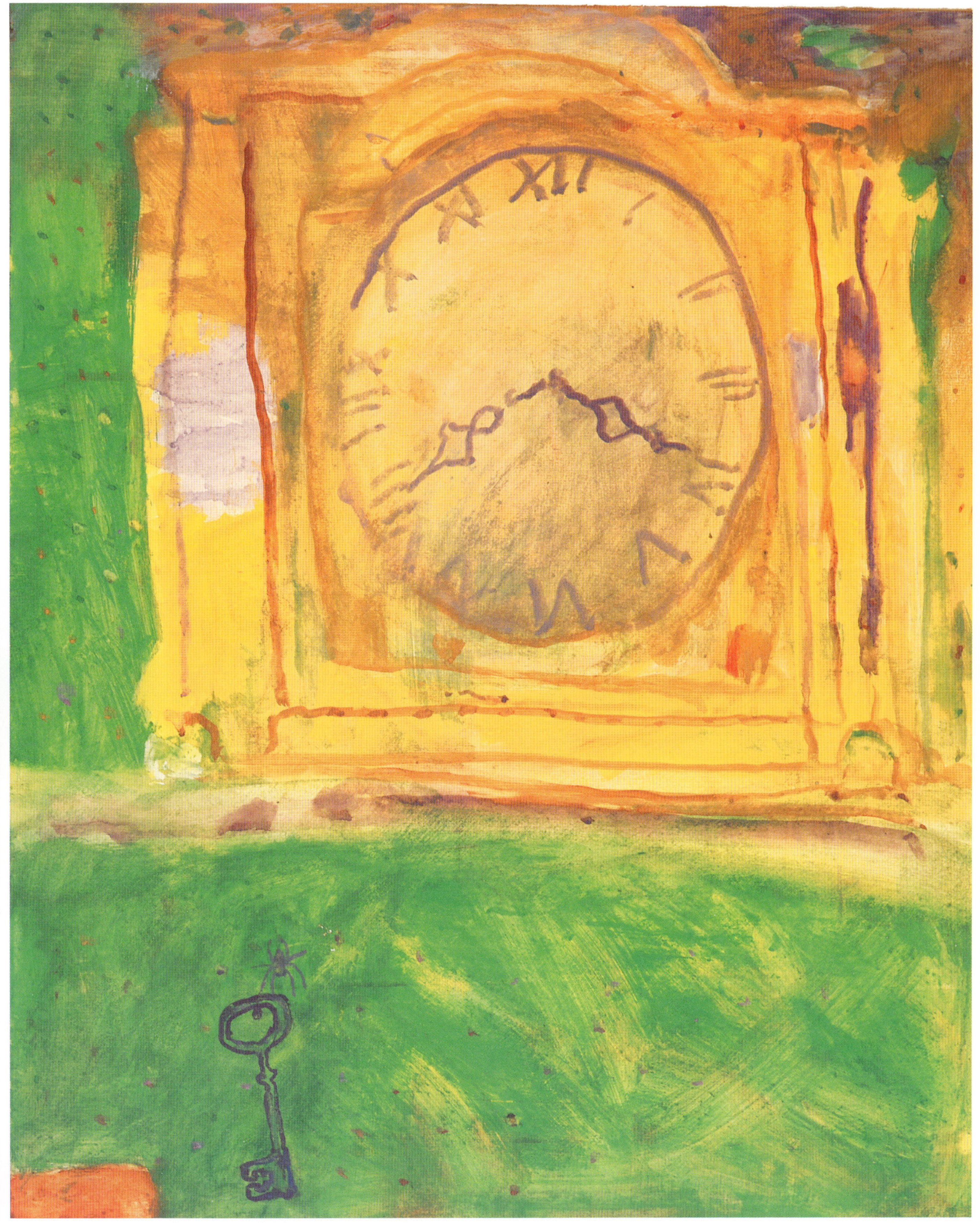

20. Rose Cottage, Vase of Flowers*

54 × 76 cm
Bequest Collection

In 1963, soon after he moved to Ermington, Ben Hartley began drawing Rose Cottage in Langbrook, a nearby hamlet. He got to know the people there and did some drawing in the house, including numerous drawings of a vase of flowers standing on a green raffia mat, as well as a view through a window. In the years following his conversion to Roman Catholicism in 1968, when he begins to concentrate in his notebooks on ideas and theories in modern art, he reaches a climactic moment in two notebooks of May 1975. We find numerous pages of writing copied out from books on Bonnard and Matisse. In addition to the usual writing about the importance of colour, we find Matisse quoted as developing a concept of 'spiritual space'. A writer on Bonnard is quoted, referring to 'his intense lavishness...the exploration of the intensity of each component...exaltation rather than opposition.' The drawing shown here marks the climactic moment when Ben equates the vase of flowers with the concept of unity at the heart of Christian belief and doctrine.

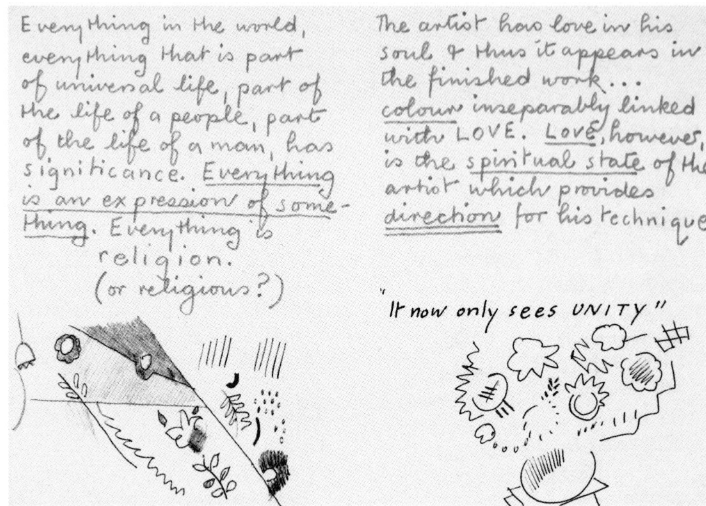

It is interesting to note that, in 1990, his friend Susan Bone sent him a postcard of a detail from Duccio's *Annunciation* in the National Gallery, showing the traditional symbolic vase of lilies, placed on a step, between the Virgin and the Archangel. He wrote back immediately saying how much he had always admired this painting. Ben Hartley's *Rose Cottage* painting is invested with a religious significance, not only in the simple vase of flowers, crudely drawn, as in the Duccio, but also through the pure beauty and mysteriousness of the colour and brushwork of the curtain and view of the garden which takes up the left-hand side of this painting.

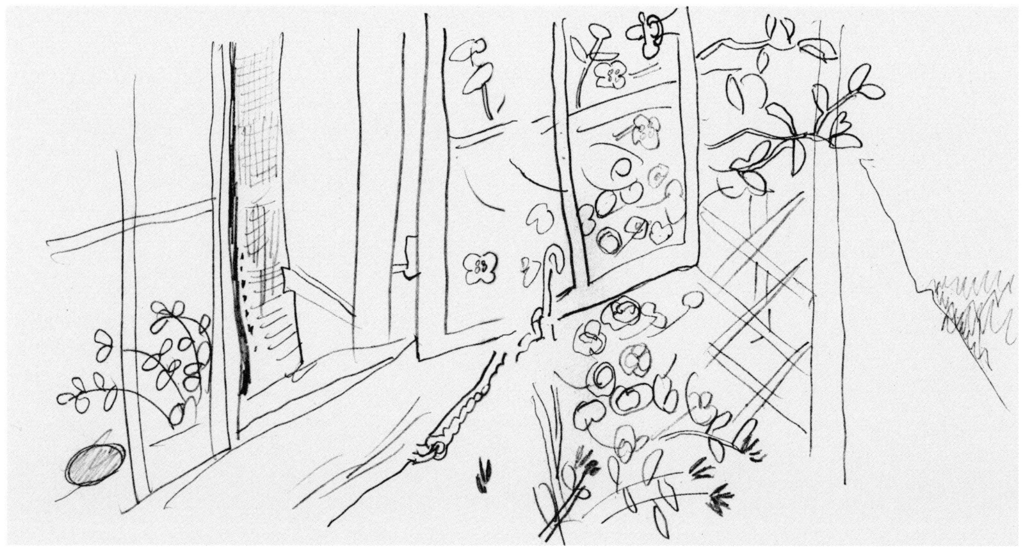

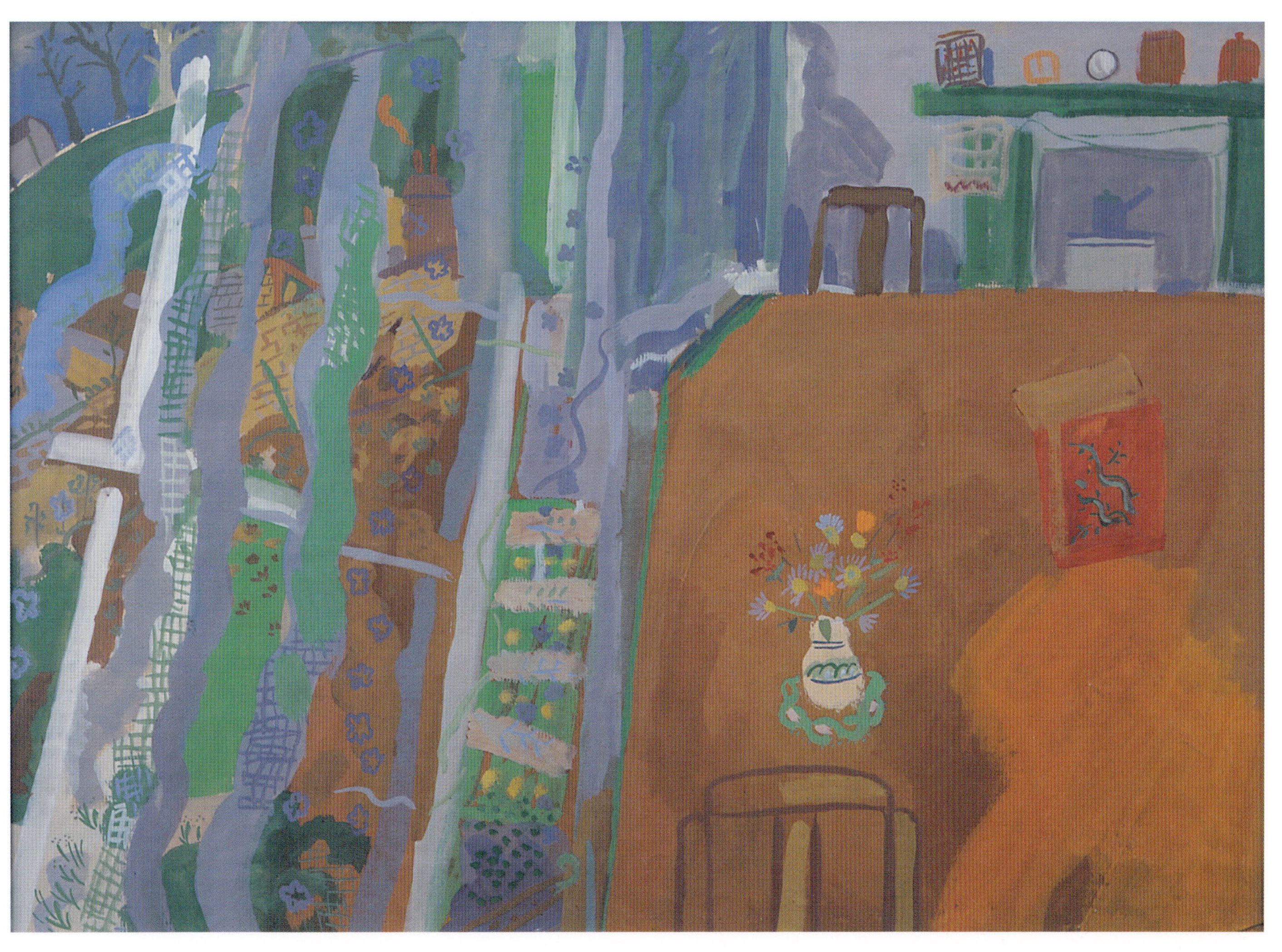

Animals, Birds, Insects

For people familiar with the work of Ben Hartley, especially the work shown in the earlier exhibitions, two things come to mind: bright, lovely colour and lots of animals: domestic pets (mostly cats and dogs) and farm animals (mainly hens, goats, ducks, geese, guinea fowl, pigs and cows). The notebooks often contain long series of drawings of the same animal. There is a particularly fine sequence of drawings of sheepshearing, another of horses being shoed. Sometimes the presence of the animals is quite unobtrusive; you have to look twice to see the brown dog in Home Economics (plate 14). However in most cases the animal is the central feature of the painting to which can then be added other motifs which give new dimensions to the overall work.

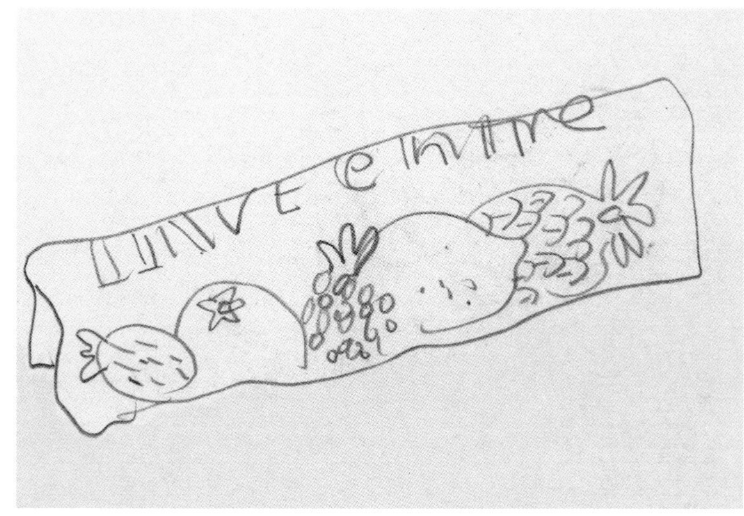

21. Dogdays

51 × 65 cm
Private Collection

Dogdays probably qualifies as Ben Hartley's most popular picture. Some people find the dog rather terrifying, but generally the gaping red mouth, the lolling tongue, the flash of white breast, the deep blue of his coat and the one great eye staring at a packet of Rowntrees Fruit Pastilles, which he might or might not grab, and the tiny toy yacht floating along above make a winning combination.

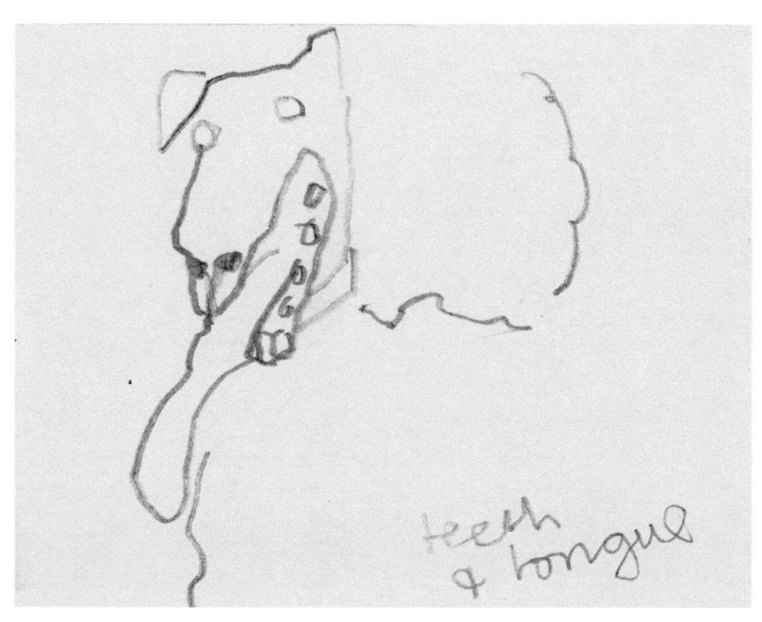

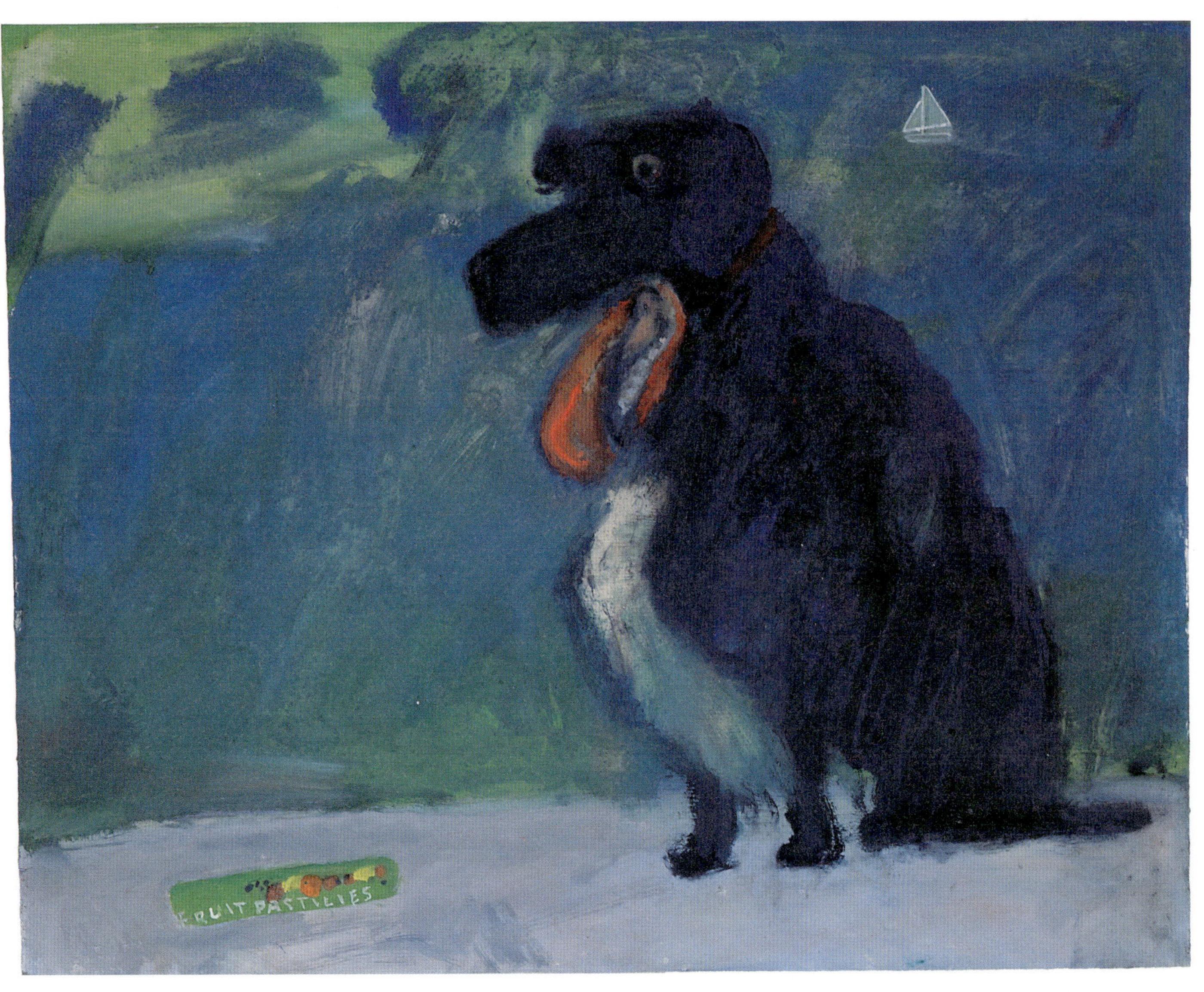
FRUIT PASTILLES

22. Cock-a-Dandy

58 × 72 cm
Private Collection

Gates, either large five-bar gates or small garden gates, are one of the most common motifs to appear in Ben Hartley's imagery. Five-bar gates, wooden or metal, with birds perched on top are one of the most frequently recurring subjects for paintings. An overall colour, here a glorious array of golden yellows, sets the keynote of the picture, a background to the characterful birds, often, as in this case, a guinea fowl.

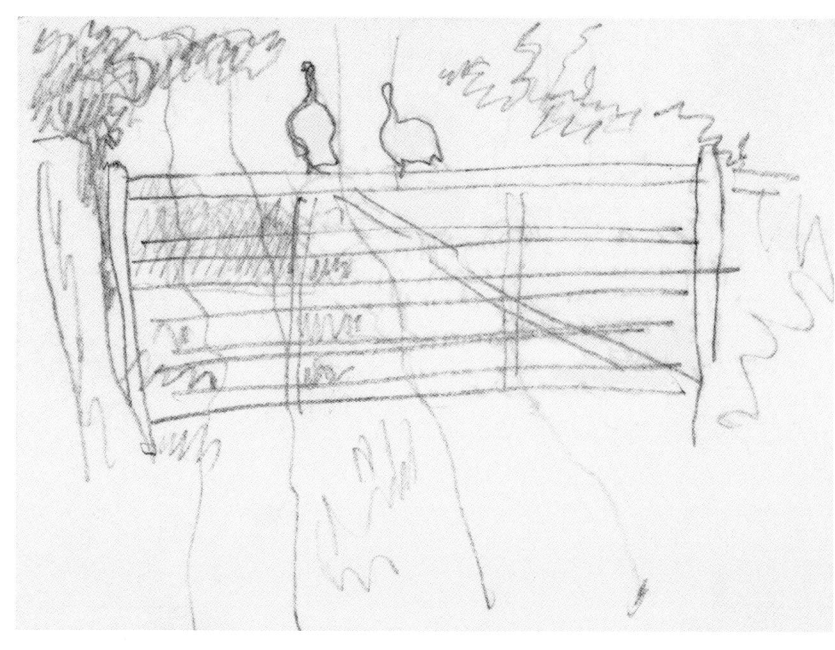

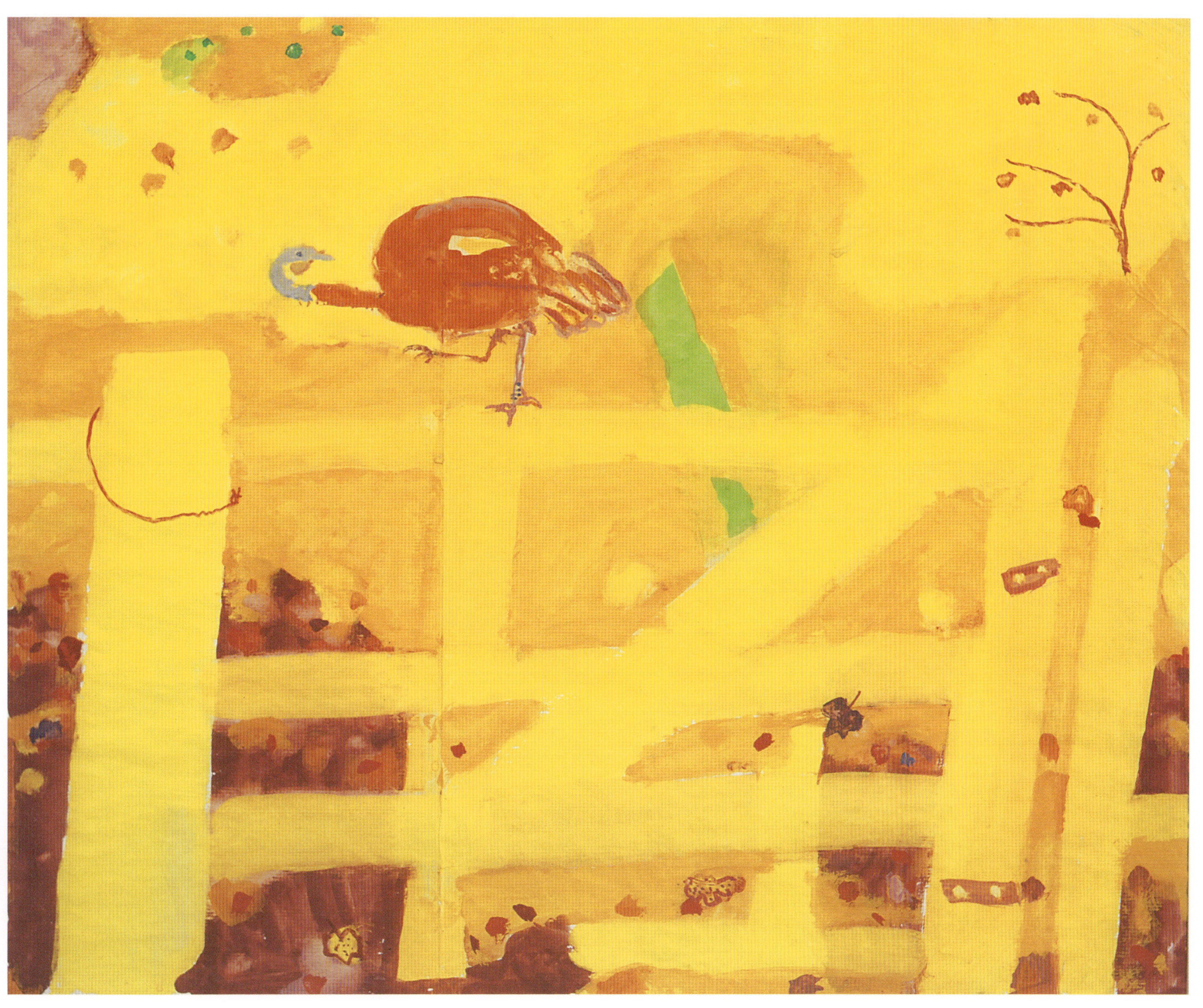

23. Cream Tea

55 × 48 cm
Private Collection

A further example of a fine work with charming motifs and deceptive strength. A bold cat, a dribble of cream, a dainty cup and saucer are the obvious subject matter. For all the charm of the motifs the great impact of this painting comes from the beautiful green and rust which could make a colour field painting. Even the white dribble of milk would have an abstract function.

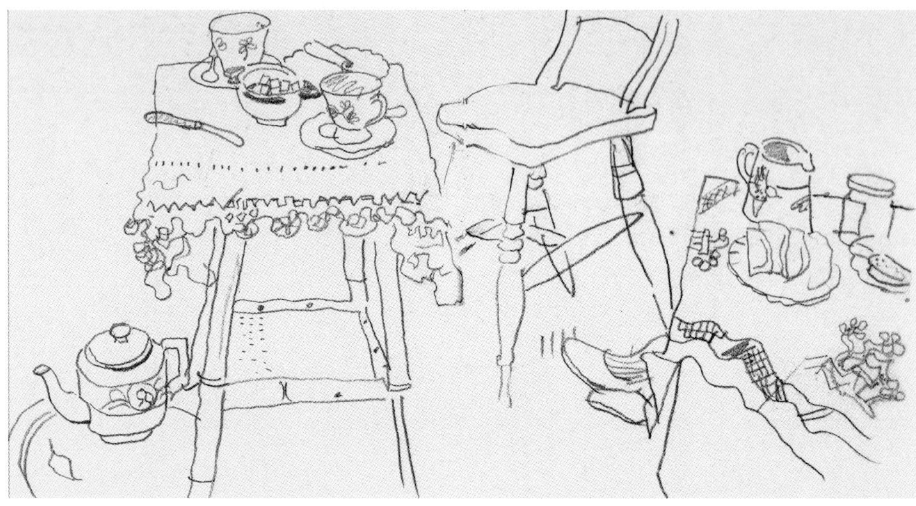

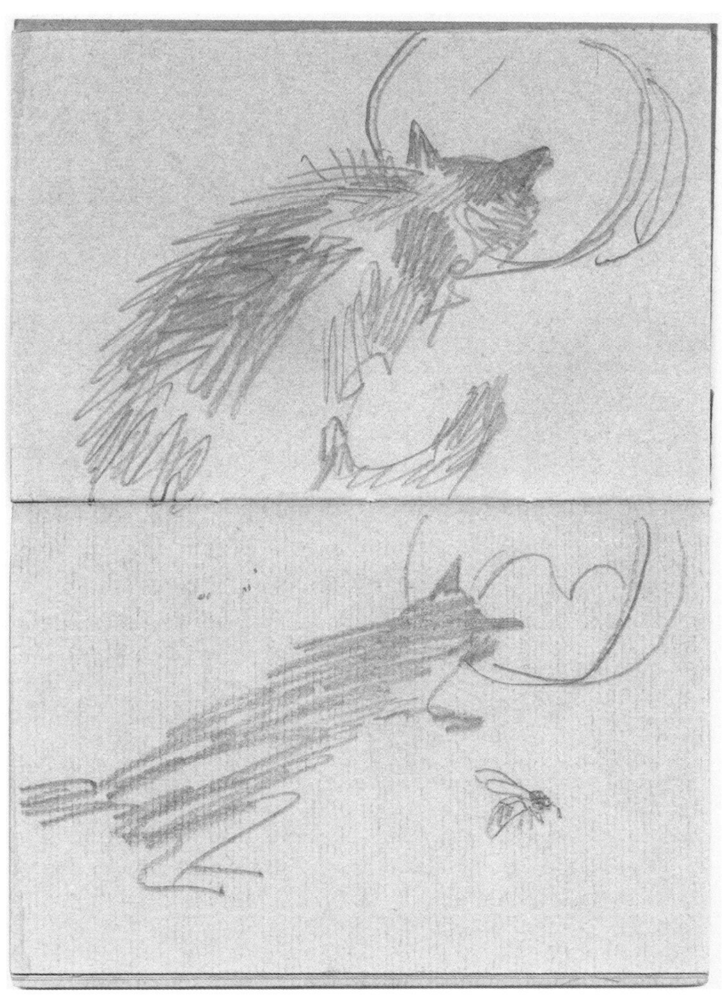

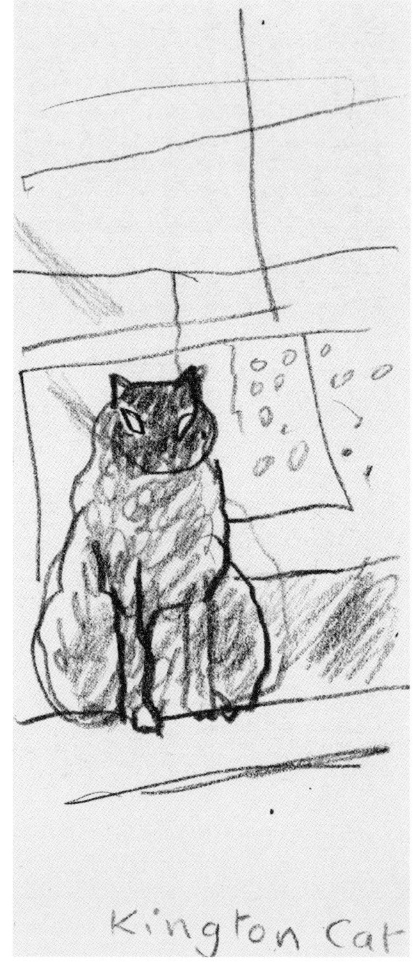

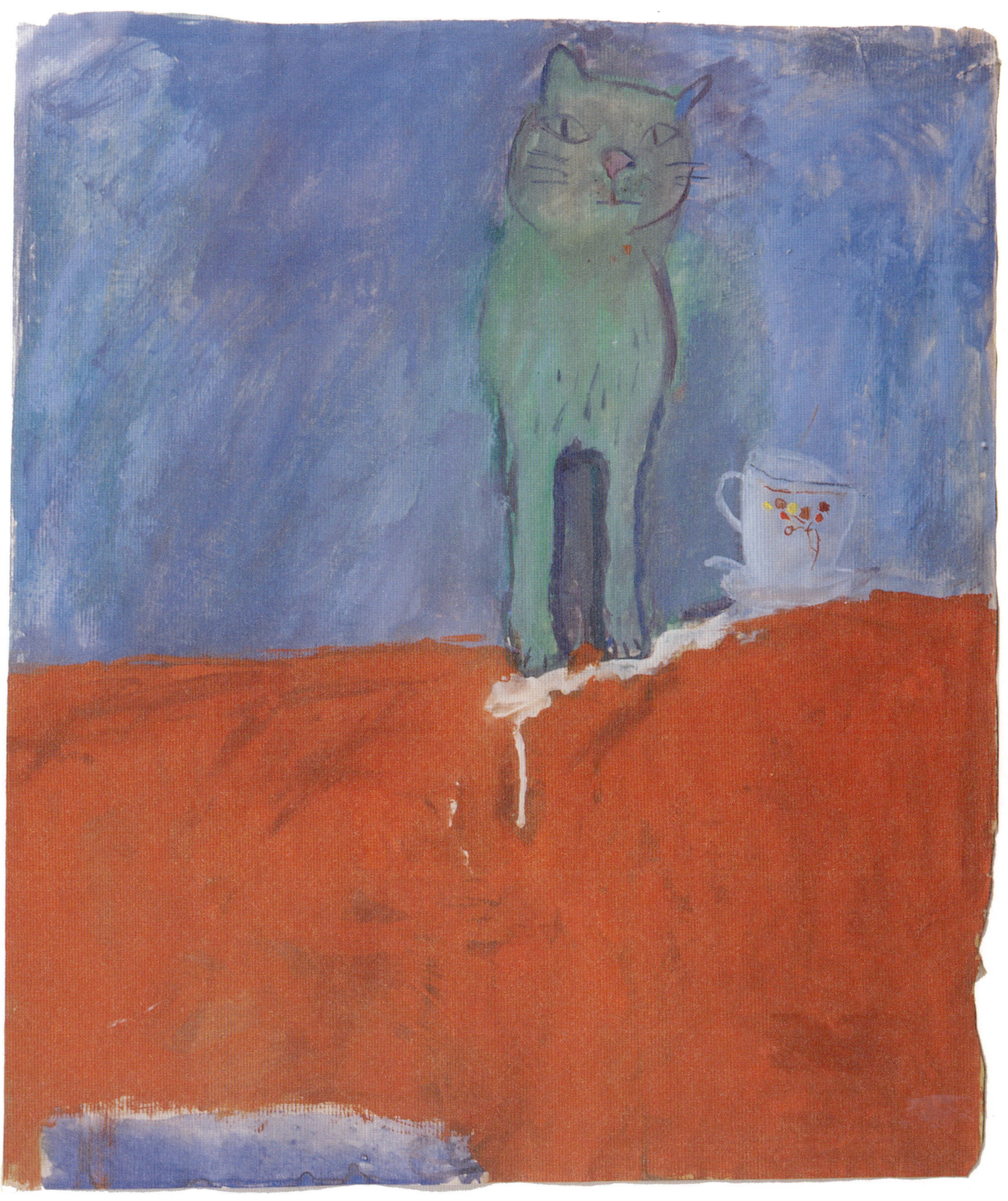

24. Dumps

53 × 64 cm
Bequest Collection

This picture was painted on a badly creased piece of brown paper, which does not prevent it from being the most deeply touching of all the numerous dogs who appear in many of the paintings. Though there are a scores of drawings of many different breeds of dog in the notebooks, there is no mention of a dog with the name of Dumps. If its identity cannot be traced, all the same this portrait is too deeply felt to be a product of the imagination. The expressive quality of this work lies in the affecting sadness and gentleness of the dog with its ruffled, light blonde coat, the hint of a wound at the top of the shoulder, the thin red line of a lead, the tail curled between the legs. The ultimate strength of the work lies in the simple but arresting composition, the green setting, the bands of indeterminate colour at the bottom and to the right and Ben's masterstroke in raising the back legs and placing them on a step.

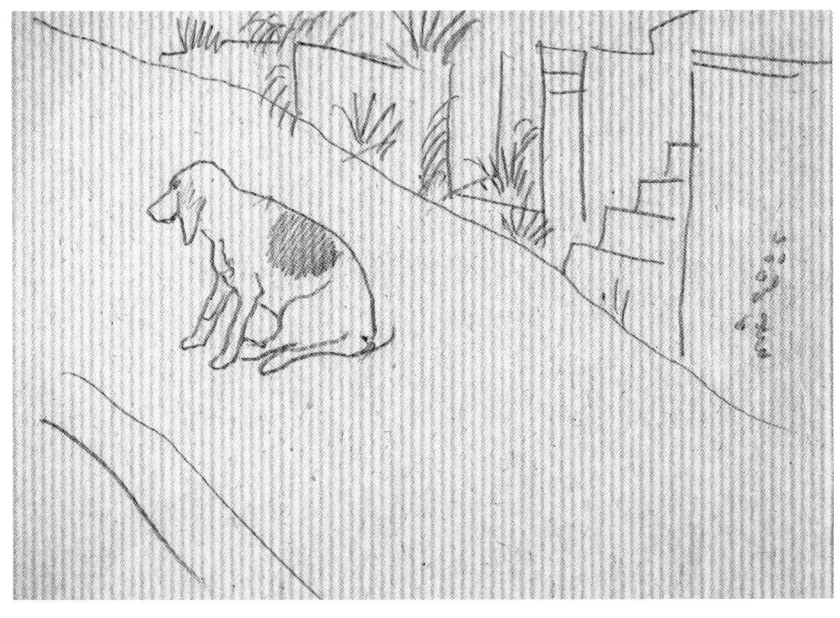

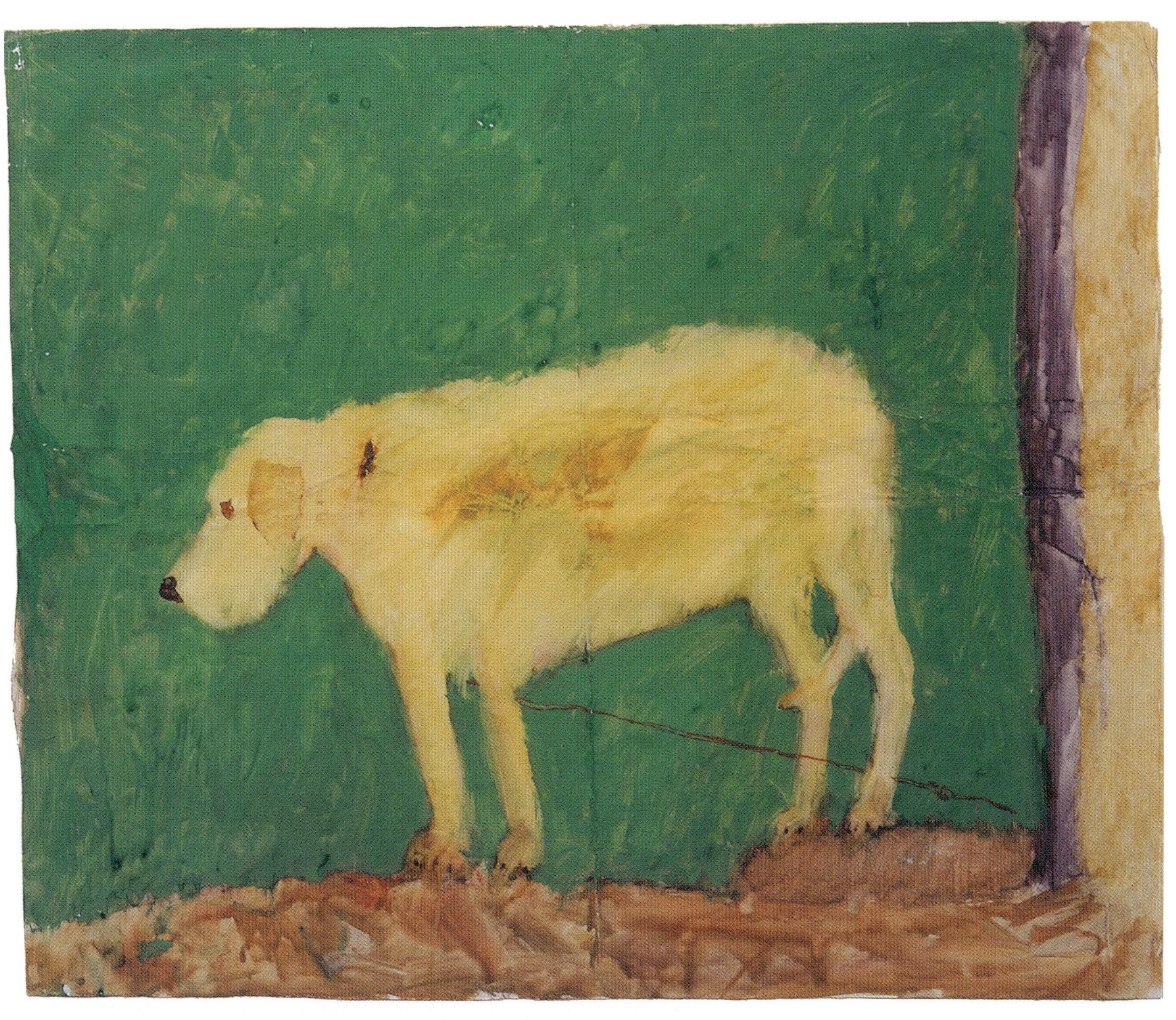

25. Jacob's Ram

48 × 61 cm
Private Collection

This picture represents one of Ben's finest animal depictions, a simple translation from an excellent drawing of this handsome breed of sheep, notable for the large dark patches on its coat. The portrayal of the ram is paired with one of the most persistent of the motifs from farm life, namely a zinc tub full of bits of kitchen waste.

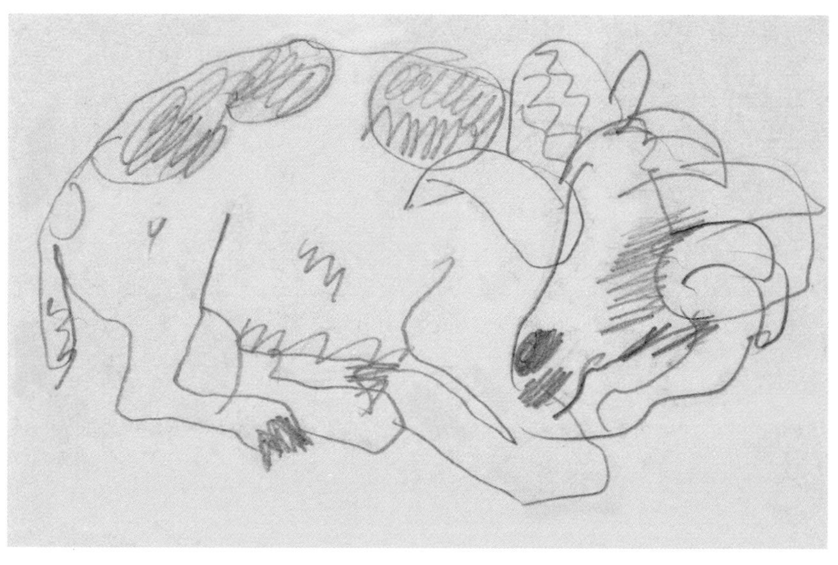

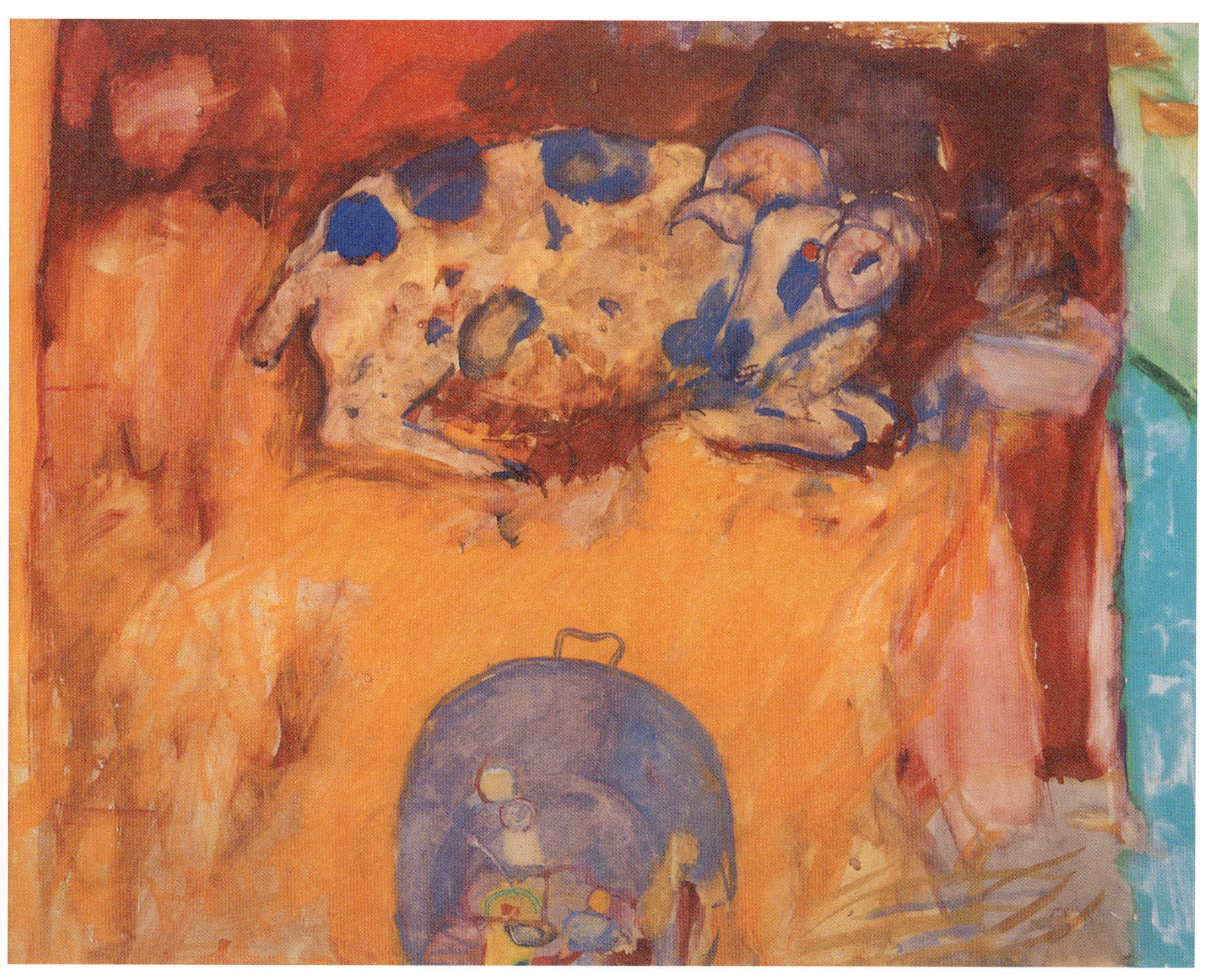

26. Kite and Swallows*

57.5 × 73 cm
Bequest Collection

In a notebook for September 1963, after Ben has returned home to Ermington from his first visit to Ireland, we find at the back of the notebook one of the rare occasions where Ben commits his personal feelings to paper. Outside his house in Ermington there were telegraph wires where flocks of migratory birds, mainly swallows and starlings, would settle. Having come back from a fascinating and enjoyable change of scenery, he now pleads with the swallows not to leave. 'Don't go. Don't leave me with sad skies.'

There were in fact eleven paintings about swallows in the bequest, mostly about their nesting habits. Here we have one of three versions, with different background colours, of the image of a group of swallows with a kite which has become tangled in telegraph wires.

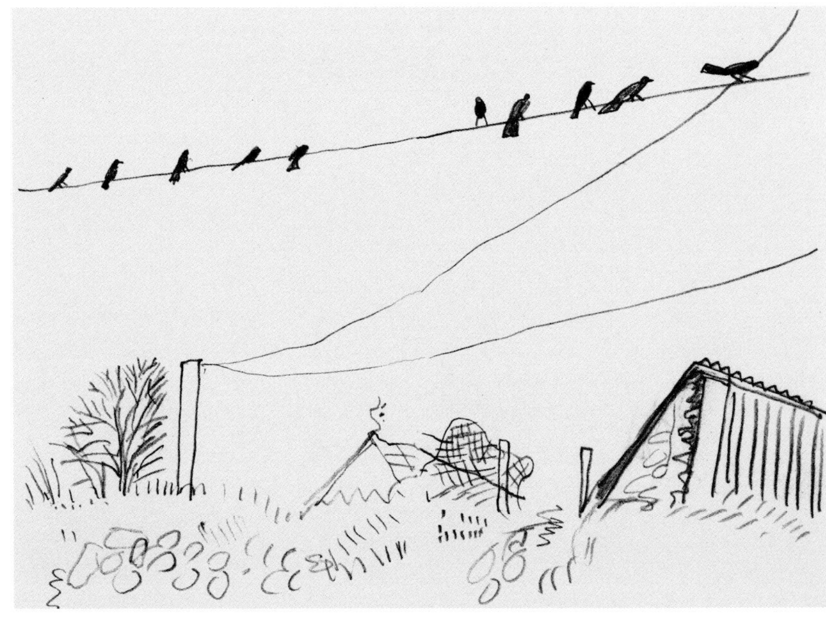

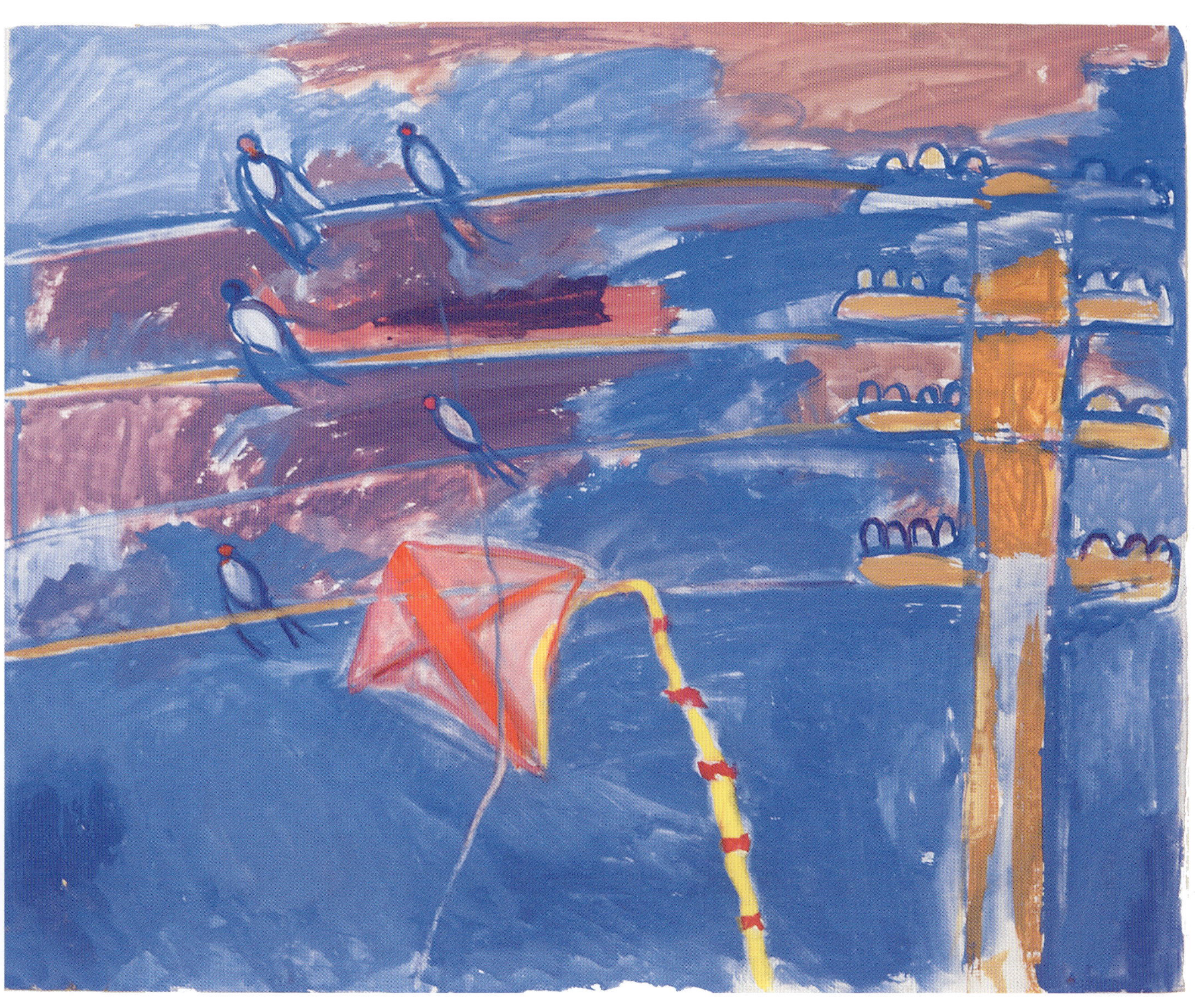

27. Bath and Breakfast

56 × 71 cm
Private Collection

Ben's eye was often caught by the untidiness of country life: the back yards of farmhouses full of abandoned machinery and old furniture. On Tod Moor, just above Ermington, he found a bath in a field; from this he managed to create one of his loveliest images. With the subtle brilliance of the colours he begins to match Bonnard, his revered master. The Heineken green of the lager can and the few brown leaves that have found their way onto the window ledge are beautiful touches; so much affection allied to so much technique.

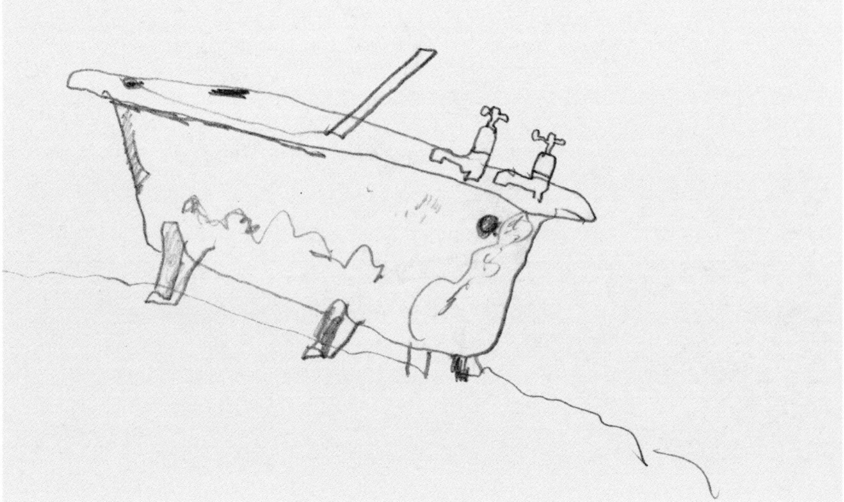

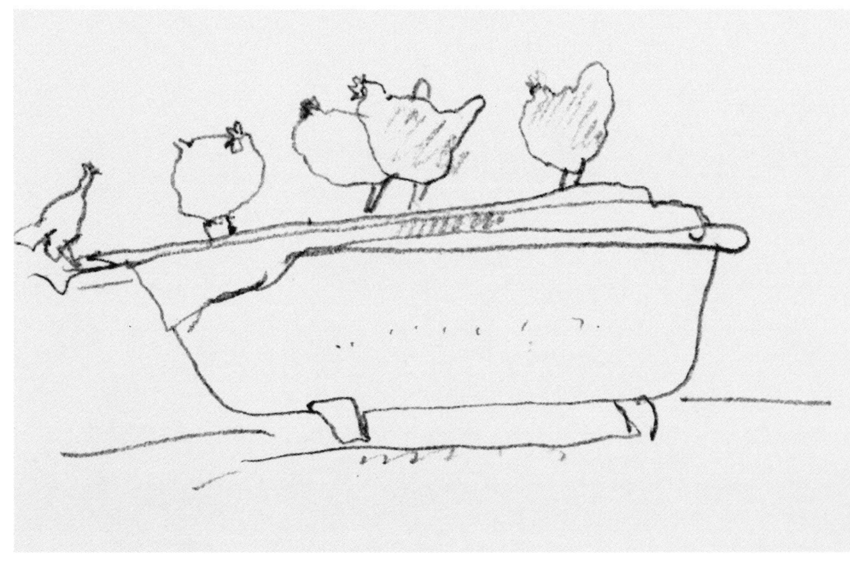

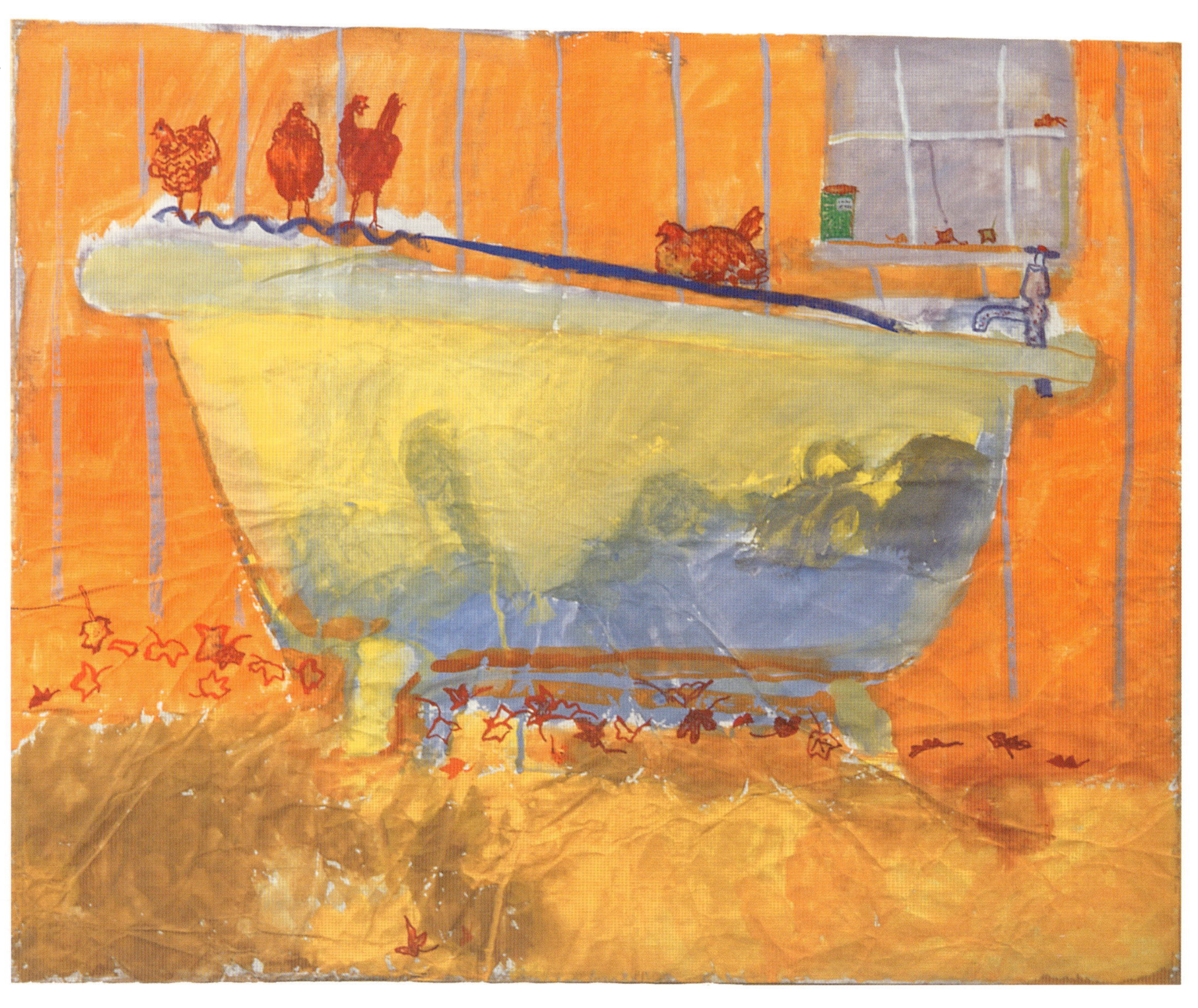

28. Comfort Corner

53 × 70 cm
Private Collection

Comfort Corner speaks about the pleasure of domesticity, a cat and a dog comfortably settled in their favourite surroundings. The chair, from a family home, appears many times in the notebooks drawn from different angles. The rich colour and the drawing of the striped covering on the armchair give this picture the flavour of Dufy.

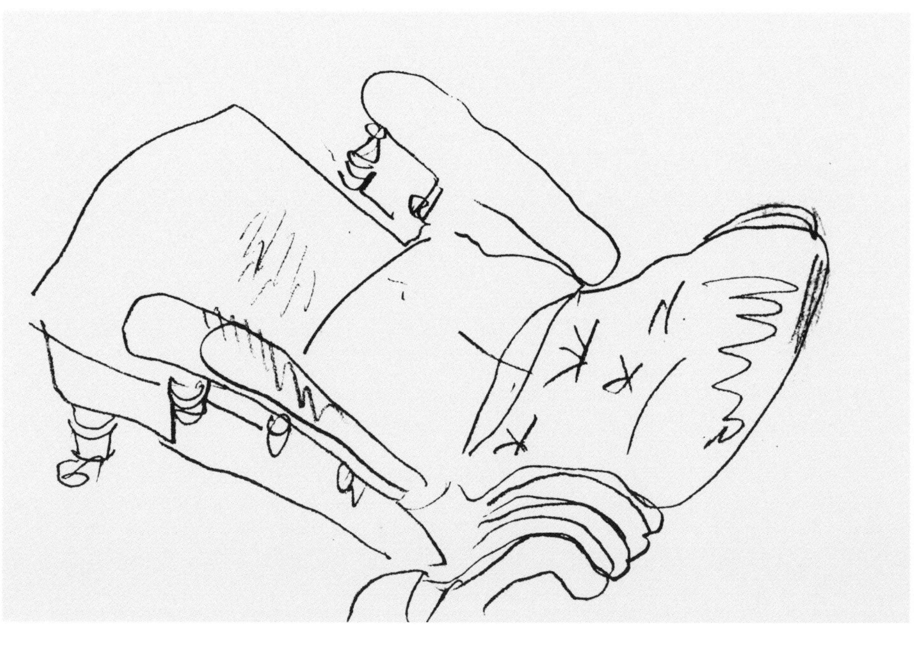

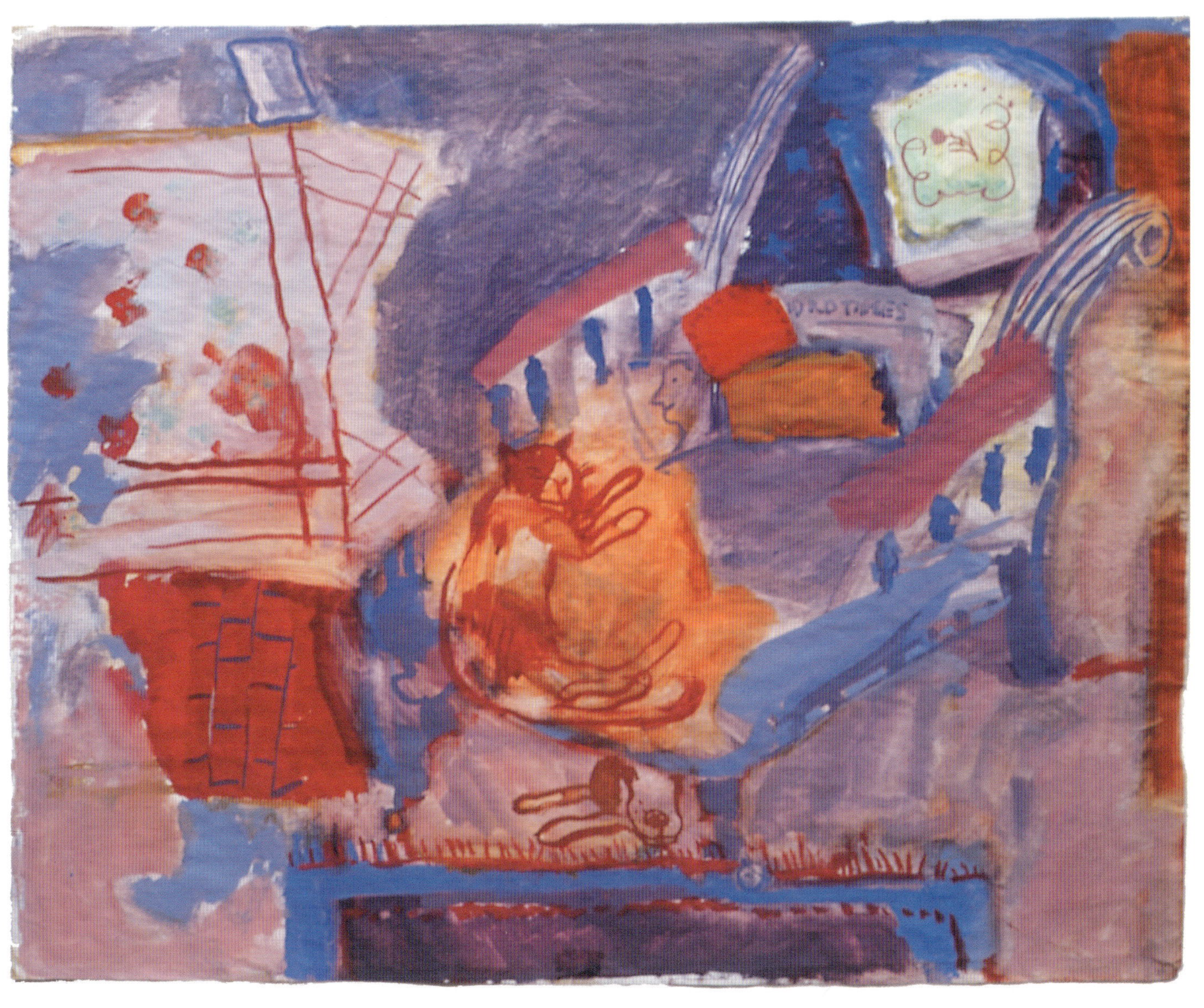

29. How d'Yer Do

52.5 × 65 cm
Bequest Collection

There must be scores upon scores of ducks in the work of Ben Hartley, but never a group of such happy and contented ducks, taking their ease on the bank of a stream, two members of the group forming a welcoming party for a toad climbing 'on board'. This is an unusual work in that it has a simple, straightforward narrative. For whatever reason Ben seems to have bestowed especial care on this painting to give a particularly grand look.

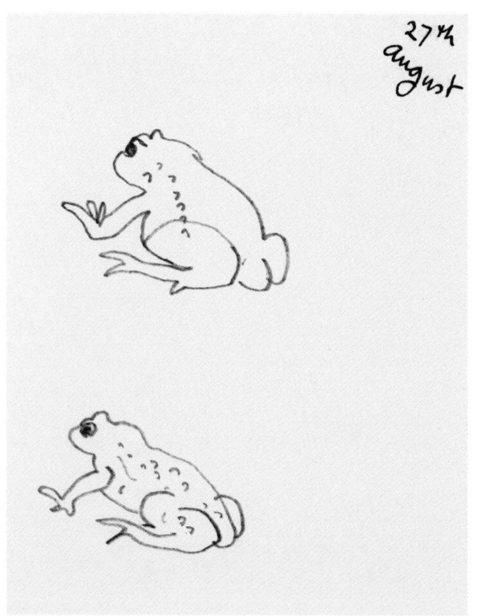

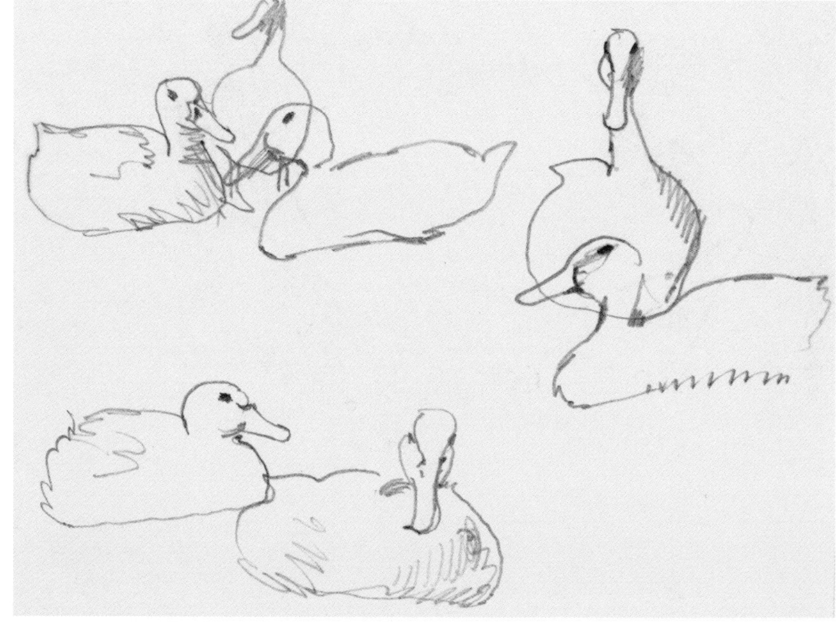

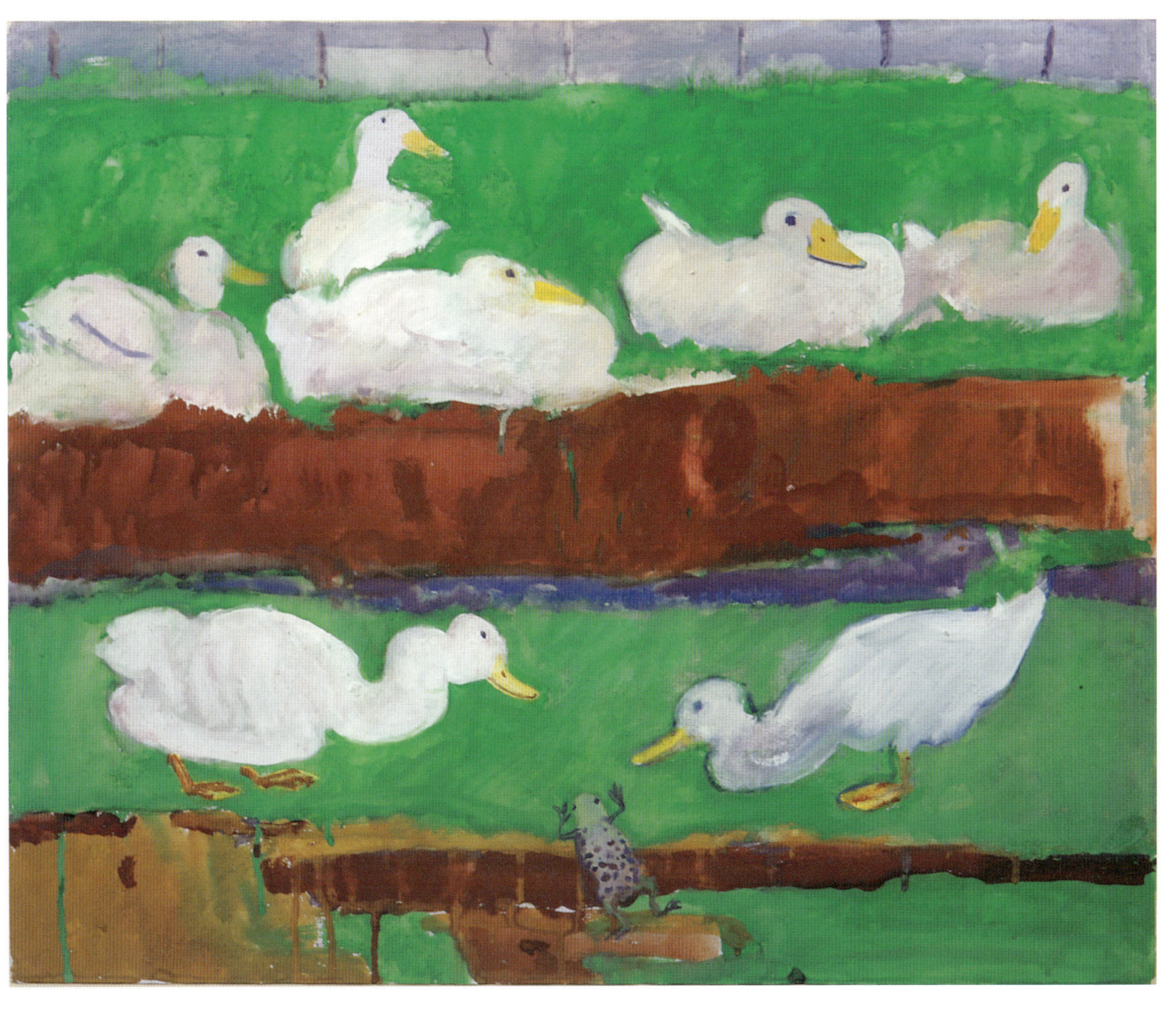

30. Billy Digger

60 × 75 cm
Bequest Collection

This psychedelically bright picture is full of humour. At the same time we find a mixture of influences. With the combination of orange and green, the colour is taken to extreme and the abstract structure and the vigorous brushwork are in themselves important. However, in addition, applied at the bottom of what looks like a wall covered in greenery is an advert for 'Digger Tobacco'. This raises the question of what relationship, if any, Ben had to the Pop Art movement that was just beginning to take hold at the Royal College during Ben's time there. Peter Blake, the most celebrated artist of the British Pop Art movement, was just one year ahead of him at the College. On the other hand there are many drawings and references in the notebooks from earlier times to all kind of everyday manufactured items, especially tobacco tins, biscuit tins, cigarette and sweet packets, all kinds of food wrapping and containers. The writer Candice Rodd had an excellent phrase when she described the novelist William Trevor as 'deeply in thrall to the poetry of brand names': words that could well be applied to Ben Hartley.

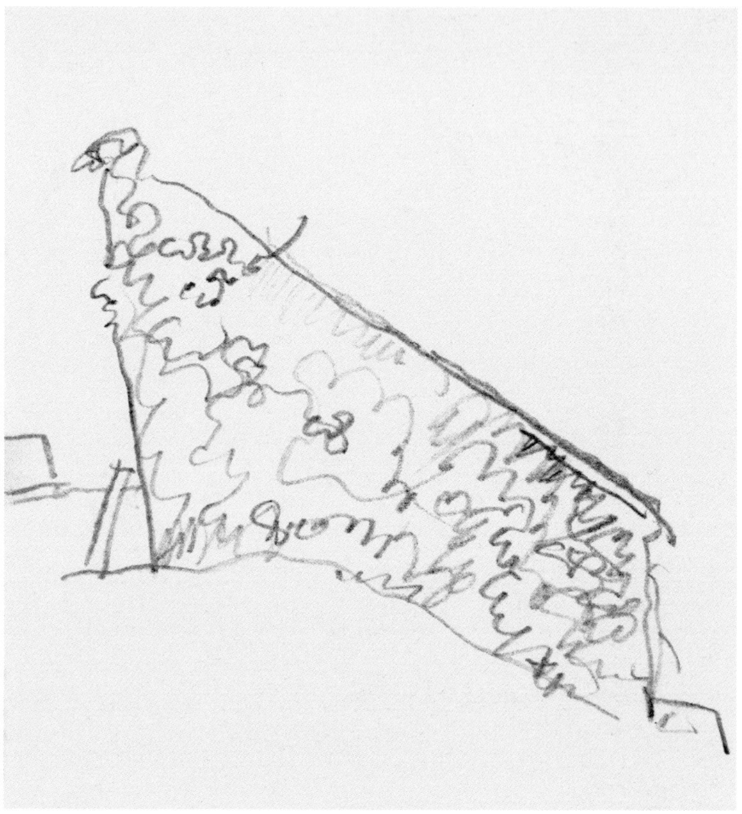

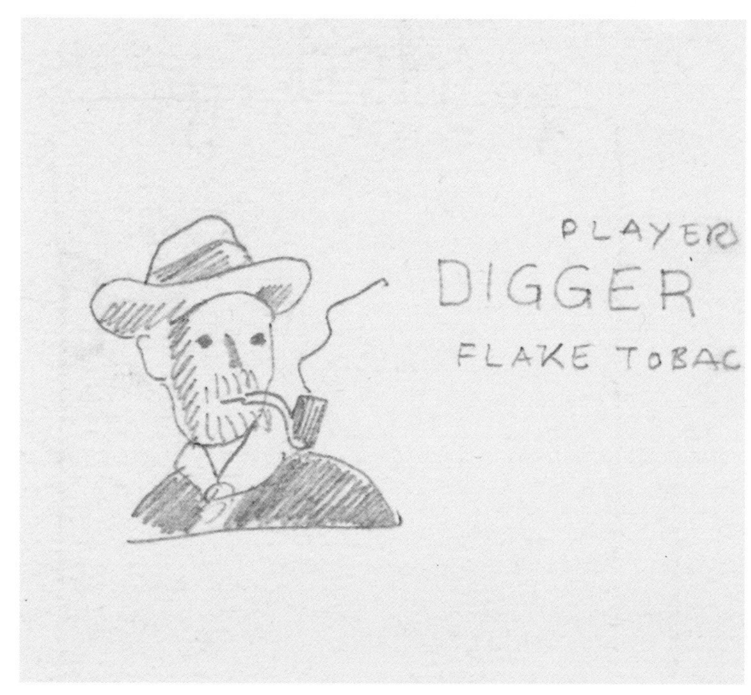

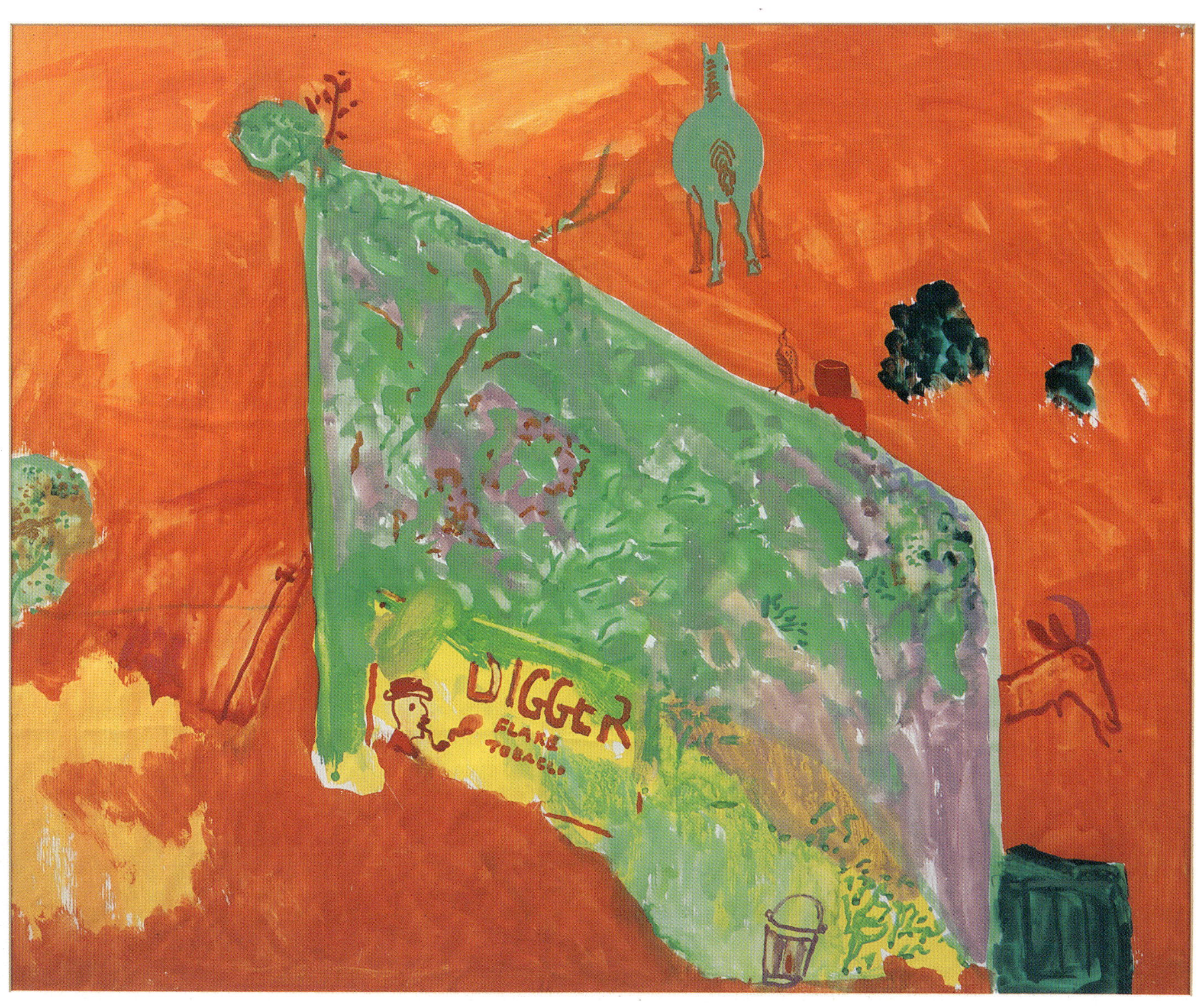
DIGGER
FLAKE
TOBACCO

31. Threesome

48 × 67 cm
Private Collection

Cows in Ben Hartley are always great beasts, which of course is what they are. There are many beautiful drawings, some of which emphasize their mountainous structure, others emphasizing their grace and serenity in repose.

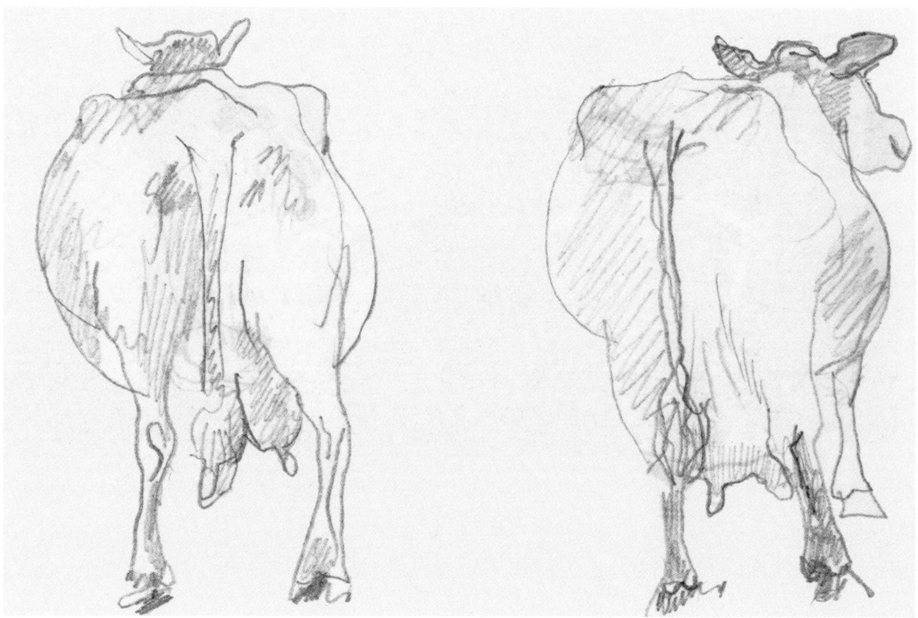

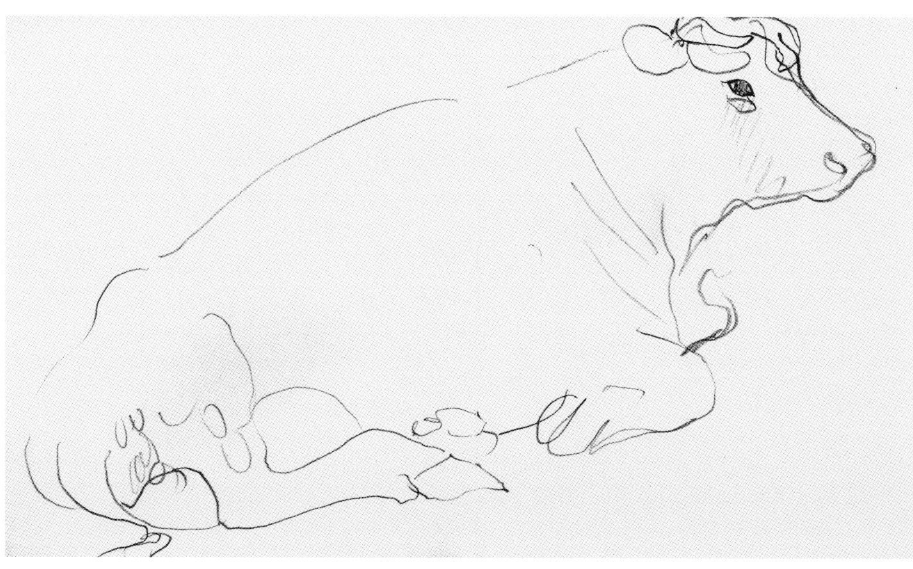

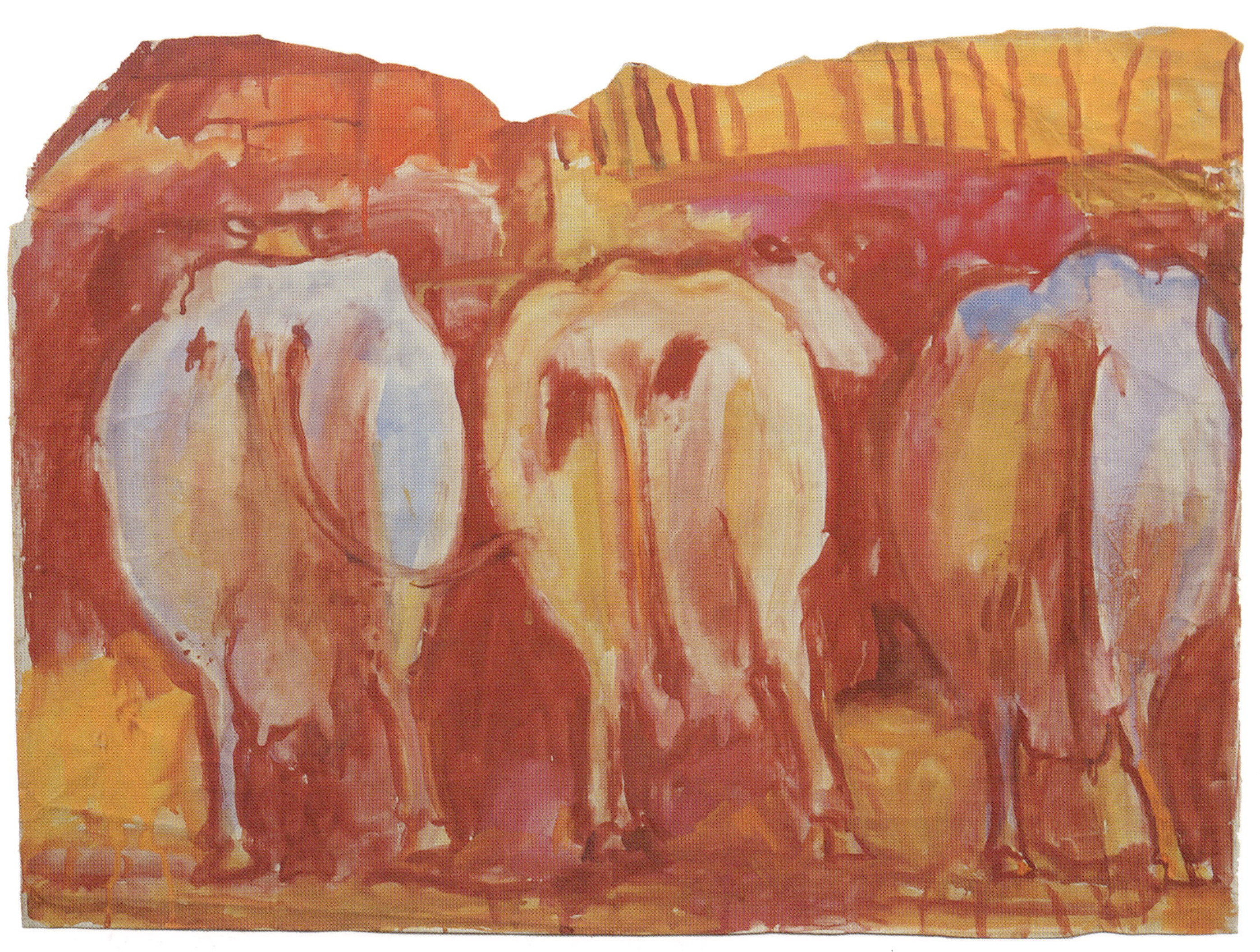

32. Magnificent Cow*

50 × 70 cm
Private Collection

For another fine view of Ben's devotion to the portrayal of the cow we turn to this memorable presence, created in the late period and which cannot be ignored; arguably conveying all there is to say on this subject.

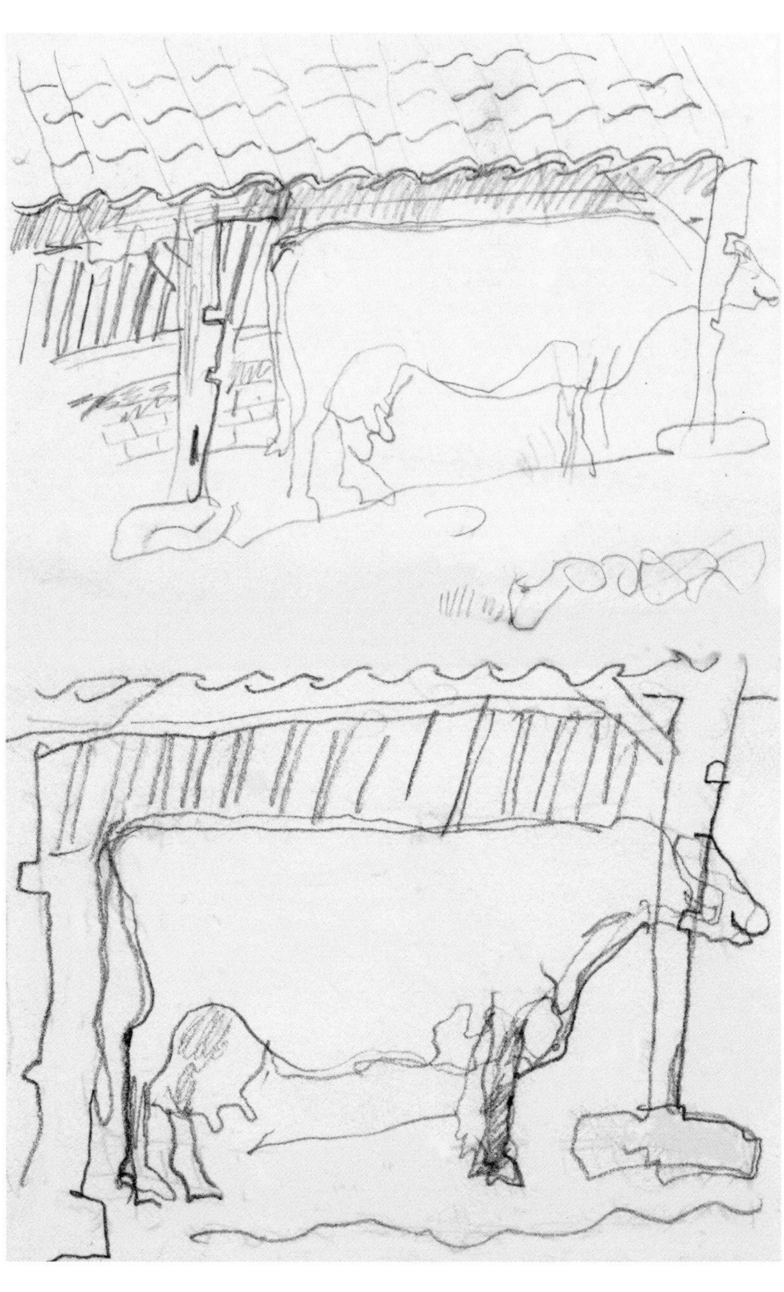

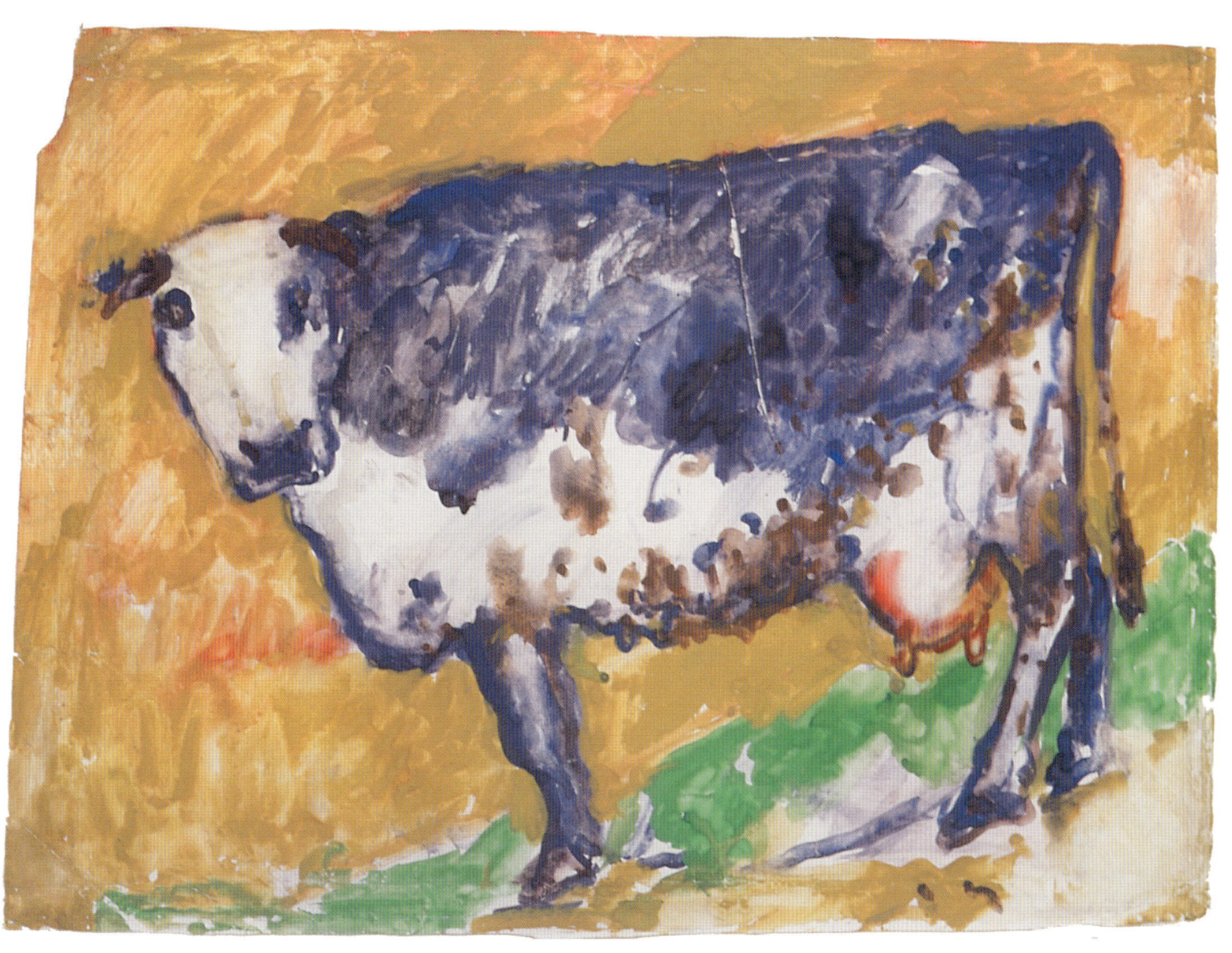

33. Workaday

52 × 69.5 cm
Reproduced by permission
of the Trustees, Dartington Hall

Workaday derives from one of the many drawings of horses in the Irish notebooks. It is one of the most poignant of the animal paintings.

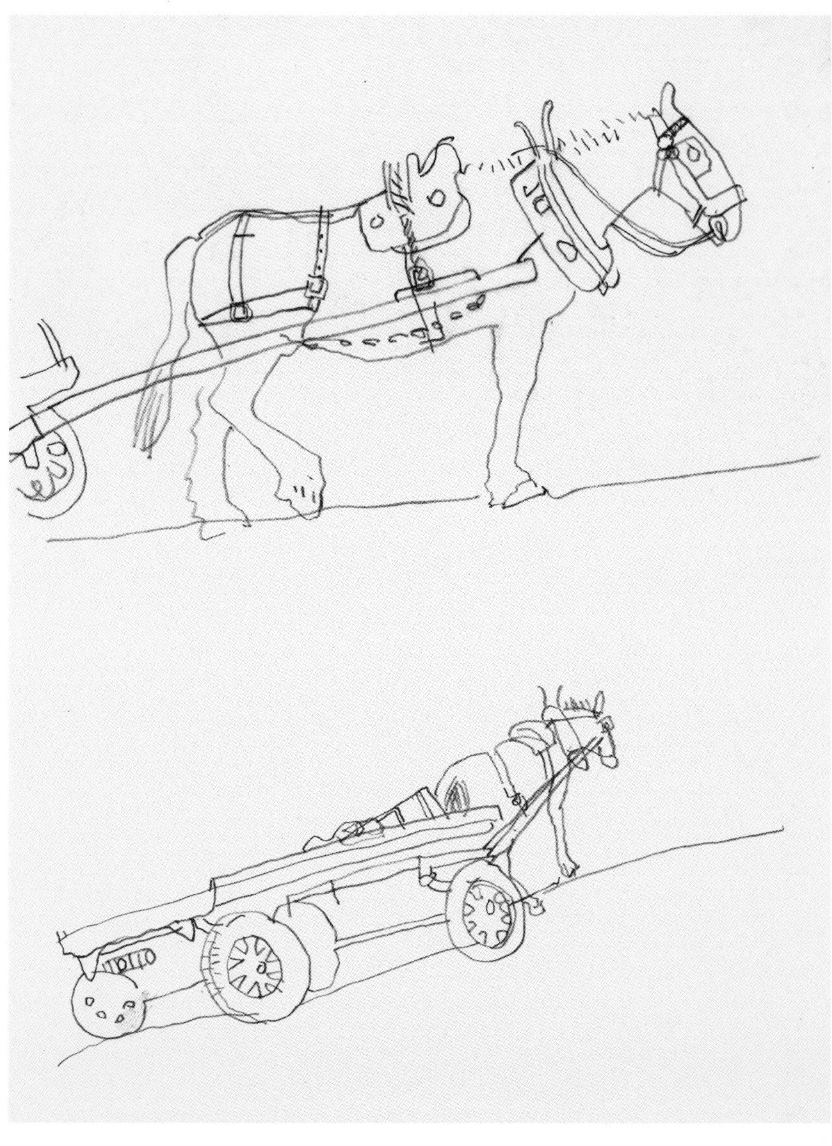

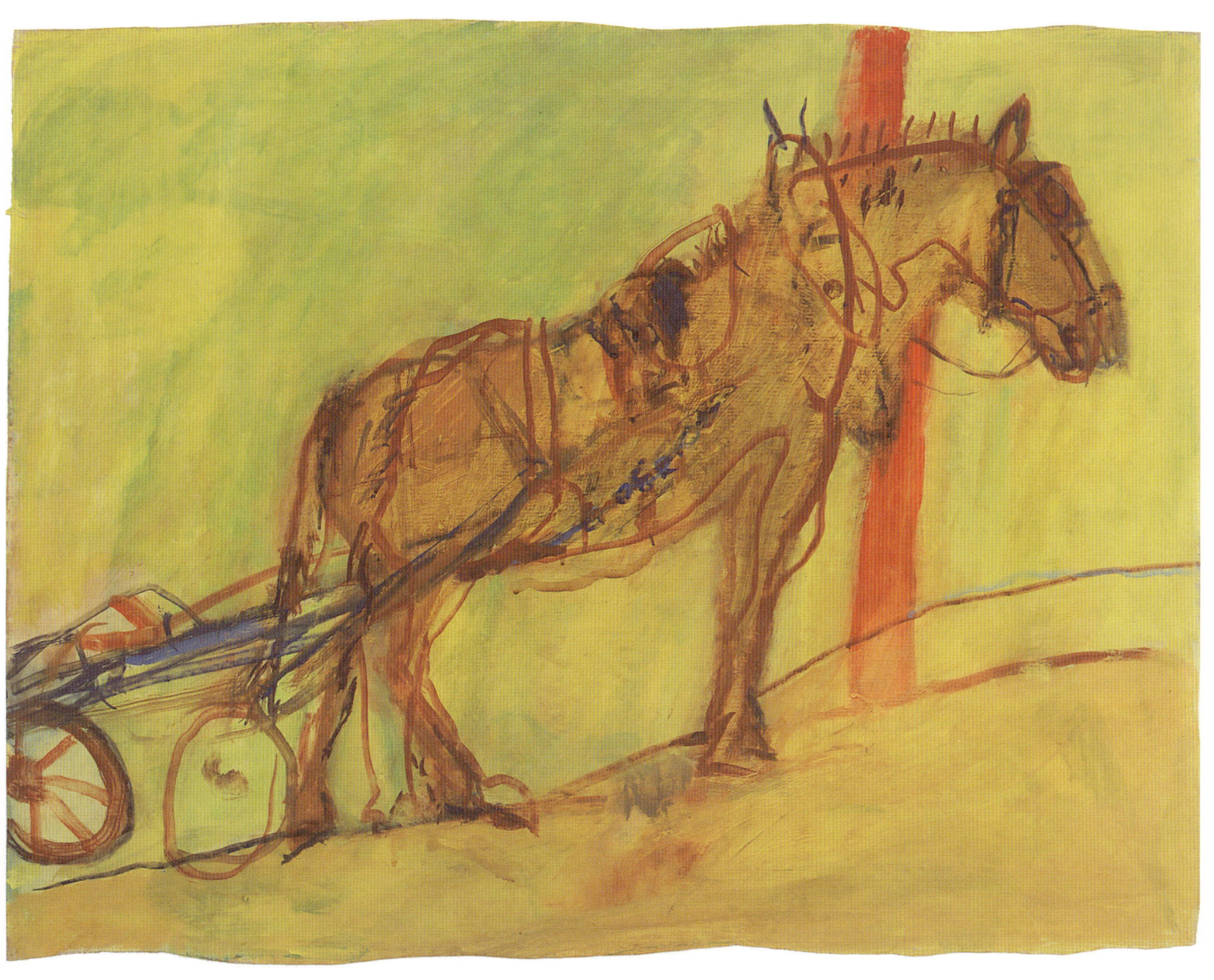

34. Outsider

49 × 68 cm
Reproduced by permission
of the Trustees, Dartington Hall

Outsider, one of many versions of the theme of the sow and her litter with one piglet on its own, is especially appealing for the richness of its colour, the mixture of deep purple, pink and khaki brown. This work was chosen by the author for inclusion in Carel Weight's eightieth birthday exhibition at the Arts Club in Dover Street in 1991. Ben himself was at a loss as to what to choose, but the event resulted in a moving letter from Ben about his admiration for Carel Weight.

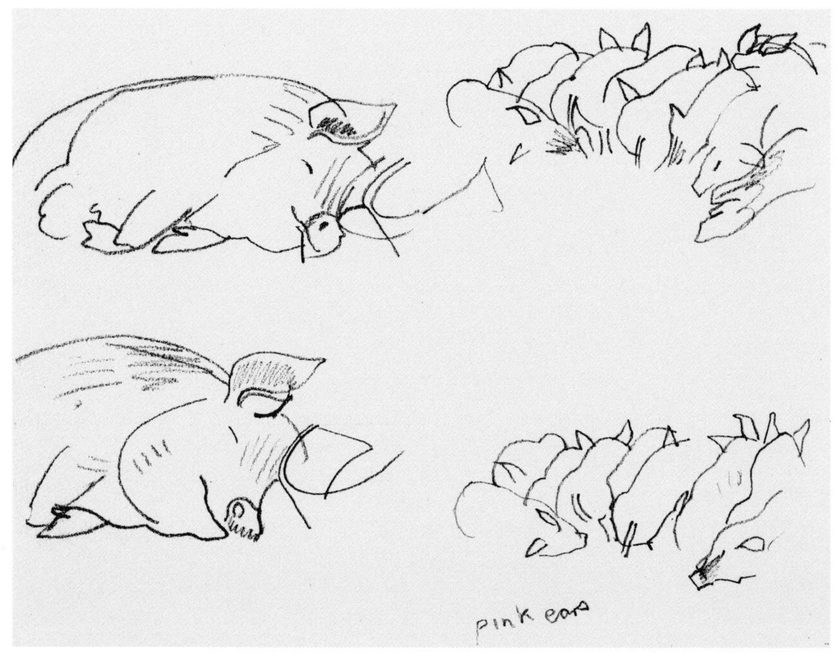

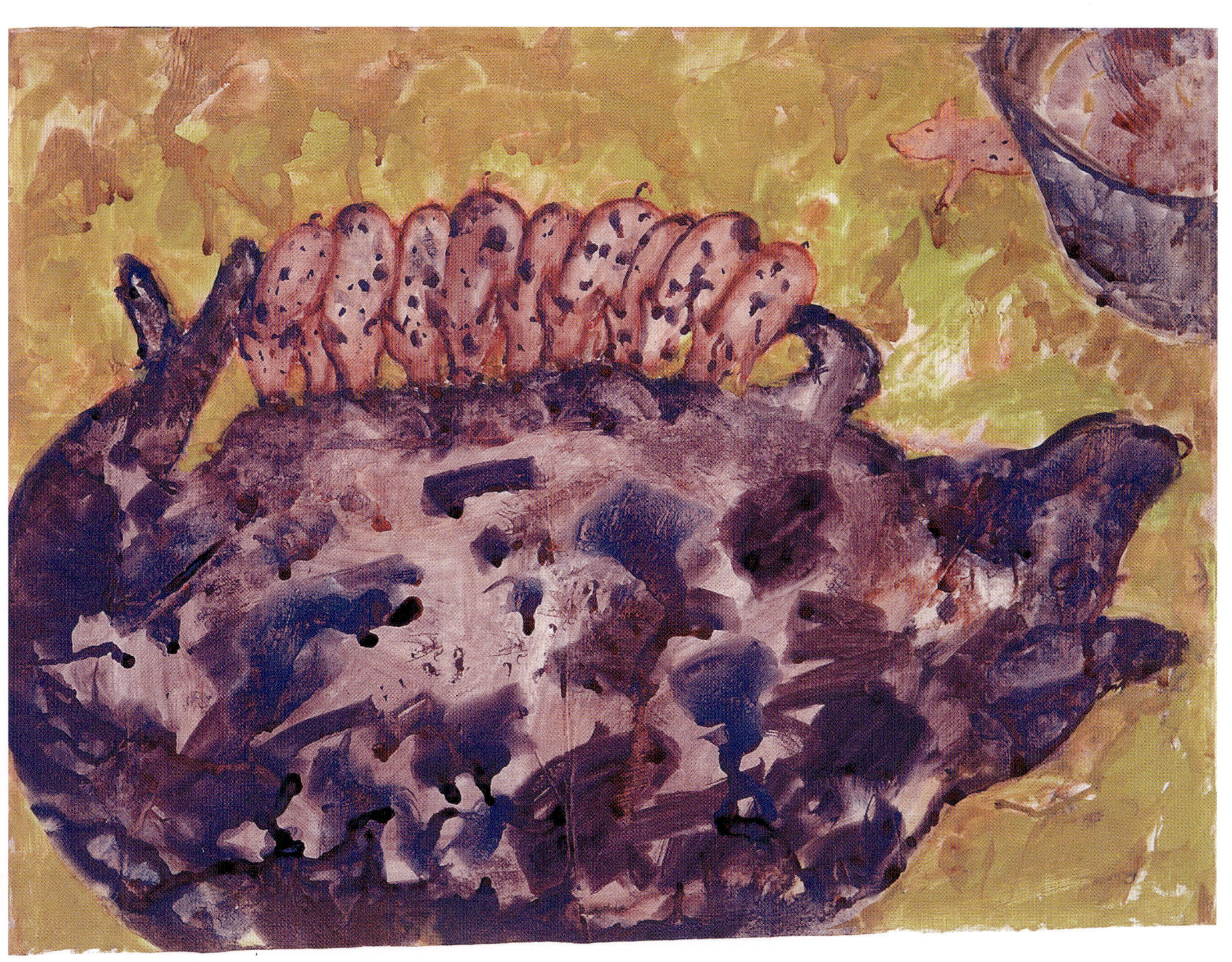

35. Triumphalist*

63 × 50 cm
Private Collection

This picture, conveying its uncompromising message from the farmyard in no uncertain terms, is one of the handful of paintings which come directly from drawings that present the final image fully formed. It came in the bequest without a title. The apt title it now carries comes from a description in a letter from the buyer.

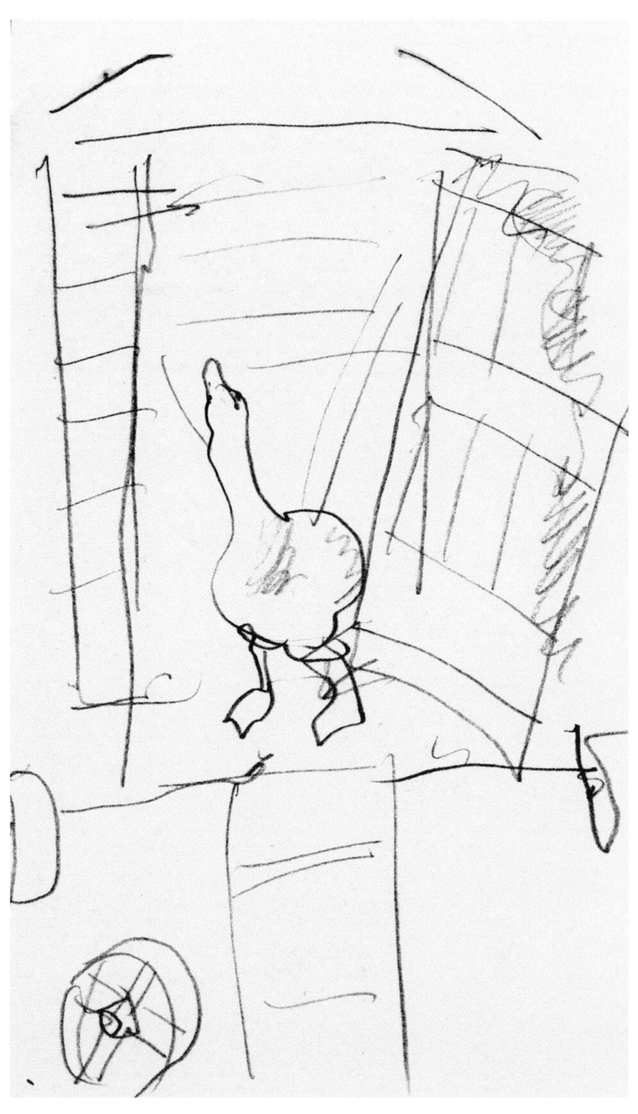

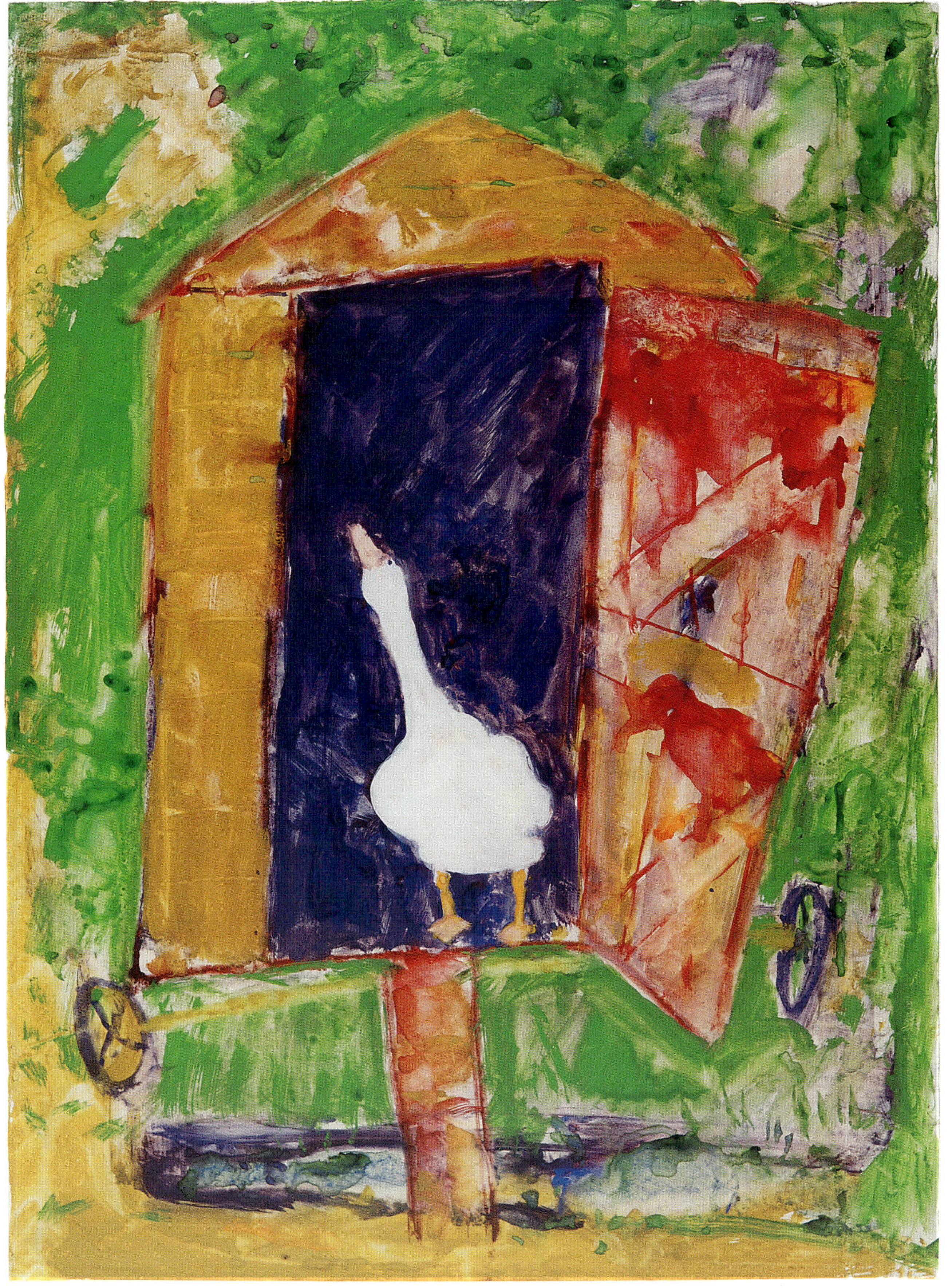

36. Dragonfly and Legs*

56 × 61 cm
Bequest Collection

Insects appear less frequently in the notebooks than animals but the dragonfly was a particular favourite. Here, in his portrayal of this most beautiful of insects, Ben Hartley excels himself.

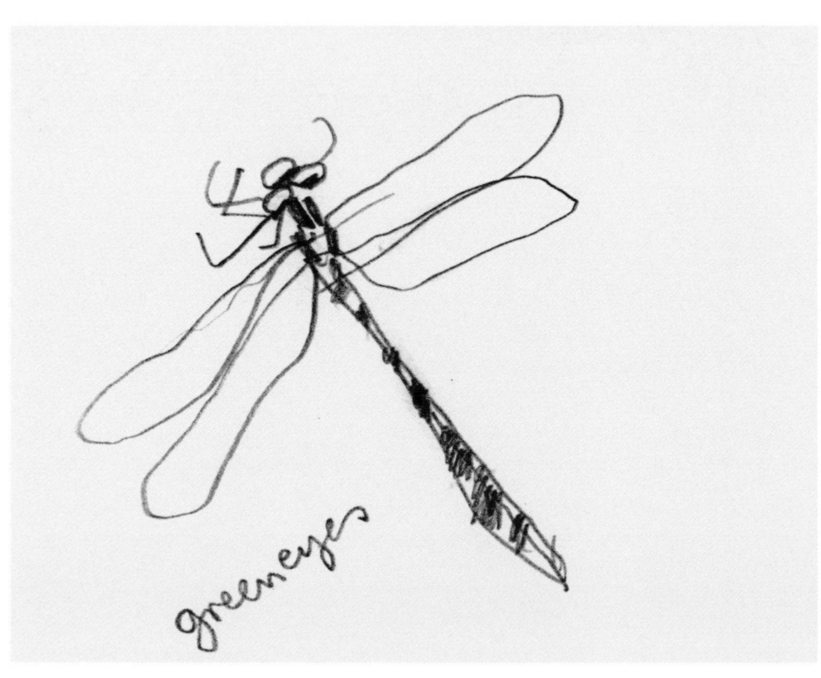

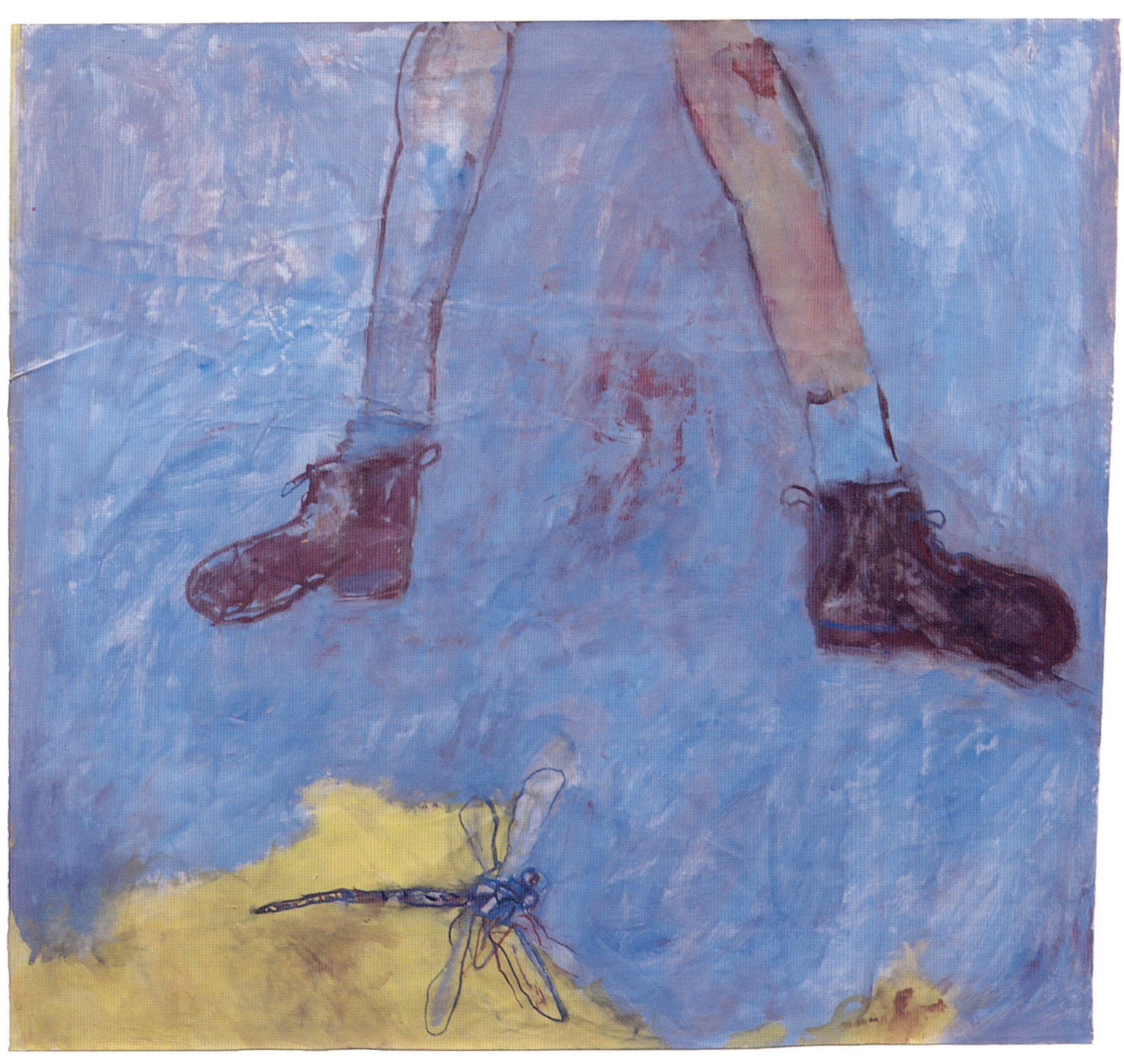

Clothes

As one would expect with someone so unworldly, the significance of clothes in the daily life of Ben Hartley was purely functional. The photograph of him at the front of this book is a detail from a group portrait taken at a garden party in Presteigne. It shows him in his usual plain tweed jacket, green or brown. The straw hat is, for him, unusually grand. Living as he did in the main street of the town, people there, few of whom knew that he was an artist, remember him as a distinctive figure, tall and thin, often dressed in winter in a long, hefty raincoat and flat cap.

In spite of his own indifference to dress, it is worth bearing in mind that his father was a tailor. It is certainly clear from the notebooks and a number of the paintings that clothes were in various ways important for him. It comes out very strongly in the early notebooks where there are scores of drawings of people. The figures have very little by way of personality. However they have a role and status and that is defined for them by their clothes. The large notebook for December 1953 has many pages of outstandingly good figure drawings where the people do have a psychological entity and their presence has a strength which derives from the firmness of the drawing of their clothes, in most cases a heavy overcoat.

Curiously, in a notebook from June 1958, there is a jotting about a Parade of British Couture held *in London at the Hyde Park Hotel. There is no indication whether he went or not. Given the rarity of that kind of information in the notebooks, this jotting has to be in some way significant. The feeling is that he enjoyed the challenge of drawing clothes, by no means an easy subject to handle.*

One particular item of personal clothing belonging to Ben features in the notebooks. He owned a peaked cap which accompanied him on his travels in Ireland and in France. The cap makes its first appearance in the notebook for the visit to Ireland in the summer of 1966. This same cap then seems to reappear, quite some years later, in a notebook covering a visit to France, hanging off the end of the back of a very nice marquetry inlay chair outside a café. The caption 'my cap has nine lives I hope' (a typical Ben Hartley pun) conjures up the story of Ben and his cap and his solitary journeys.

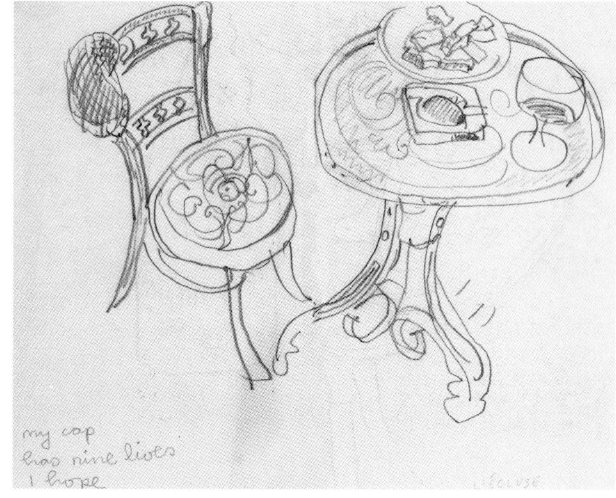

37. Check and Stripes*

58 × 75 cm
Private Collection

Checks and Stripes is a variation of a picnic painting of which there are several versions; in this case the motifs are a dog, two baskets, a teapot, a bottle of wine, all spread out on the ground, with the picture plane virtually taken over by two jackets. The watercolour drawing of a green jacket comes from a notebook from the summer of 1970. Huish, Witchcombe and Spriddlescombe are all farms Ben would have passed by and occasionally visited in his daily walks and cycle rides in the vicinity of his house in Ermington.

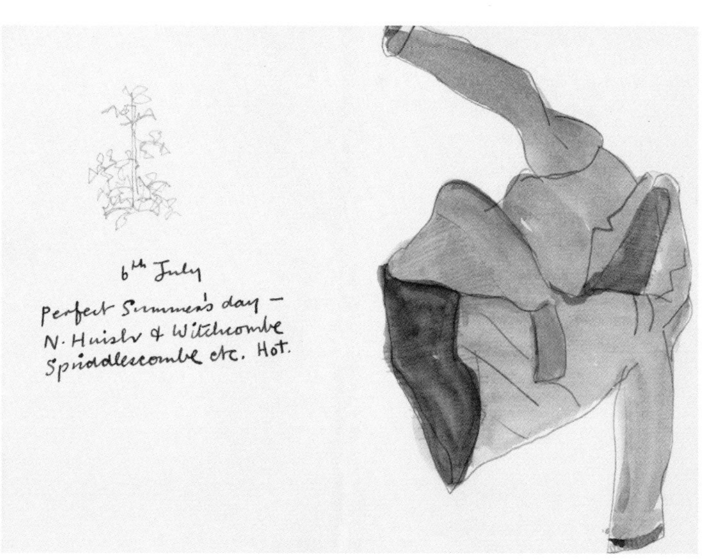

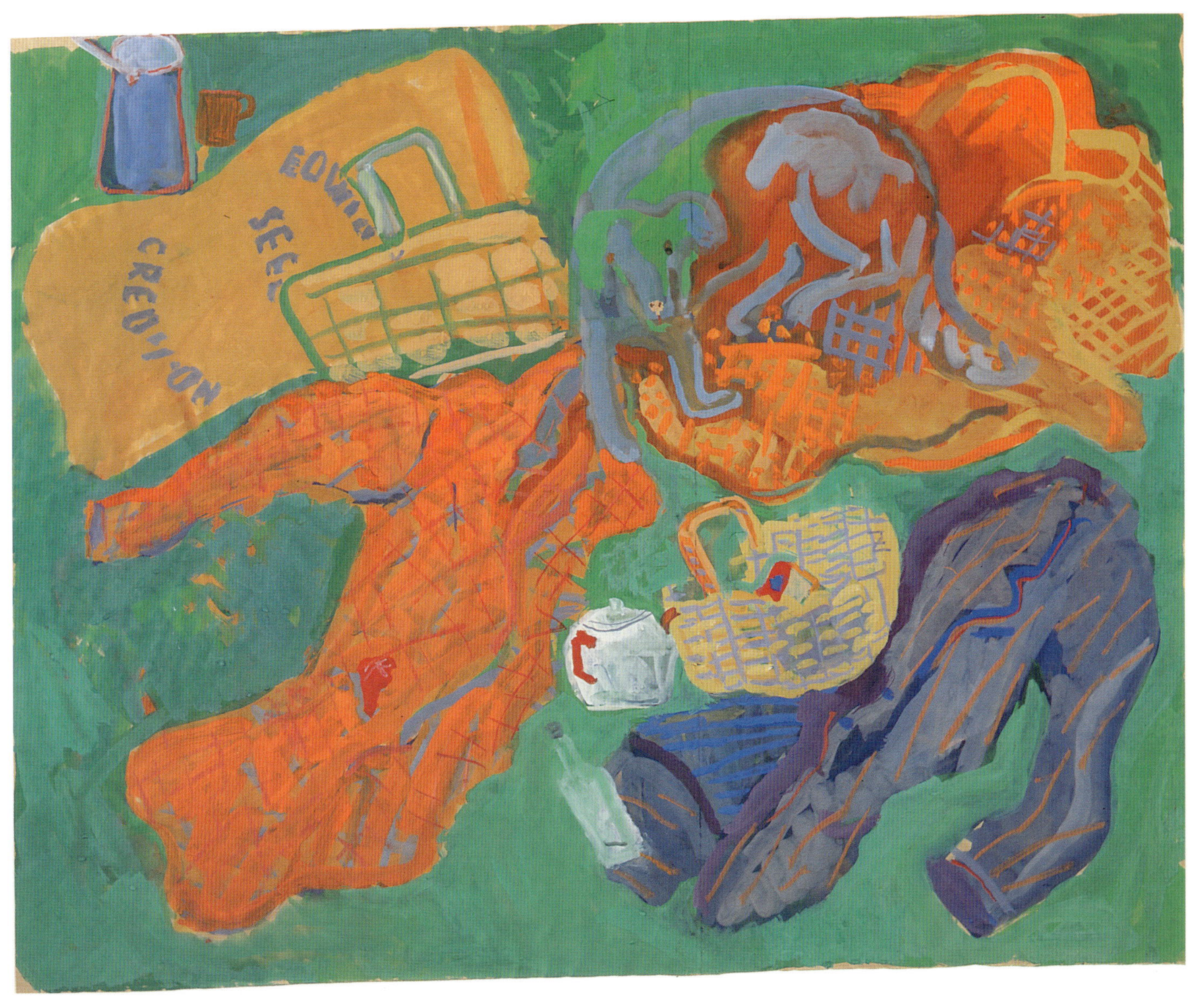
CREDITON

38. Summer Hat*

57 × 60 cm
Bequest Collection

Summer Hat is taken directly from a drawing, delicately executed in coloured crayon, in a notebook for the summer of 1971. Ben has set out on 10th July for his customary vacation time visits to his family. His first port of call is his sister and her family in Herefordshire, just across the border from Presteigne; his first action to attend mass with the Carmelites in Presteigne, followed by picnics on successive days. A day later he is in Hay-on-Wye, 'the book capital of the world', buying a copy of *Piers Plowman*. The diary entries are full of place names, a kind of poetry that reminds us we are in that line passing through Shropshire, Warwickshire and Worcestershire, on through the Wye Valley to Gloucestershire and the Severn, home, in so many ways, to many of the finest of English poets and composers.

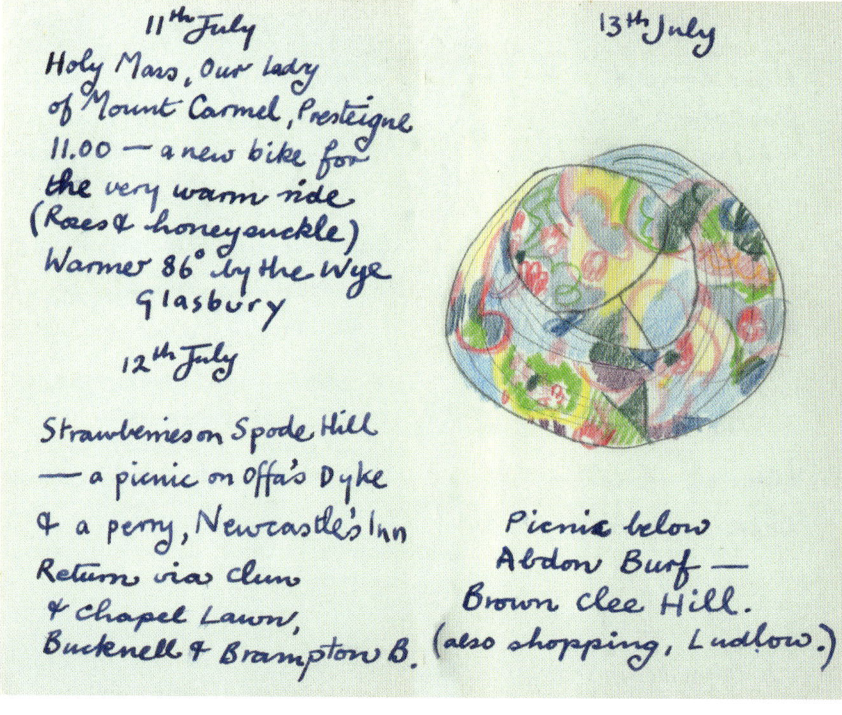

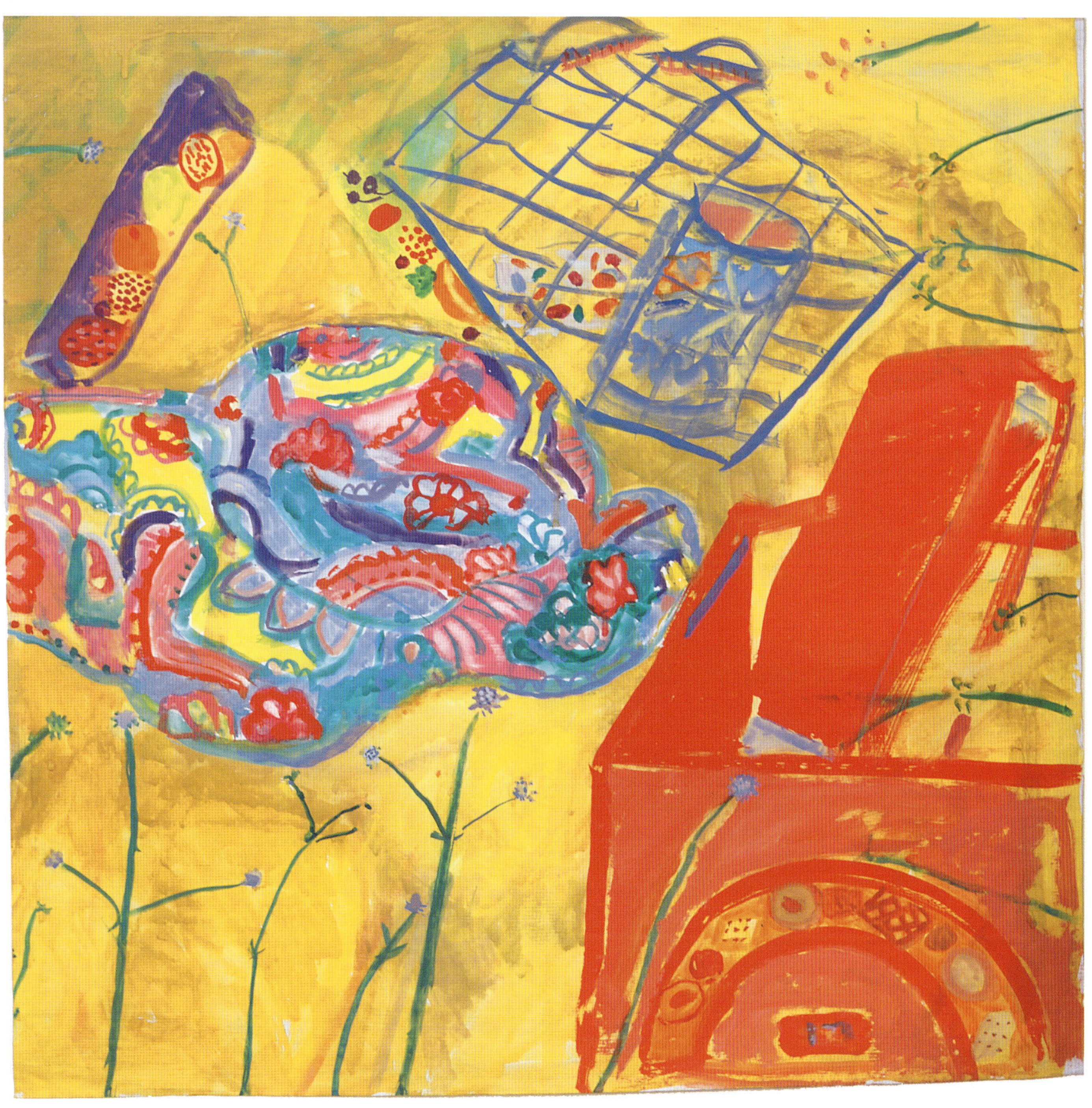

39. Finest Attire*

53 × 62 cm
Bequest Collection

Drawing figures starting from the knees downwards was one of Ben Hartley's more idiosyncratic ideas. Shoes, boots and slippers appear in a number of paintings and drawings. Ensuring he was well shod was important to him, essential for his devotion to walking in the countryside, both a pastime and the source of inspiration for his work. Here, based on a drawing in a notebook recording a visit to his parents in the summer of 1964, but almost certainly painted quite some years later, we find best quality footwear and hose belonging to some prosperous Derbyshire farmer, with elegant dogs to prove the point.

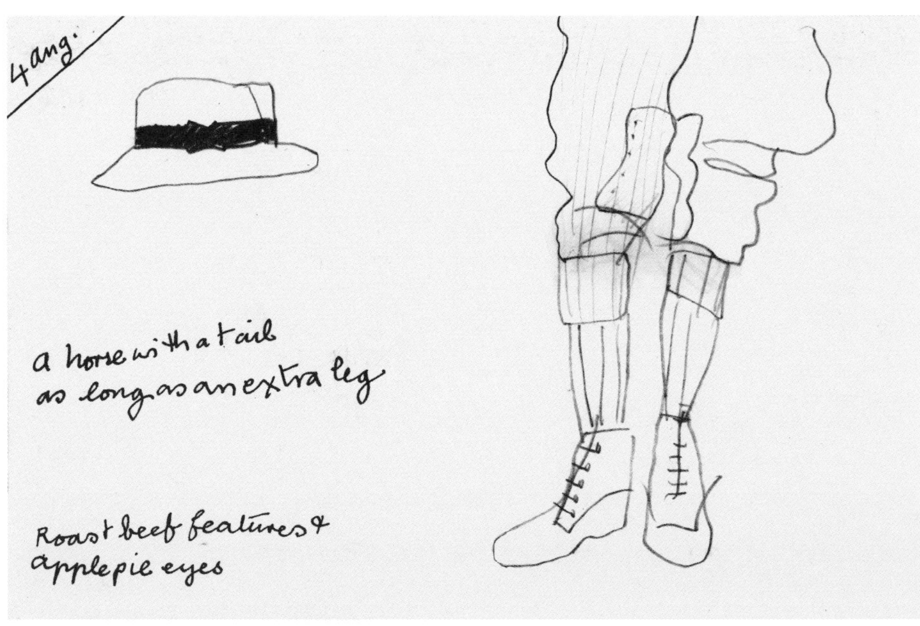

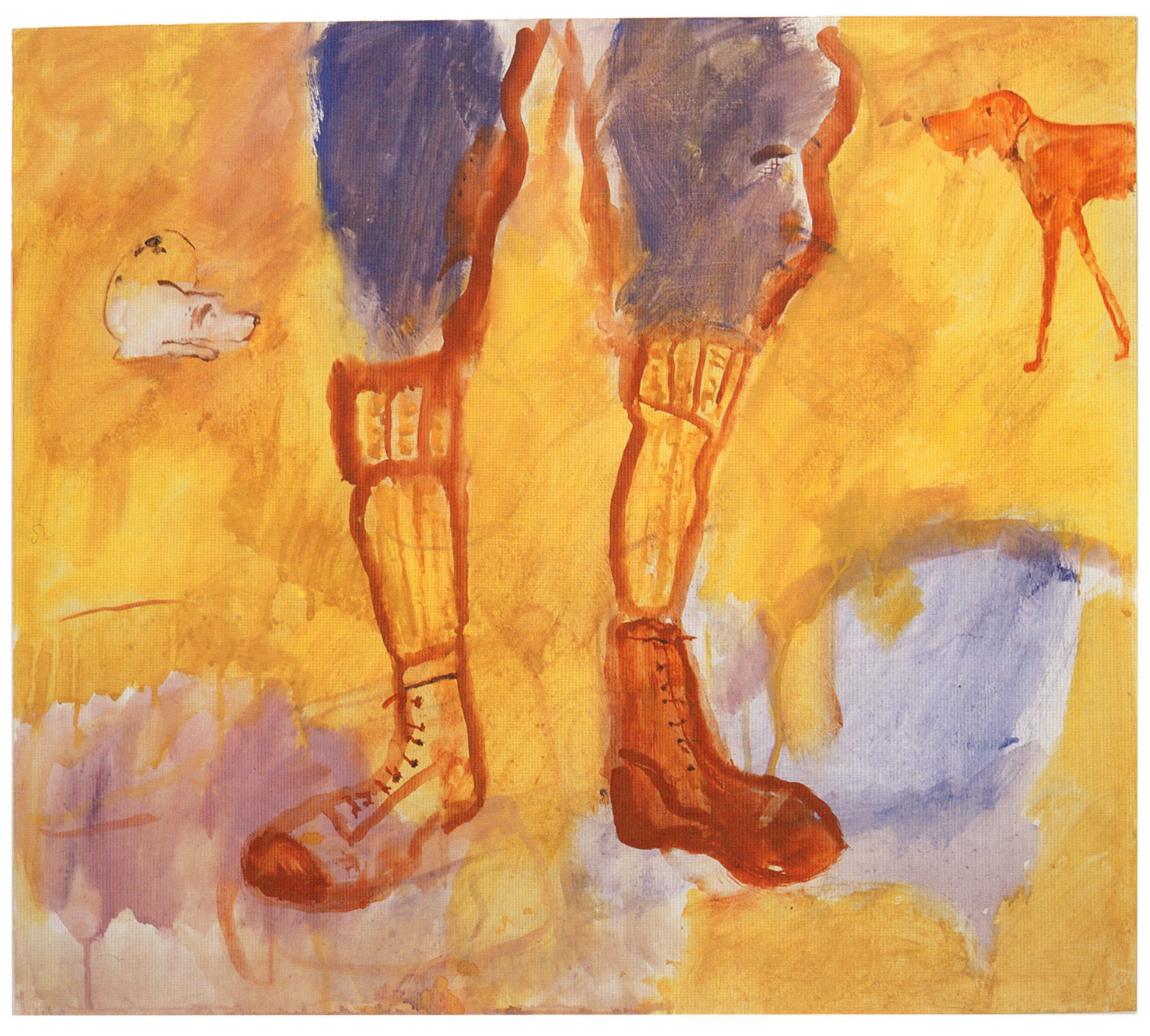

France

As can be seen from the introductory memoir to this book, Ben Hartley had a great love of French art and French literature and visited the country many times. Despite the many notebooks from visits to France and the fact that he managed to reach a large number of major cities, towns and villages spread out wide around the country, there is only a relatively small number of paintings that were inspired by these trips. Not surprisingly the main qualities that come through in these paintings are wit and elegance. In the notebooks Ben is at his most observant, especially about people, many of whom he drew whilst he was travelling on trains. He seems to have been fascinated by the characterful faces, particularly of older people he came across.

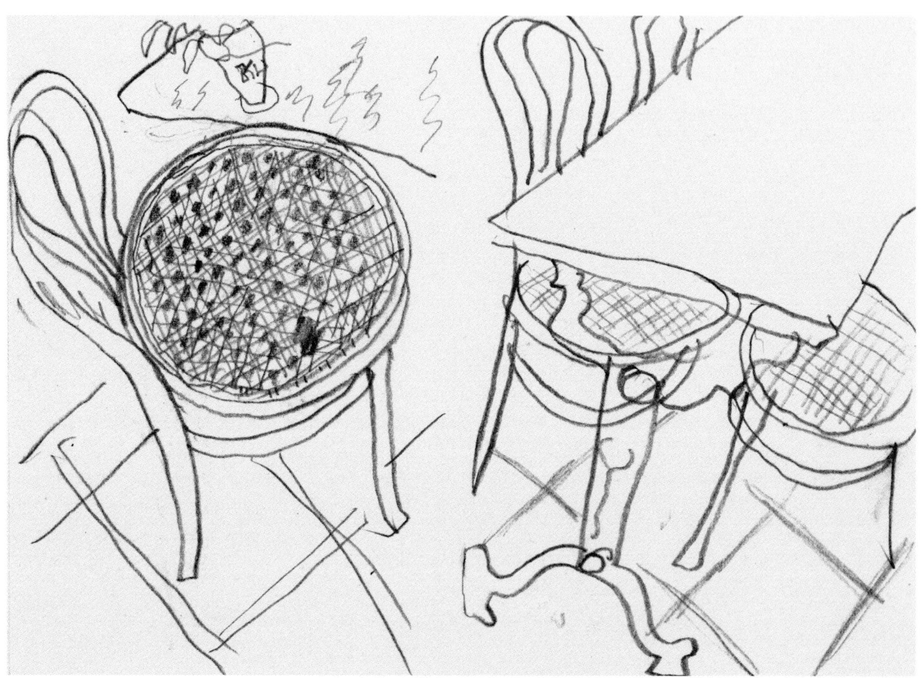

40. Bonheur de Vivre*

48 × 55 cm
Private Collection

Like any enthusiast of French life on tour in the country, Ben found a great deal to record about café life, the people, the distinctively stylish furniture, the brand names on bottles and ashtrays and so forth. This drawing comes from a notebook about Paris and Chartres, mostly Paris. The phrase 'bonheur de vivre' occurs as a jotting in one of the notebooks.

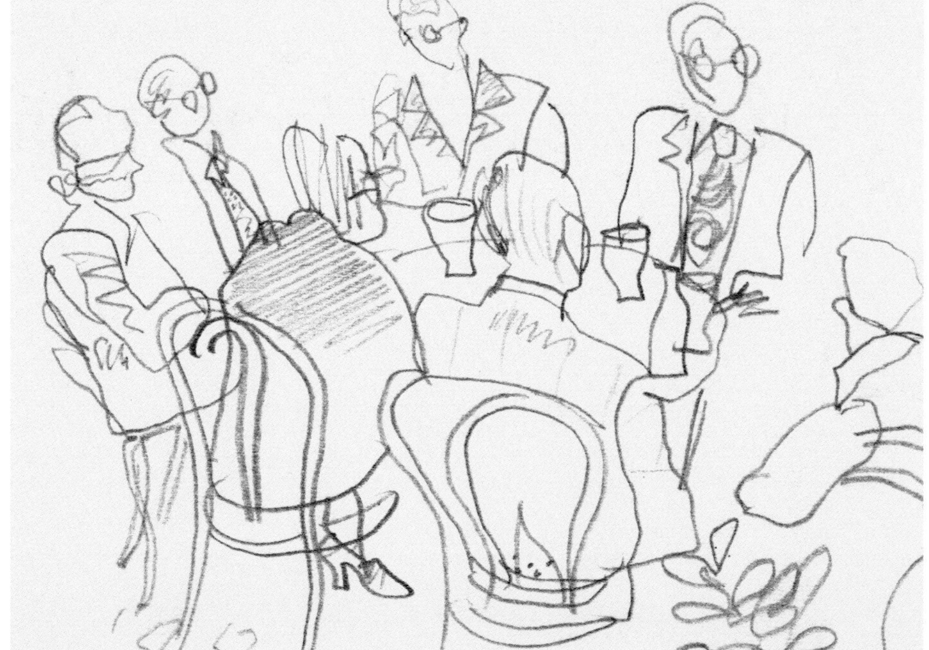

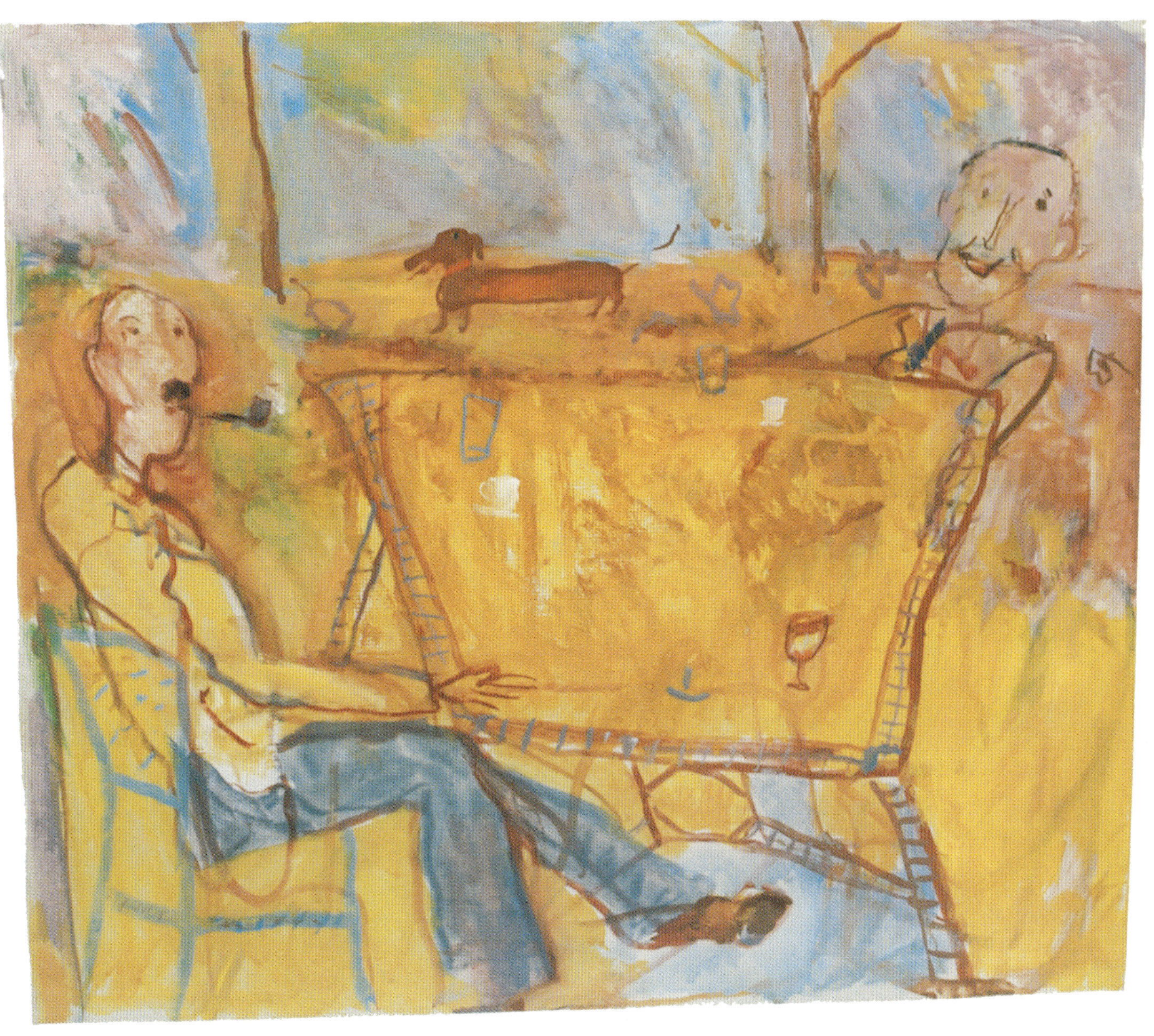

41. Clientèle

50 × 52 cm
Bequest Collection

Clientèle derives from a page in a wide-ranging notebook, taking in Perpignan and Carcasonne in the Southwest, Aix and Marseille in Provence, Annecy and Grenoble in the east and Amiens in the north. Amid some drawings referring to Annecy we find a page simply taken up by the drawing of the name of a hotel set into the floor of the entrance hall. The subtlety of the colour of this work is exceptionally beautiful, the whole effect of the picture set off charmingly by a dainty pair of feet and an impudent little pug dog.

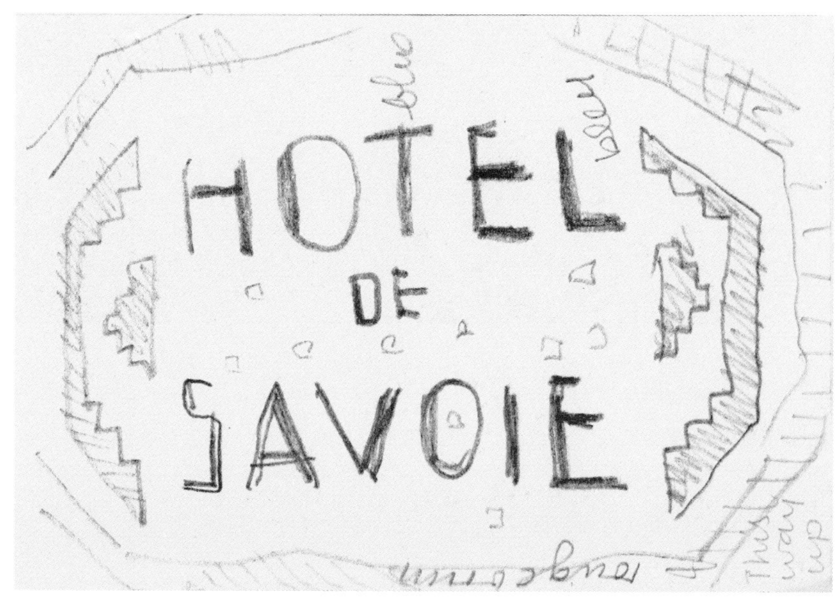

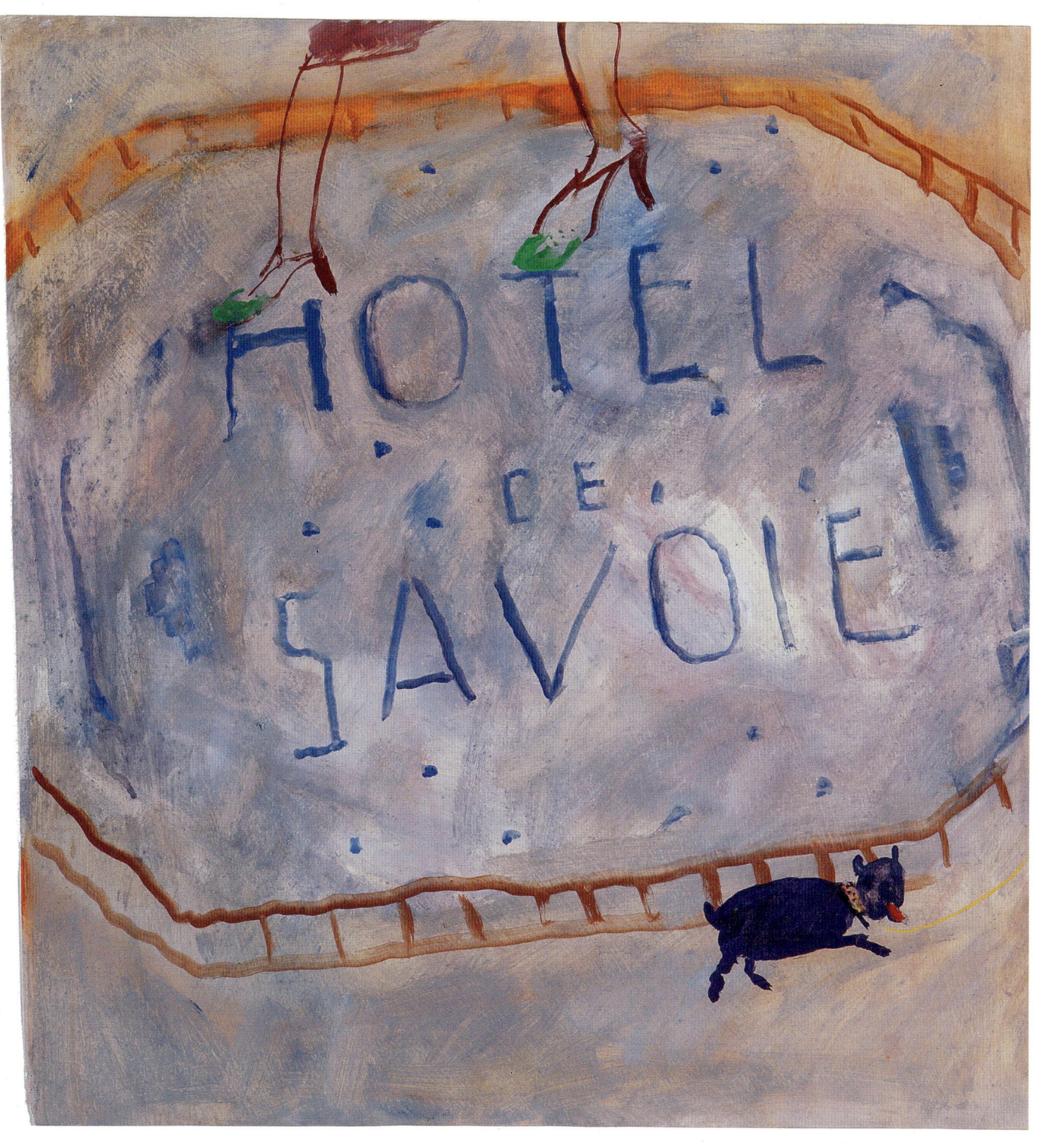
HOTEL
DE
SAVOIE

42. Madame

60 × 46 cm
Private Collection

Madame, one of the most brilliantly coloured of paintings, appears to be an imaginative rereading of the recurring motif, a lady pulled along by her dogs, that first appears in one of the earliest notebooks from the 1950s. It is illustrated here from an undated notebook, most likely from the 1980s, transformed in the painting into a picture of the epitome of French chic and style. Appropriately enough this work was bought by an English couple living in Paris.

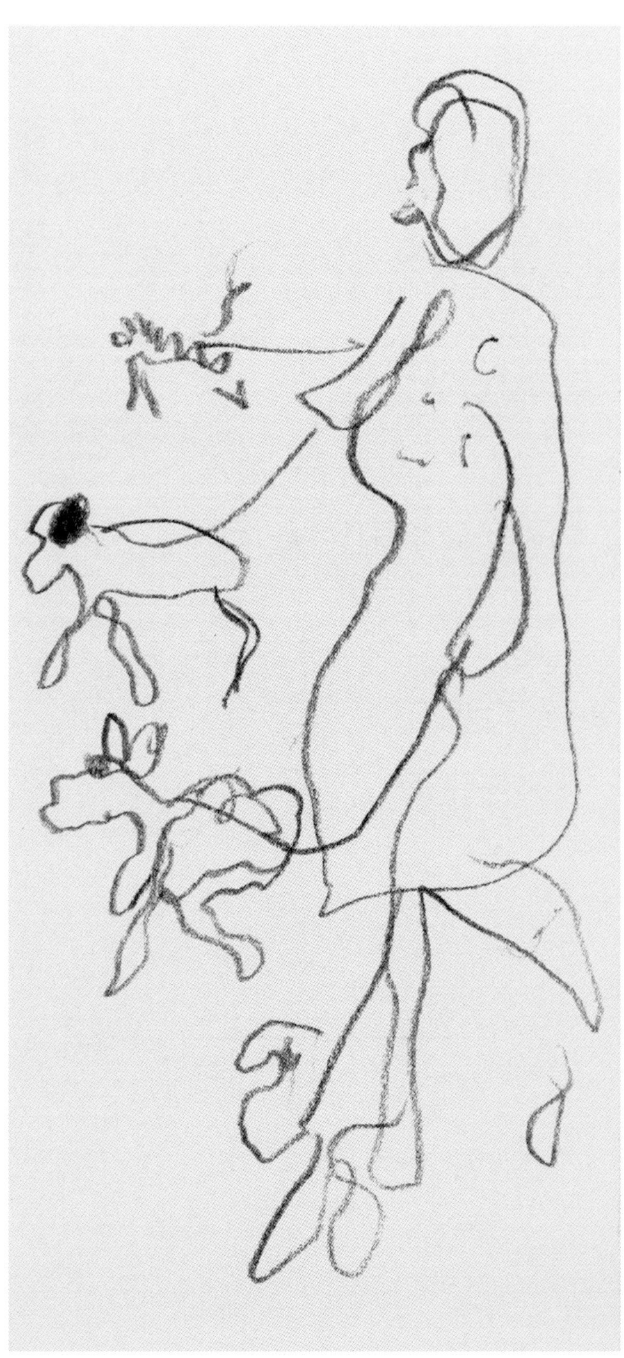

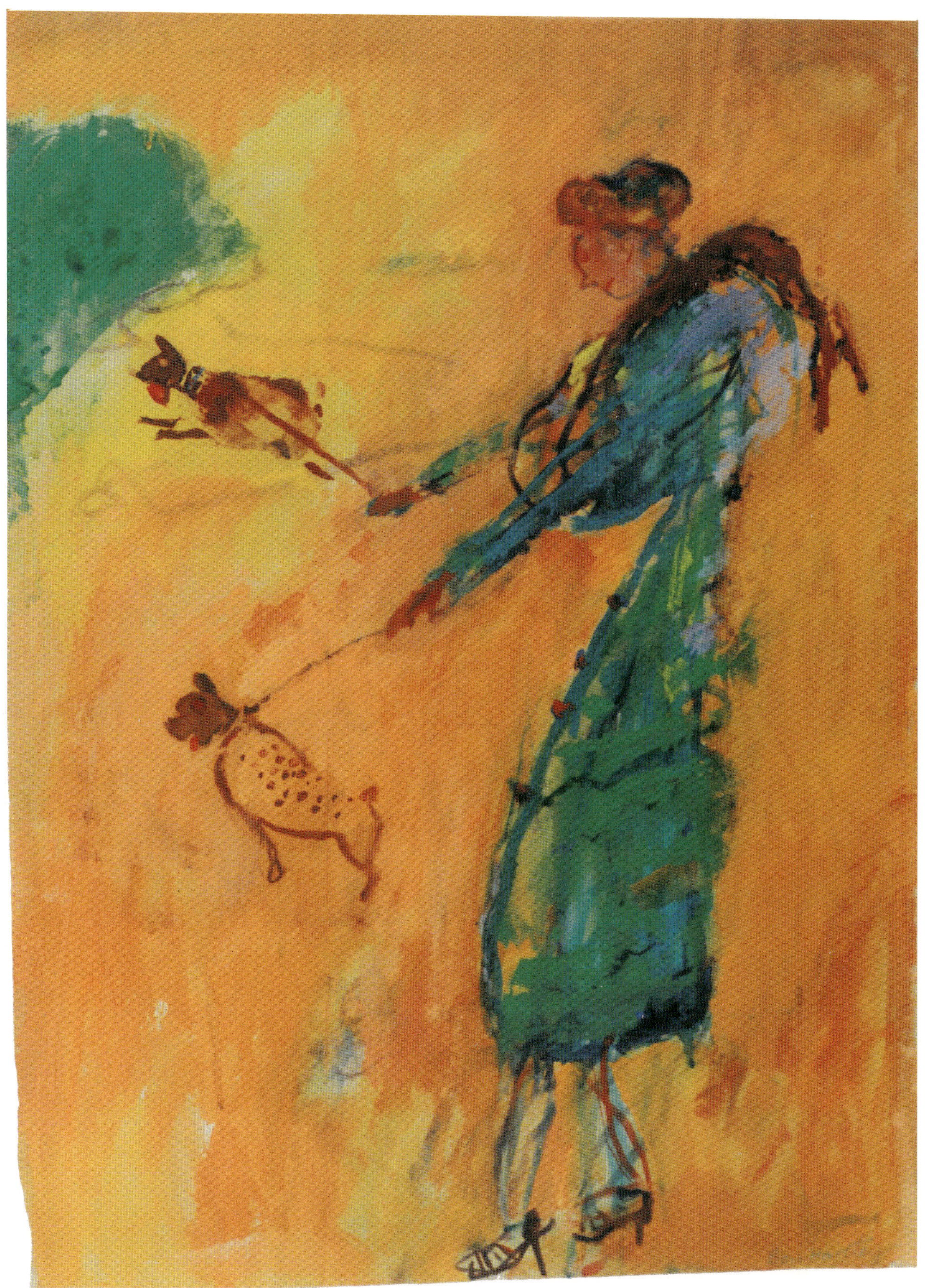

43. Napoleon Noneother*

66 × 61 cm
Bequest Collection

This statue is a well known landmark in the centre of Rouen. The drawing is one of a group of drawings in a notebook made on a journey exploring Normandy some time during the days when Margaret Thatcher was making herself 'popular' in France. (Ben noticed a sign saying 'Faudra-t-il brûler Thatcher?')

Before he sets off on his trip abroad he calls in at the Tate and records the pleasure of being able to see Bonnard's *Nu dans le bain* – all to myself at last'. The drawings in this notebook, people, poodles, old folk on the way to church on Palm Sunday, the facades of antique shops, the engraved front windows of a patisserie, have the speed and vivacity of his beloved master.

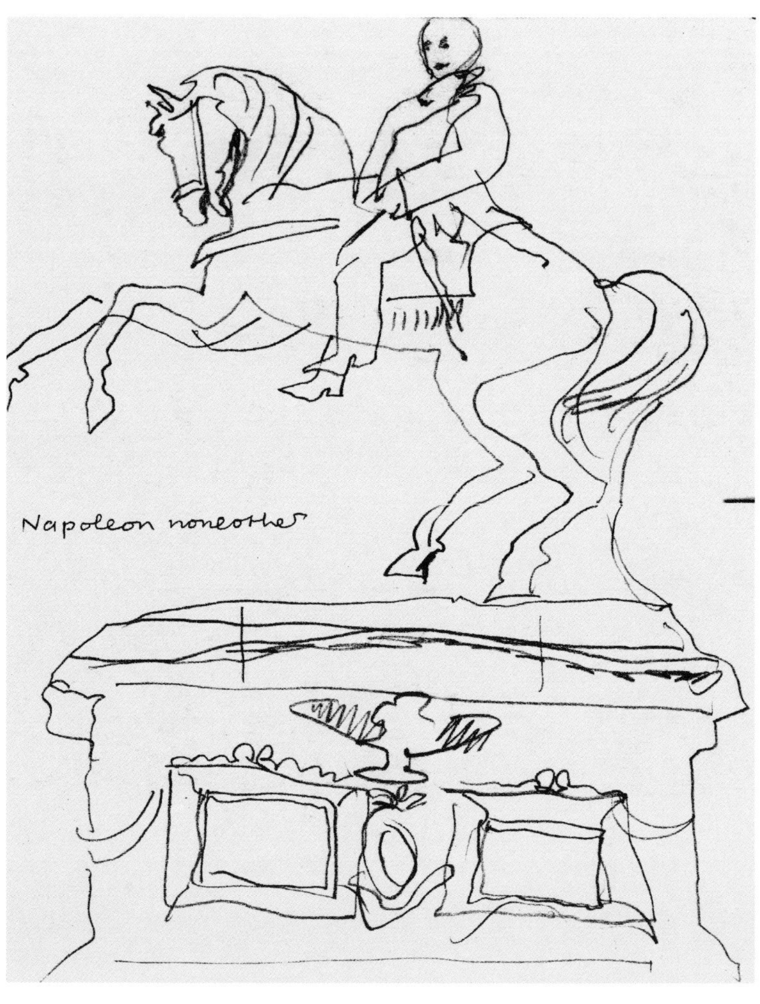

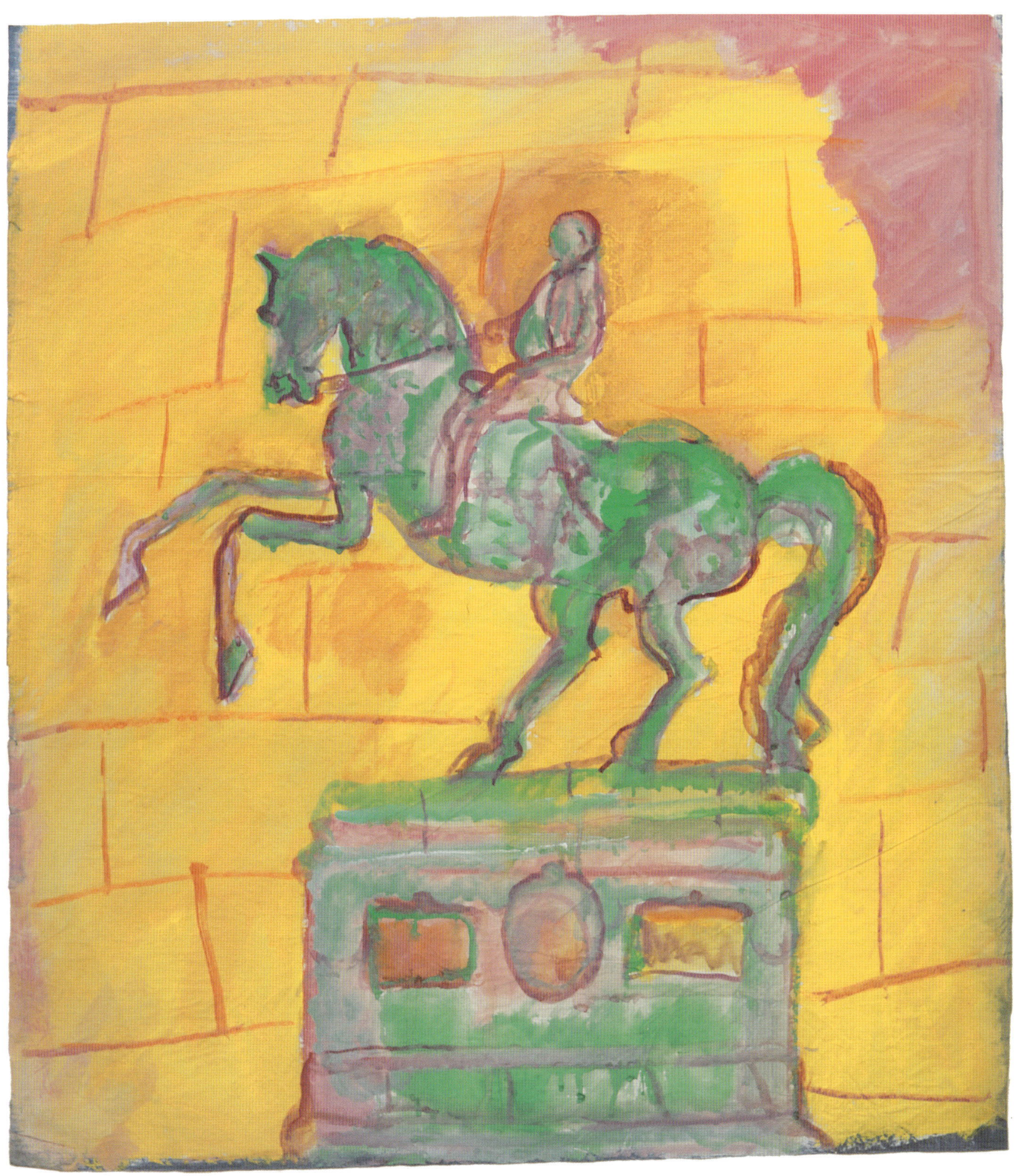

44. Penitent

68 × 53 cm
Bequest Collection

Penitent was probably the most astonishing single image to come to light in the entire bequest. The notebook for this painting comes from a journey covering a large area of the south-west of France, not far inland from the Mediterranean, made in 1983, four years after he gave up teaching and the year in which he moved to Presteigne. This image is a late work and one of the very rare occasions (see 'Dogdays' plate 21) when the humour of a scene, here an old lady storming along on her funny little feet on her way to church, stick and handbag flailing around, turns to something more menacing. Some of the colour may be bright but the mood is distinctly grim. The vulture-like posture of the bent old woman, the wasp-shaped lower half in bright green, the V-shaped shawl in lurid purple is closer to Francis Bacon than Ben Hartley.

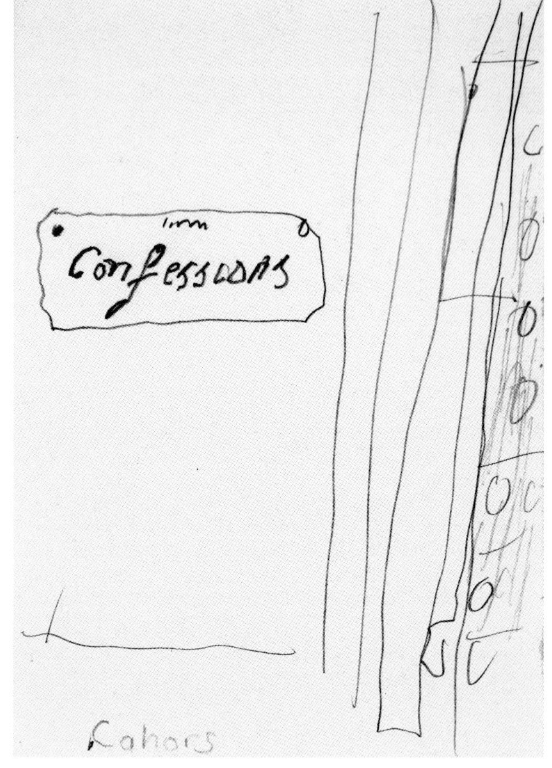

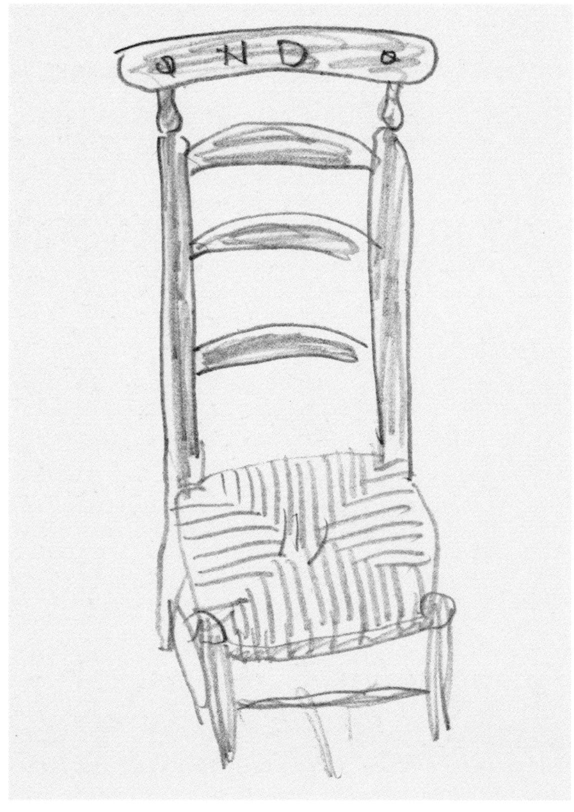

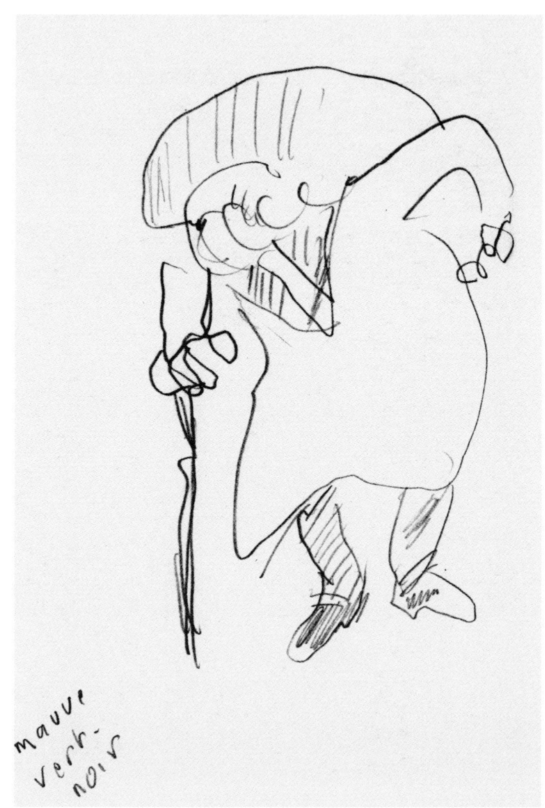

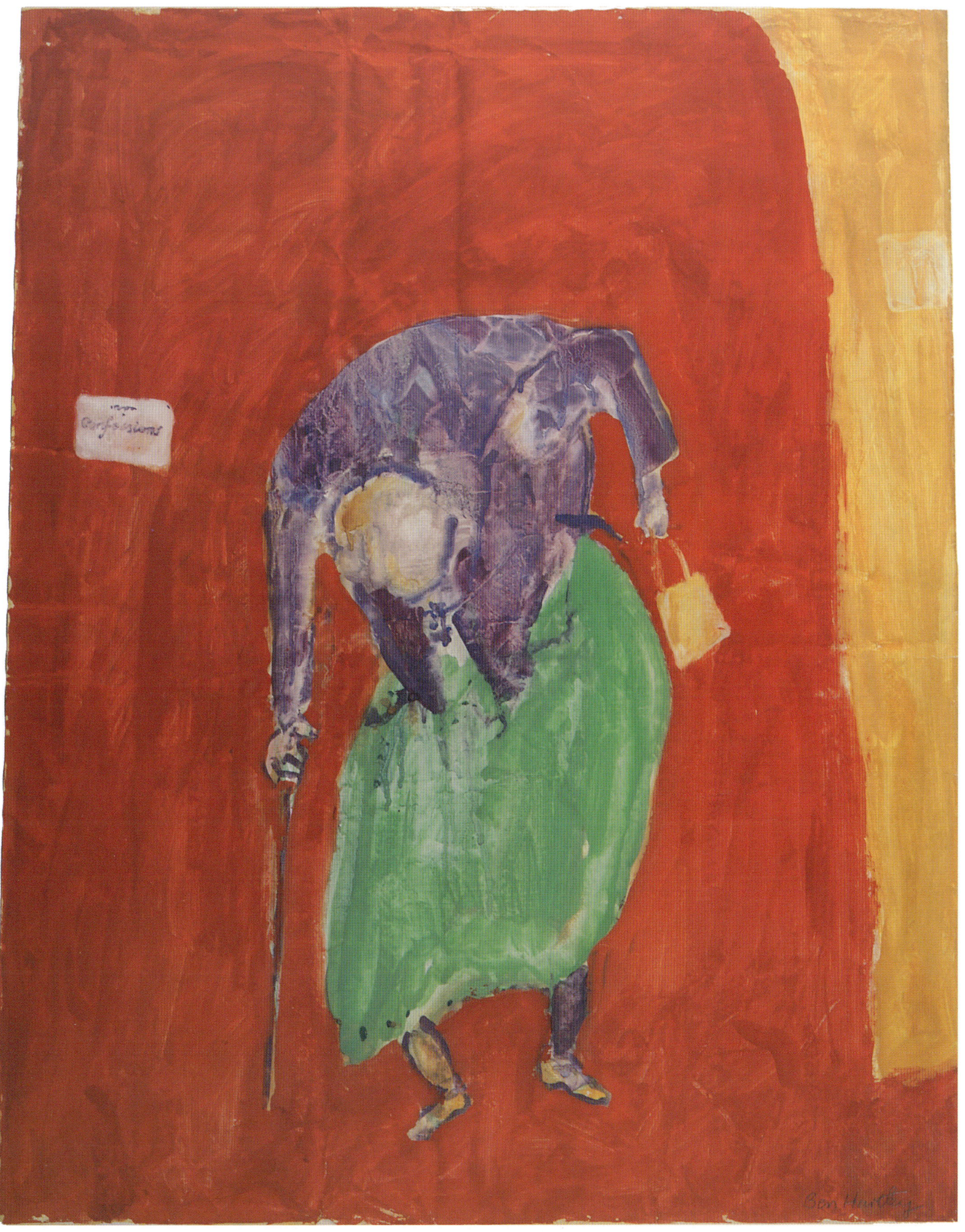
Confessions
Ben Hartley

The Seaside

The seaside, the place of treasured childhood memories, appears extensively in the notebooks and there are many pictures about seaside holidays. The drawings of the seaside are especially lovely. It is doubtful whether Ben was able to go in the sea like other children but he was certainly able to cast his poet's eye on the scene.

There are two paintings about the seaside, Picnic Shore, Strawberry or Vanilla *and* Reading Belle, *which are quite unique. They are both very light in tone, using very much the same colours, blue and a pinkish cream representing sand. This combination of colours occurs nowhere else in the work. More importantly these two works seem to inhabit a special, almost mysterious part of the imaginative world of Ben Hartley.*

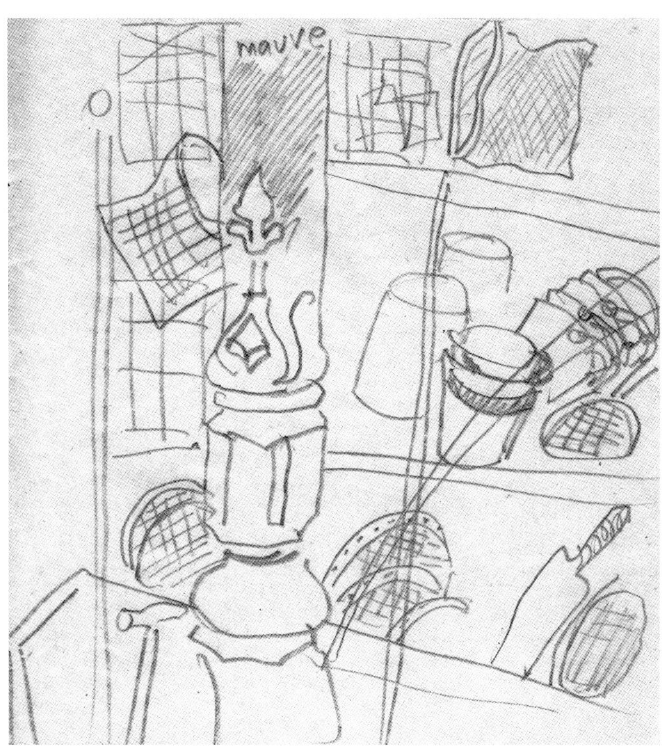

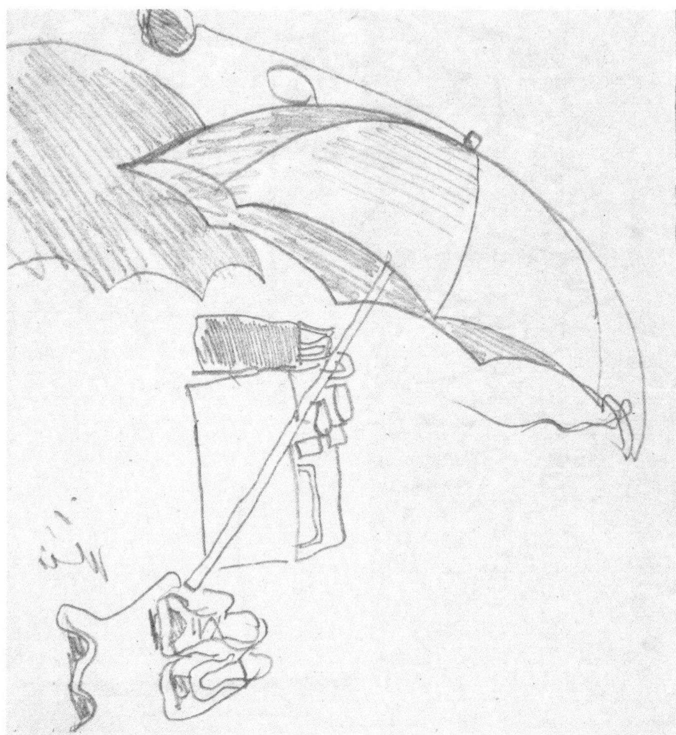

45. Reading Belle

62 × 57.5 cm
Private Collection

Reading Belle is clearly constructed from a number of drawings and motifs in an exceptionally lovely notebook, full of observations of people, grown-ups and children and a dog at the seaside; it is undated but looks as though it comes from around 1970.

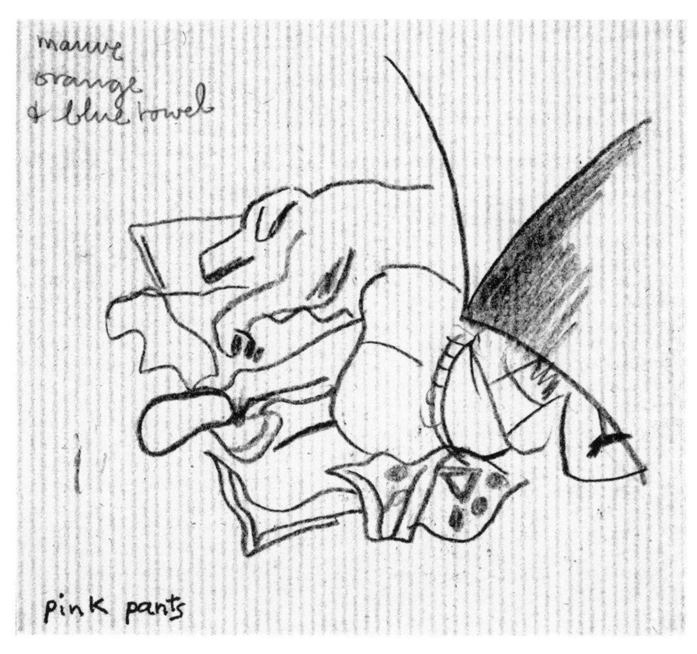

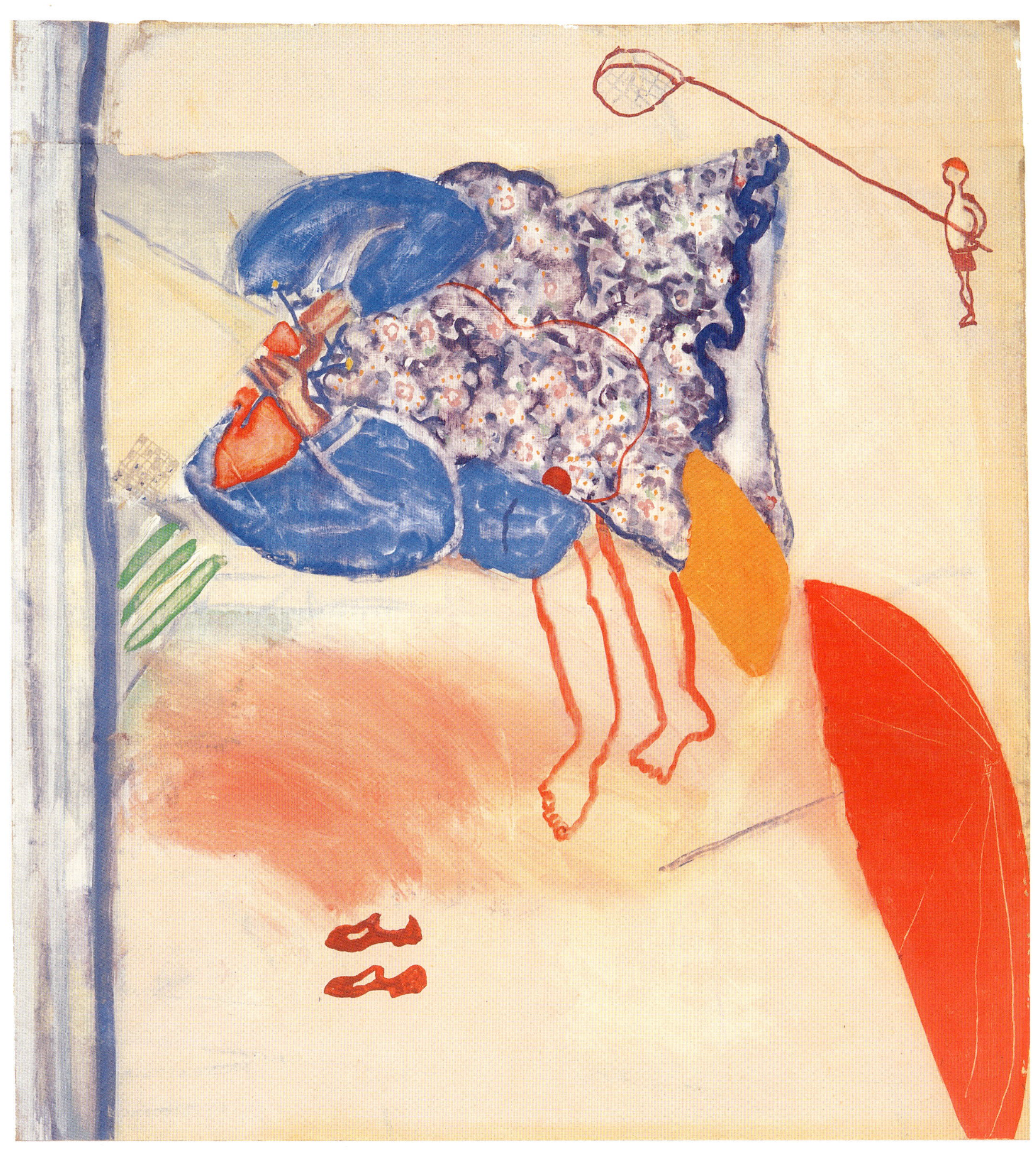

46. Picnic Shore Strawberry or Vanilla

57 × 70 cm
Bequest Collection

Like *Reading Belle* (previous plate) *Picnic Shore, Strawberry or Vanilla* seems equally to want to deceive the viewer. The area in the middle – is it a mound going upwards or is it an arm of the shore going out into the sea? Is the surrounding blue the sea or the sky? Aside from odd little doodles in the notebooks for the lemonade bottle on the left and the little deckchairs at the bottom, there are no drawings relating to the main motif of this picture. The central mound appears to have come straight out of Ben's imagination. However in one of the Irish notebooks, from the visit to Sligo in 1966, there is a descriptive note, (just words, no drawing, which is unusual), that reads like a short prose poem:

'The endless sea's motion against the little coloured plastic game of buckets and spades in the seaside stores. Tinned holiday food and grown up's golf. The bright packet of empty sweets. The sea going bluer. The tin can caravans. The empty golf course. A baby lotion bottle a rusted tinned can cheap bright knick knacks'.

On the next page there is a little jotting – 'a seaside icecream' – but no drawing to go with it. Whilst the painting of the Roman Catholic Church at Sligo (plate 10) was probably done soon after visiting the town, *Picnic Shore* must have come some years later. It is interesting to note that during the course of this visit Ben did some drawings of the church at Drumcliffe, the burial place of the poet W.B. Yeats, just a few miles north west of Sligo.

It has already been suggested that two paintings *Fawns Autumn* (plate 7) and *Rose Cottage, Vase of Flowers* (plate 20) inhabit the realm of the mystical. The same can also be said of these two seaside paintings.

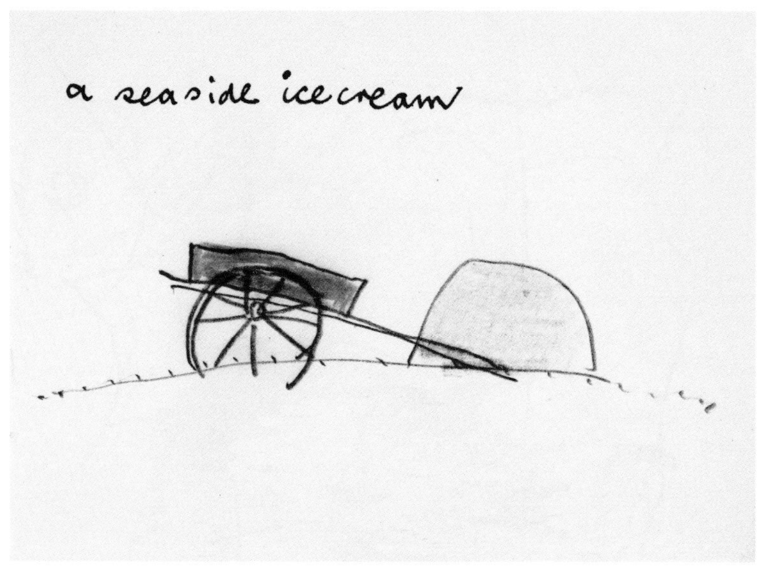

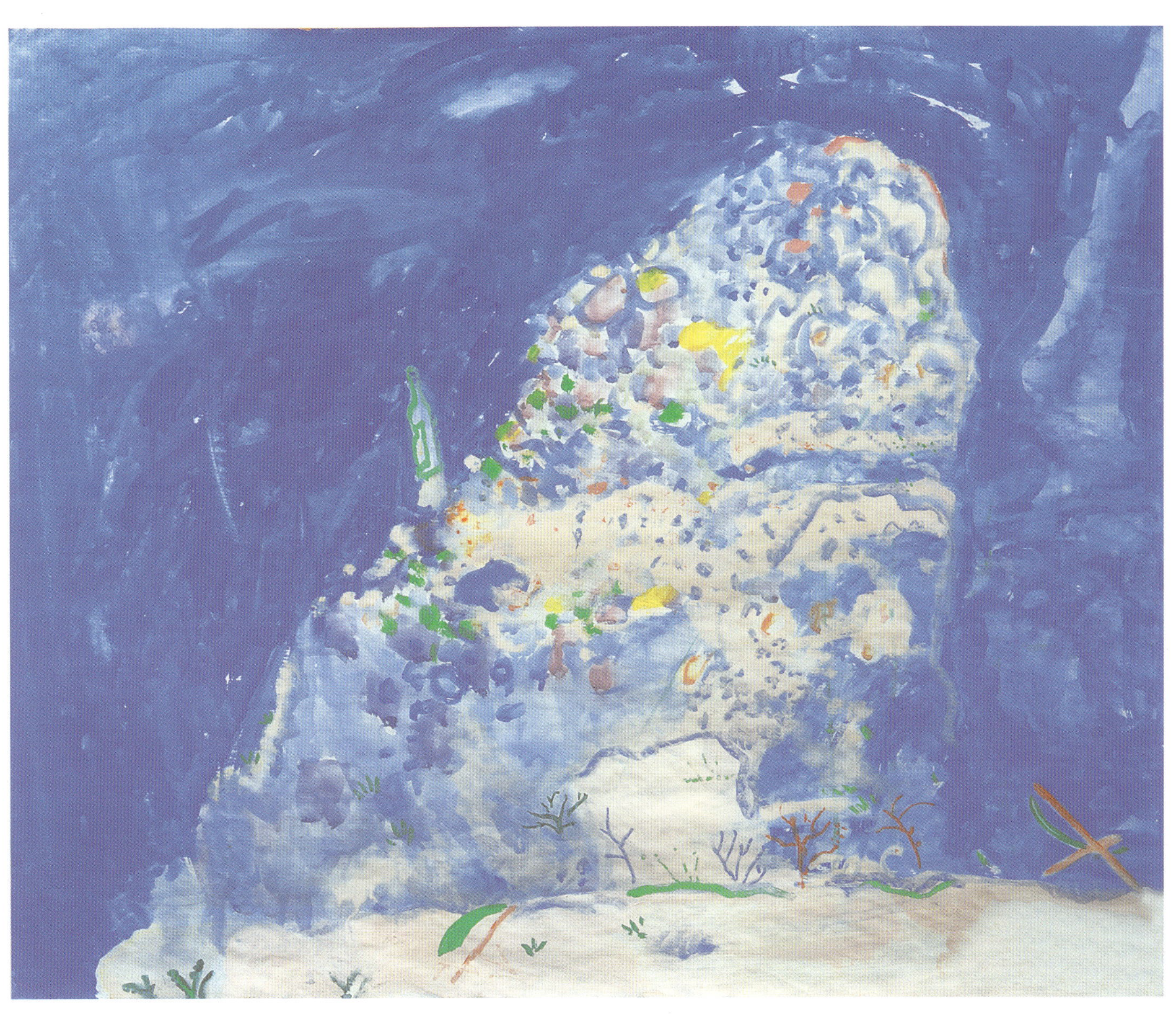

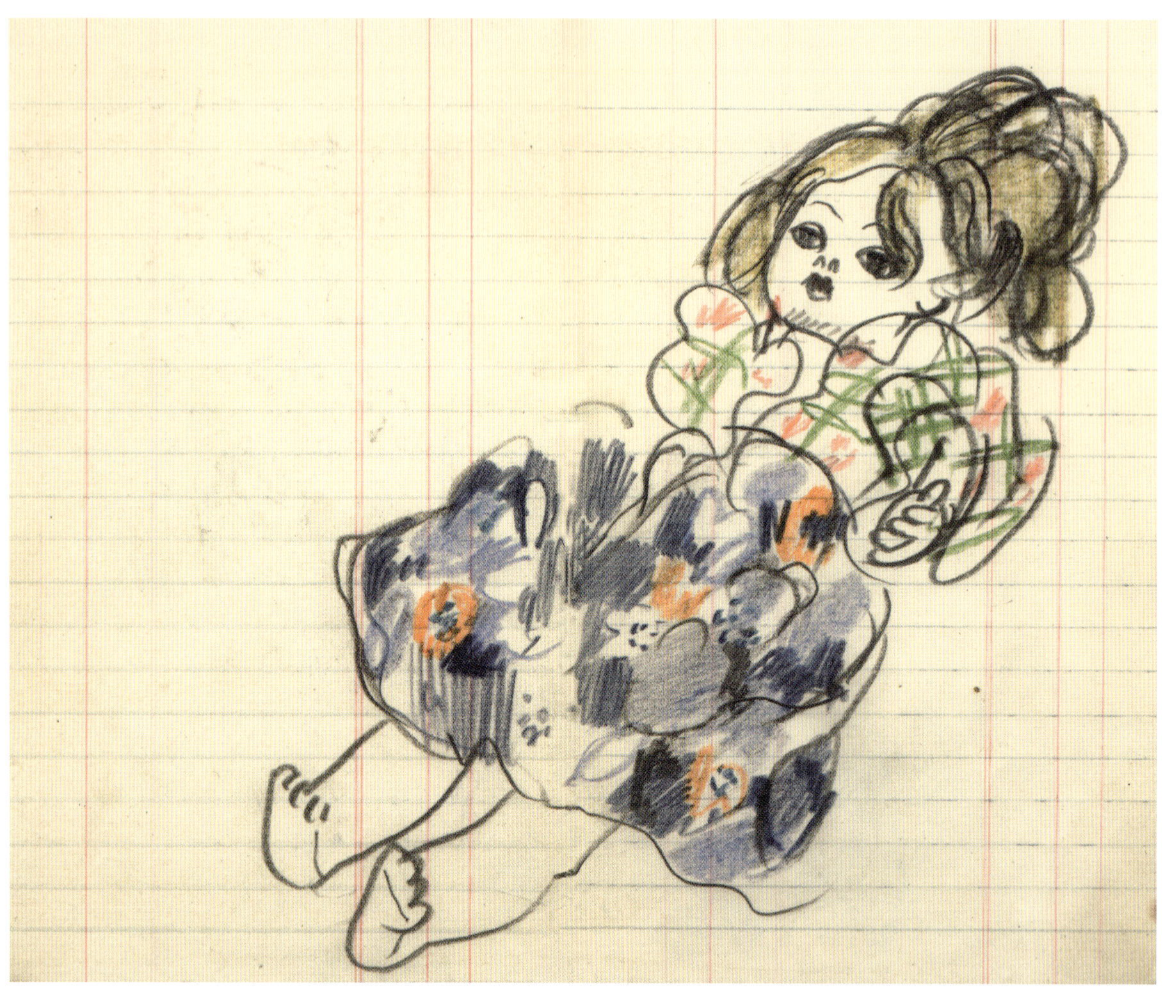

Drawing of a doll in coloured pencil from a notebook dated June 1959

Childhood

The question of the nature of childhood experience is central to the aesthetic of Ben Hartley's work, regardless of what the subject matter of the image may be. However, children themselves often appear in the notebooks, children in prams, children in uniform on the way to school, children at play, climbing trees, having fun on a river and so on. It is very clear from various letters and photographs, as well as from the work itself, that children meant a great deal to Ben and, in a familiar situation, he could feel at ease with them. He was also very acutely aware of their vulnerability. One of the most moving discoveries in the bequest was the extent of his contact with UNICEF. He was deeply affected by knowledge of the suffering of children in the Third World. He made donations and empathized with their plight, possibly to the point where he denied himself for their sake. At the same time there is nothing in the least sad about his portrayal of children in his work, the notebooks or the paintings.

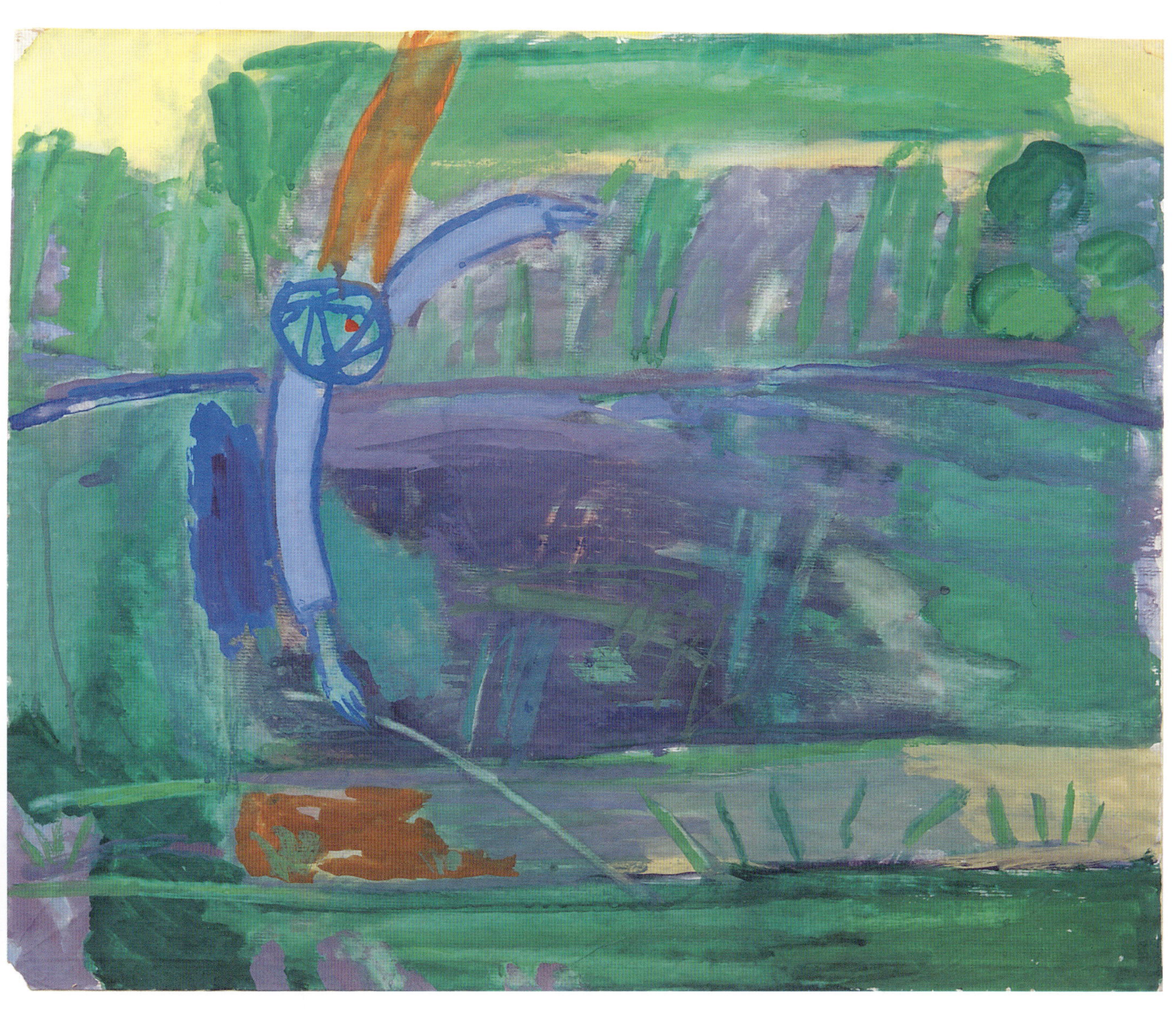

50. Swinging Belle*

57 × 60 cm
Bequest Collection

Swinging Belle is certainly one of the wildest paintings, the girl at the top of her flight with her view of surrounding houses and gardens shown in strip form on each side of the picture. Like the rest of Ben's work this picture has no date. Late middle would make sense. This picture displays the extreme brightness of the middle period allied to the freedom that comes from complete mastery.

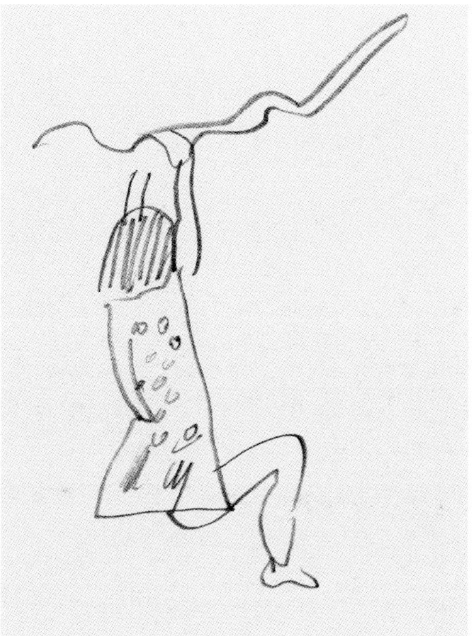

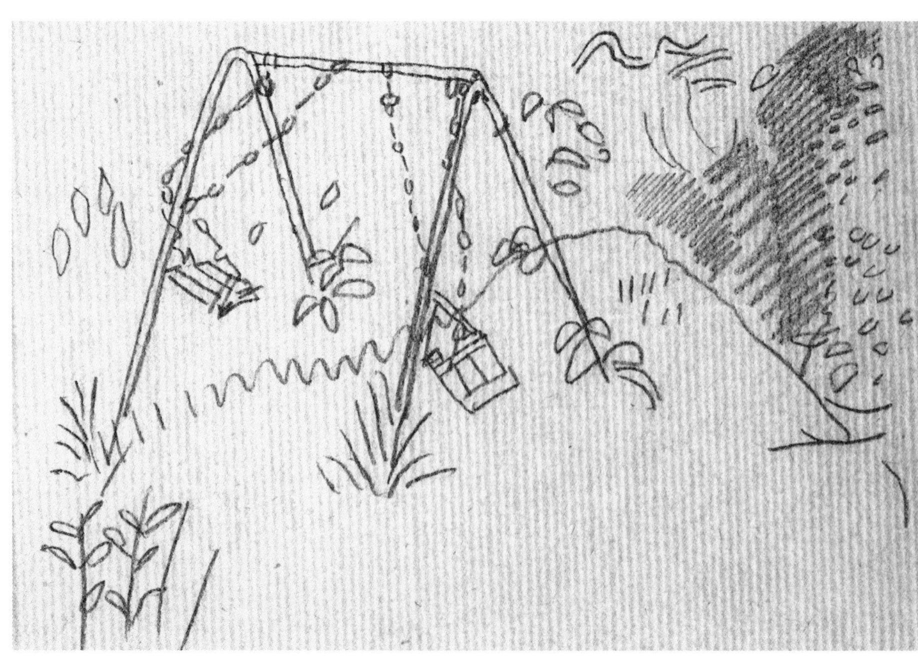

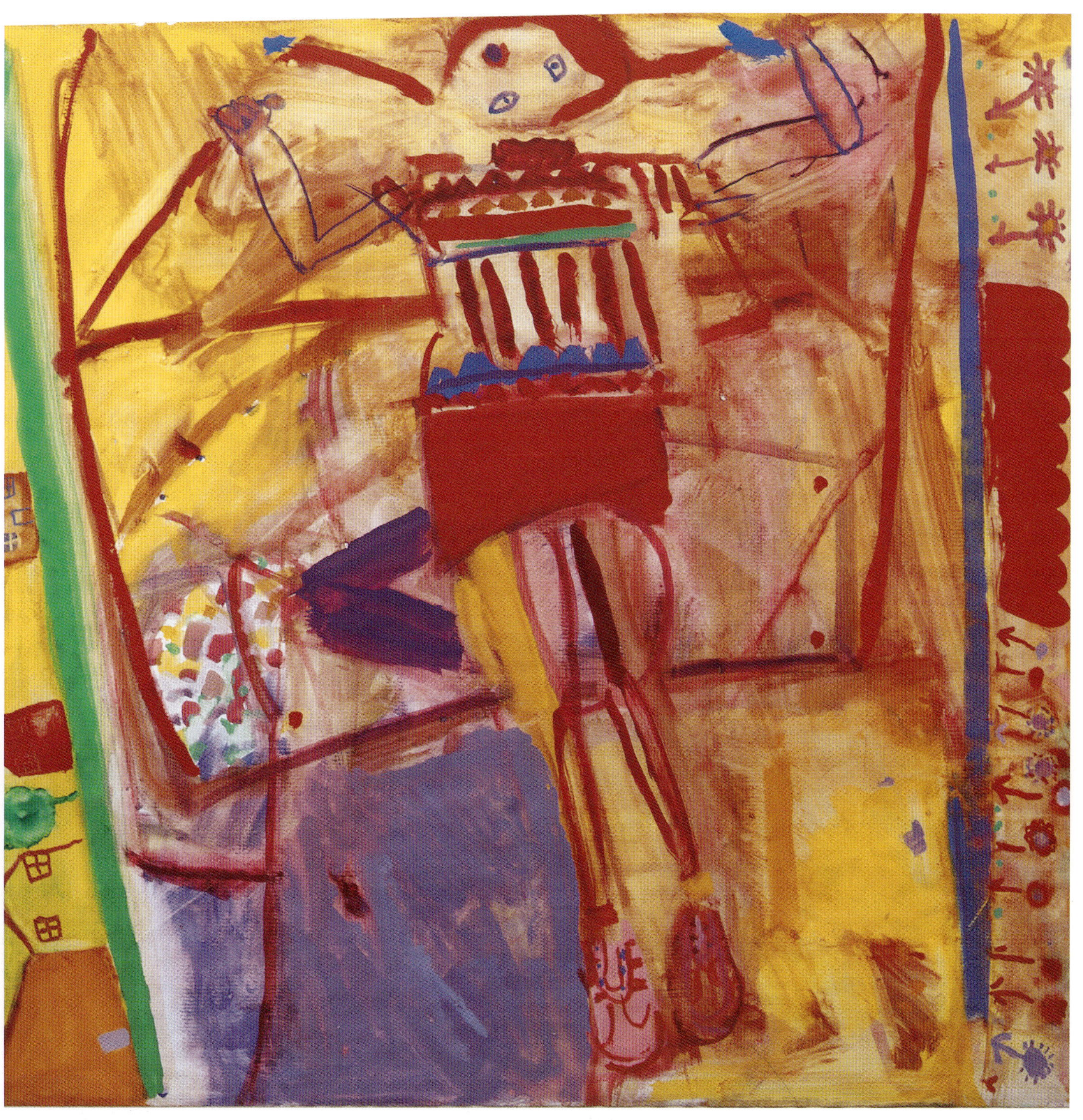

51. Us and Henrietta

52 × 63 cm
Bequest Collection

Though the drawings relating to this painting come from early notebooks going as far back as 1957, this is a late work which is as fresh and carefree as anything Ben ever achieved.

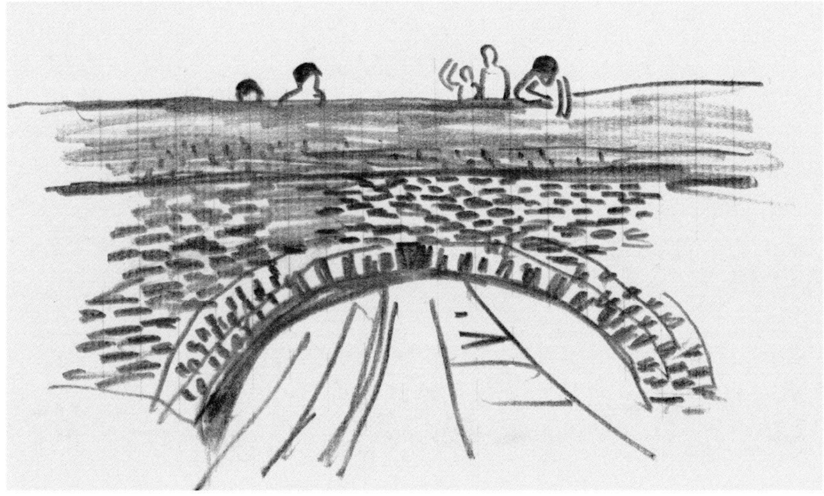

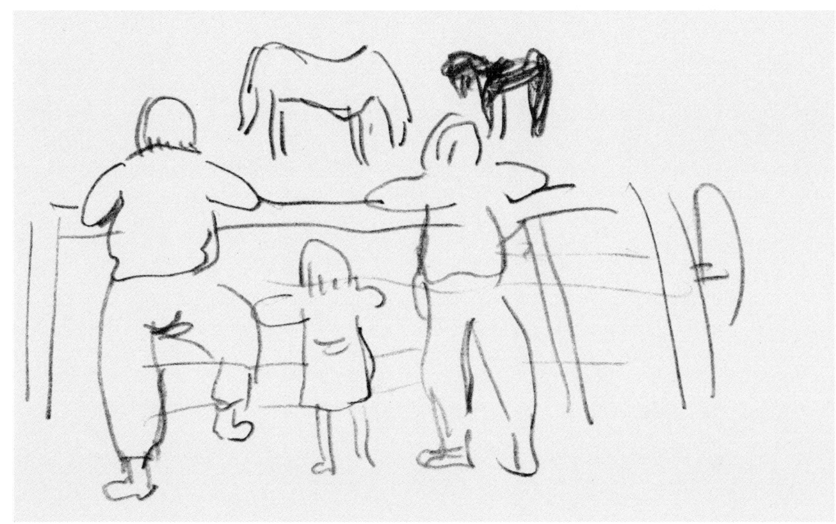

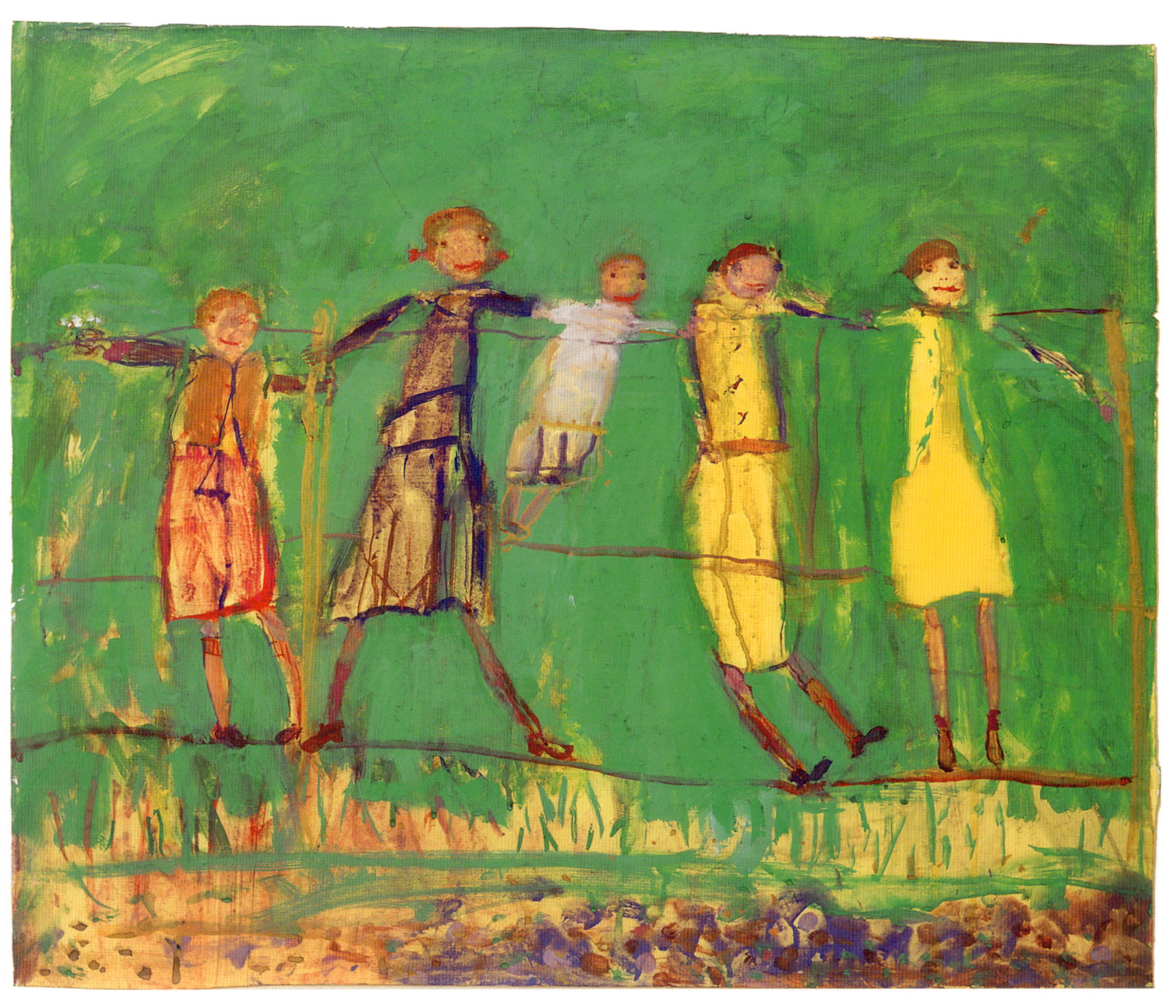

Self-portraiture

Though emphasis has been placed on Ben's retiring nature, like many artists, not least Bonnard, he was fascinated by the idea of himself as a presence in his pictures. As one might expect, his approach to the subject was oblique.

This drawing comes from a notebook which was begun in the winter of 1966 and carries on through to mid-June of that year. The notebook has a wonderful feeling of lightness, one could even say a sweetness of spirit, with entries from Ben which read like poetry. Whereas a drawing of a shadow may suggest something slightly sinister, it is not the case here. On the immediately preceding pages we find drawings of groups of cows in a field in which Ben highlights his fascination with the shadows cast by the cows.

The single figure of an elderly man very much at home, his jacket off, maybe wearing a waistcoat or just in shirtsleeves, his trousers held up by braces, wanders in and out of a number of paintings. The figure on the left in Home Economics *(plate 14) in cloth cap and waistcoat, one slipper on one slipper off, is a good example. We are never given a clue as to who these people might be. They could be relatives or friends, or simply a generalized recollection of domestic life. At the same time we cannot rule out the possibility that this is Ben projecting himself into some kind of home, or even a form of self-image. At one point, writing about his own childhood, he said he never really had a childhood. It is possible, even likely, that once he got beyond a certain age he always thought of himself as being old.*

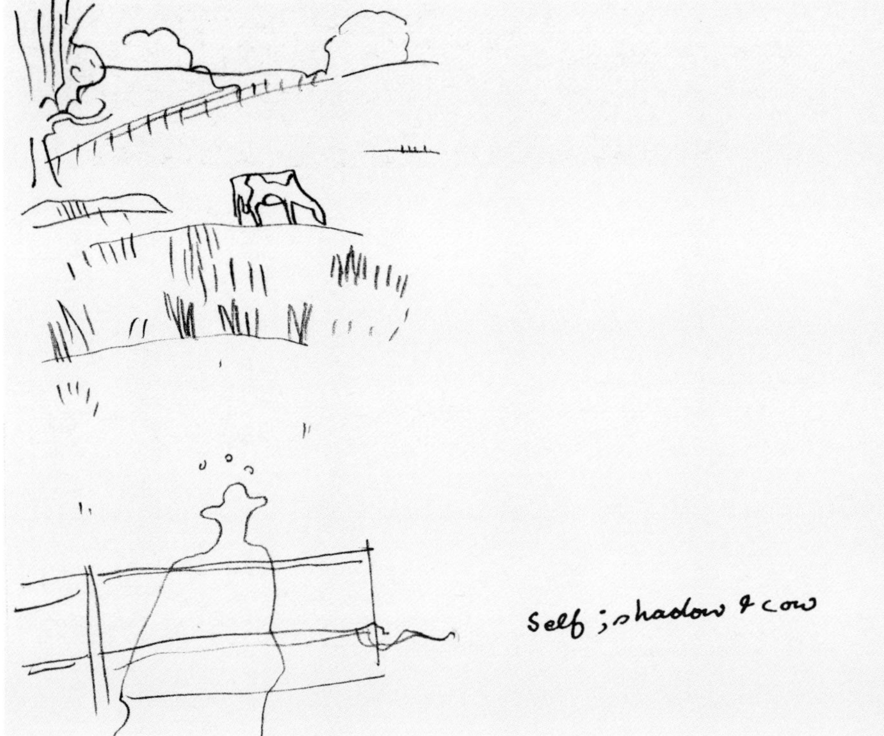

52. Backitchen

56 × 66 cm
Bequest Collection

For the most part, regardless of his real underlying feeling, Ben saw the representation of these elderly figures as an opportunity for comedy, nowhere more so than in *Backitchen*. The old-fashioned fireplace is very much like the fireplace in his cottage in Ermington. But here Ben has gone for much more homeliness and ornament. Colourism, the strong yellow, the vigorous blocks of reddish brown, pink and blue, has a large part to play in the way the picture works. Centre stage however is our perennial unidentified personage, a thin old man, bending over tying a shoelace, his charmingly painted cap still on his head and his beloved marmalade cat stretched across his back on the fork of his braces; hence the punning title of *Backitchen*.

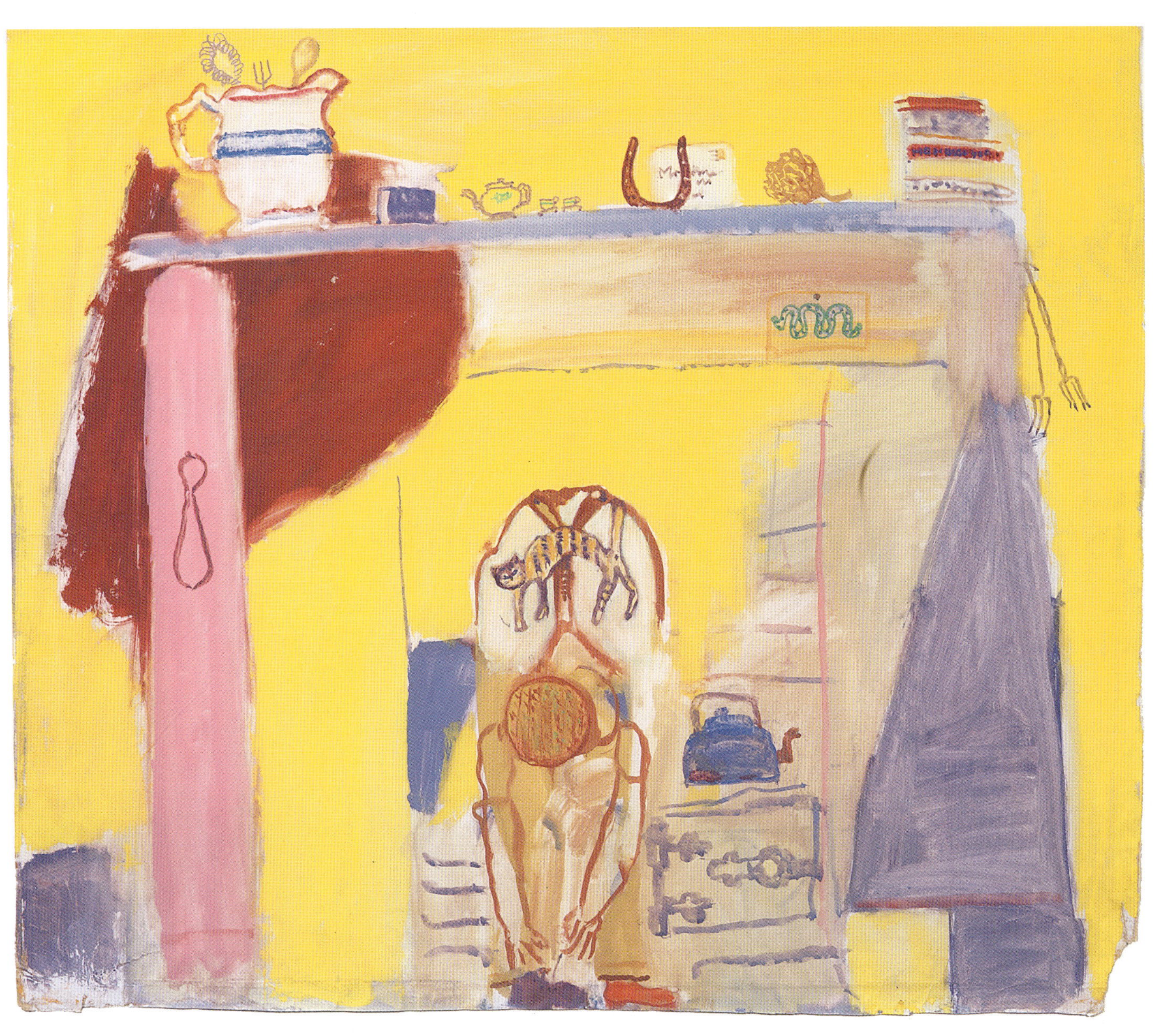

53. Collected Legs

52 × 67 cm
Bequest Collection

Ben appears to have been especially conscious of the fact that he had long legs. As a result we have a quite a number of drawings in the notebooks in which they feature. In *Collected Legs* (Ben's and various domestic companions') the trousers come out blue, in another similar work they come out bright yellow. Though the figure is invisible from the legs upwards, these legs and bony knees can only be Ben's.

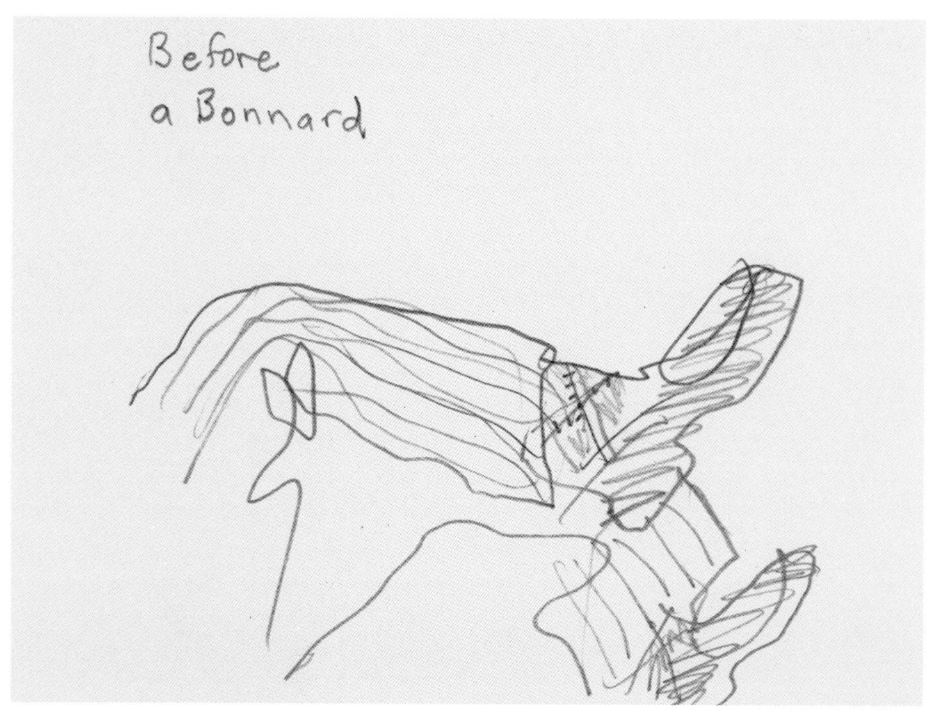

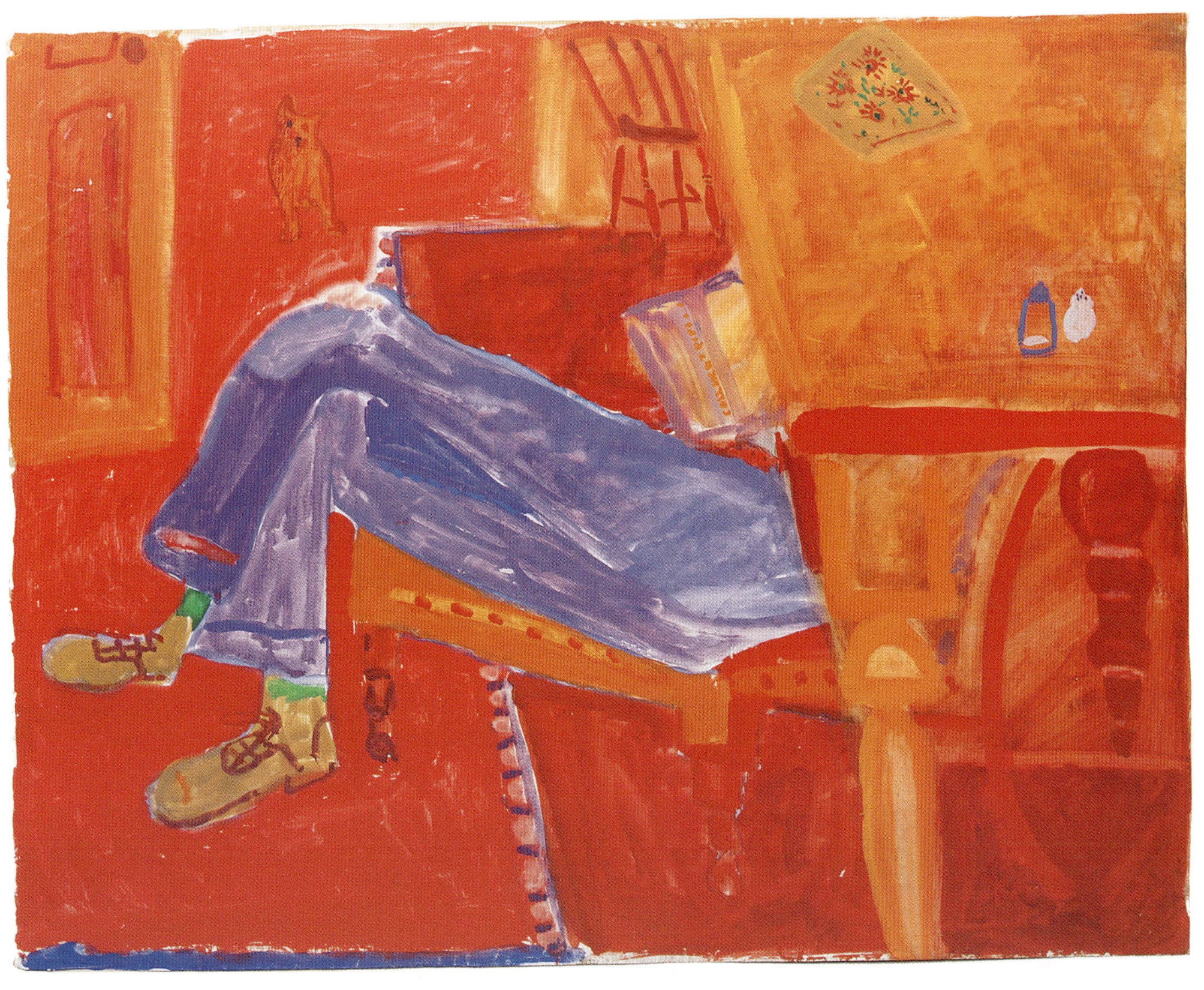

54. Cocoa Quiet

not known

Cocoa Quiet is the most heartbreakingly sad picture Ben ever painted. It has Ben's usual, lively array of colour and a chaos which at first glance might be amusing. But this picture is in deadly earnest. For once we almost see the face, but all we are given is a blank oval, the spread-eagled legs under the table bespeak distress. The title leaves us in no doubt as to the meaning of this picture. It was sold in around 1980 to an architecture student who came to Plymouth Arts Centre as a technician with a touring French mime company. The price, by present day standards, was very modest, less than £100; all the same it seemed a lot of money for a student to find, but find it he did. The picture can no longer be traced. Attempts to track it down via an address in Paris have sadly come to nought. Fortunately the painting was recorded on a 35mm slide which is the only source for reproduction.

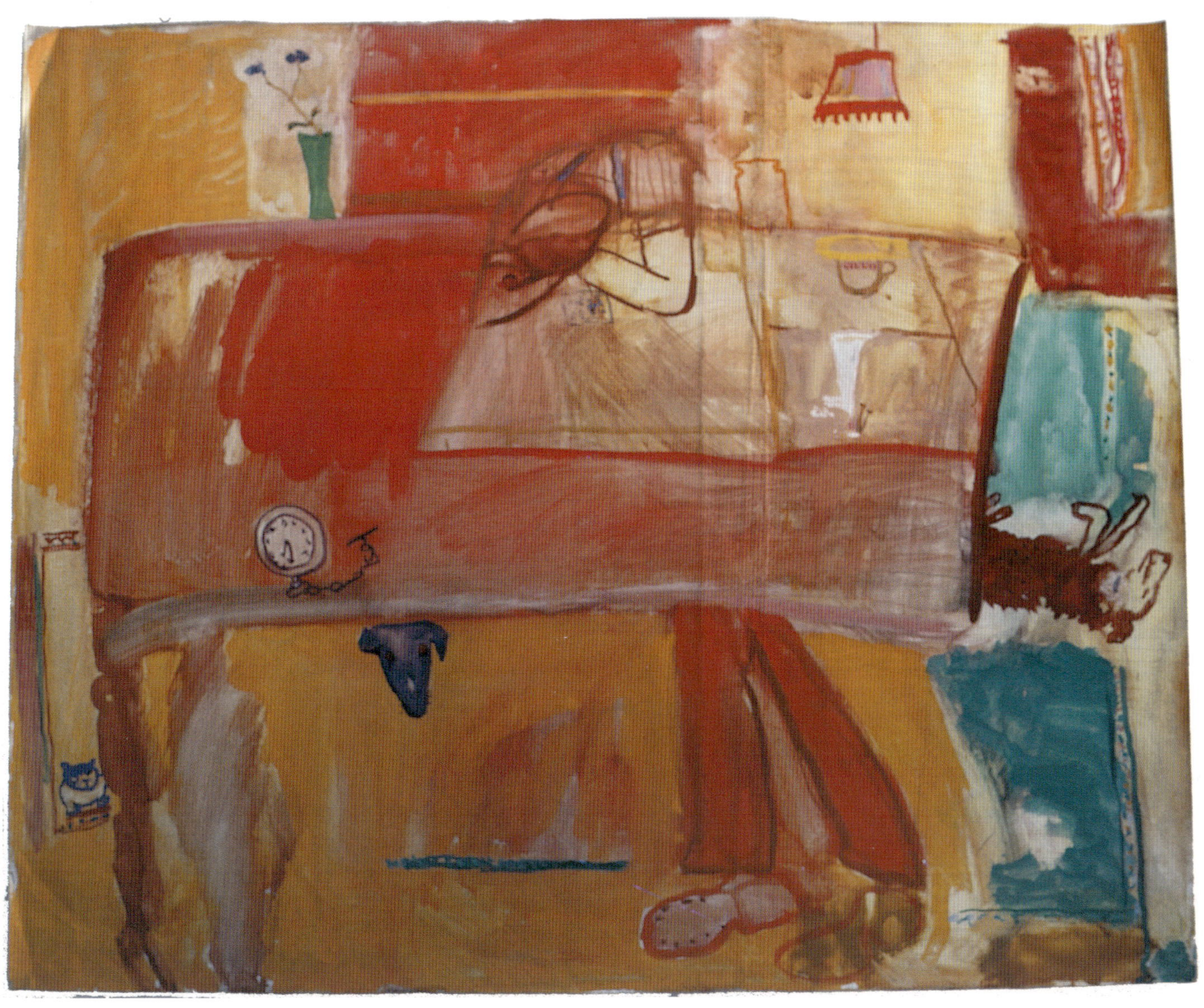

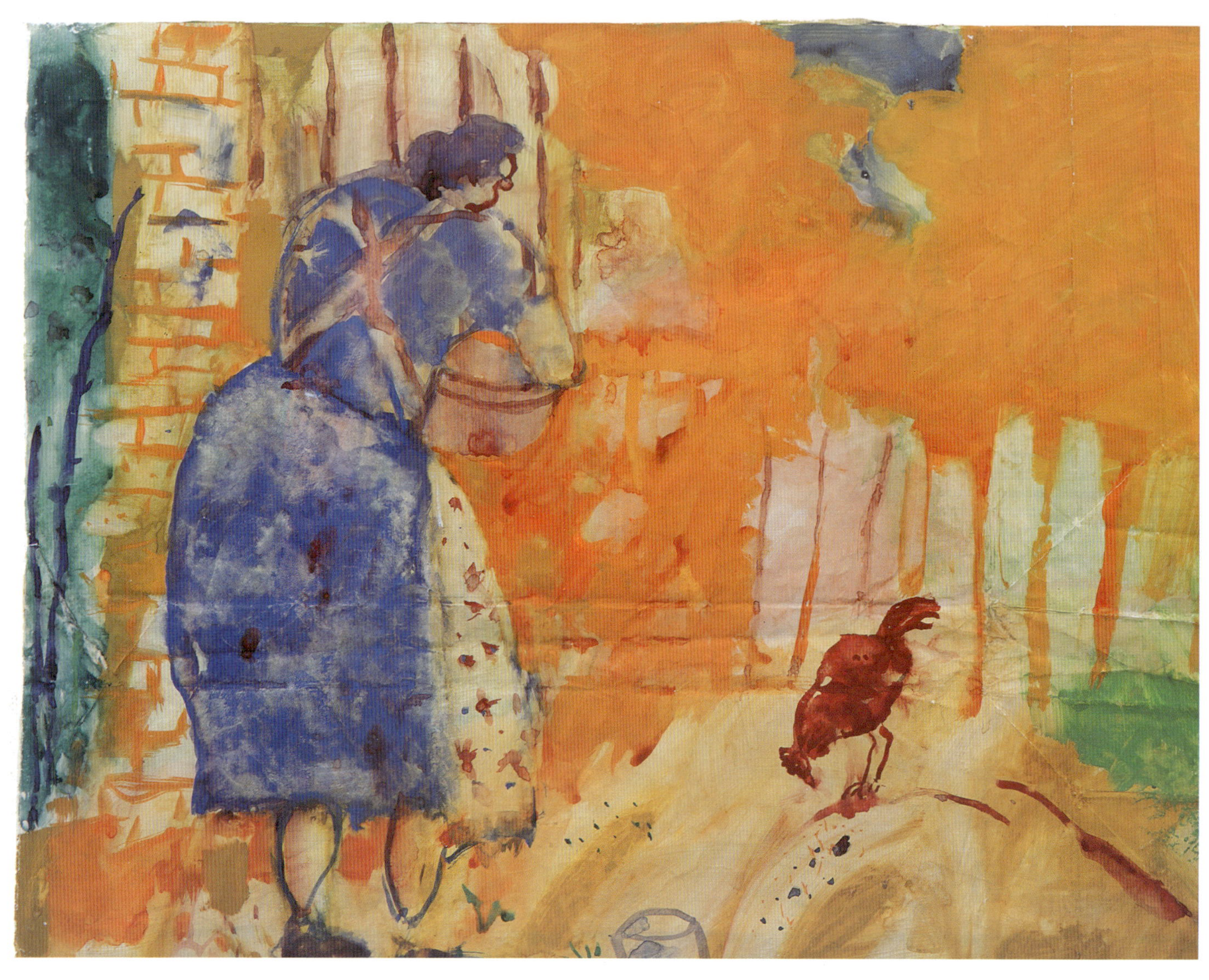

55. Chuck-Chuck-Chuck

54 × 71 cm
Bequest Collection

Late work

The chronological division of Ben Hartley's work into early, middle and late is quite easily discernible. There is a distinct difference between early and middle, partly because of the change of palette, partly because of a more adventurous approach in the middle period to constructing the imagery. The difference between middle and late is not quite so distinct. There is a degree of carry-over of the imagery of the middle period. The main break comes with the move to Wales in 1983. Technical changes occur which alter the surface appearance of the work. The gouache is much thinned down, looser and allowed to dribble. Occasionally other material is added: grit or eggshell. Then we find an extraordinary move to the use of different paper. Instead of his beloved brown parcel paper, Ben began using material from a papermaking factor in Hereford: not the paper made to be sold by the manufacturer but poorer paper that had been overprinted to be used for parcelling. This change may account for the difference in the use of gouache. Whatever the technical background, this period coincides with the most deeply moving development in the work, showing all the qualities we associate with the notion of late work as an uplifting, final flowering.

In May 1989 Ben wrote to Susan and Quentin Bone, friends from his Plymouth days with whom he kept in regular contact. Susan Bone had been a student in Ben's class in Plymouth. In this particular letter he begins by thanking her for a postcard of a view of Nice by Matisse. But by now Ben is depressed and has been for some time. He begins to talk about how life has changed in Presteigne since he moved there in 1983. He then goes on:

'...Alas my inspirations dried up months ago. I feel quite a distaste for portraying all my old farmyard friends, ducks, hens, dogs, cats, cows and sheep etc. Noah's Ark is out and what is left? All the old-style farming ways have been superseded and the old-style people too. I doubt if more than one or two are left: and they have to be hunted out. Perhaps I have joined that regime? Old boots, old stick and old coat. ...Perhaps I too have to be hunted out.'

These observations and the profoundly elegiac mood of this letter convey all there is to be said about the underlying feeling to the late work. For all Ben's protestations in his final years about not being able to paint, we have the evidence to the contrary in our hands. The very people whose way of life Ben deemed to have disappeared became the central subject of the work of the final years. Though some of the pictures have titles, such as *Phoebe*, *Jarge*, *Smiler*, these are probably just generic names. Whereas with the work from earlier times it is almost invariably possible to locate relevant motifs somewhere in one of the notebooks, with these paintings it is rarely the case. True there are many wonderful drawings of old farming folk in the notebooks, but somehow not the particular people we see here in these paintings, each portrayed with the force and impact of his or her character. On the other hand, in a sense, Ben had drawn these people scores of times. Here, however, they have been brought to life through memory and imagination and for that reason they are all the more moving.

As so often with an artist's late work, Ben has simplified his method of communicating what he wants to say. He has abandoned the customary complexity of so much of his past work in order to create imaginary portraits: single figures with just a simple motif to provide the subject with an identity, a hoe, a beer mug, a bucket, a brolly, a walking stick and so on. Ben's humour has by no means disappeared. These people have been captured in a moment of time but by their very anonymity they acquire a quality of timelessness. Hence the poignancy so many people have found in these paintings. At the same time each of these figures in his or her way conveys a mood of joy, and even hope, to make an appropriate ending to this book.

56. Lady in Red*
71 × 58 cm
Bequest Collection

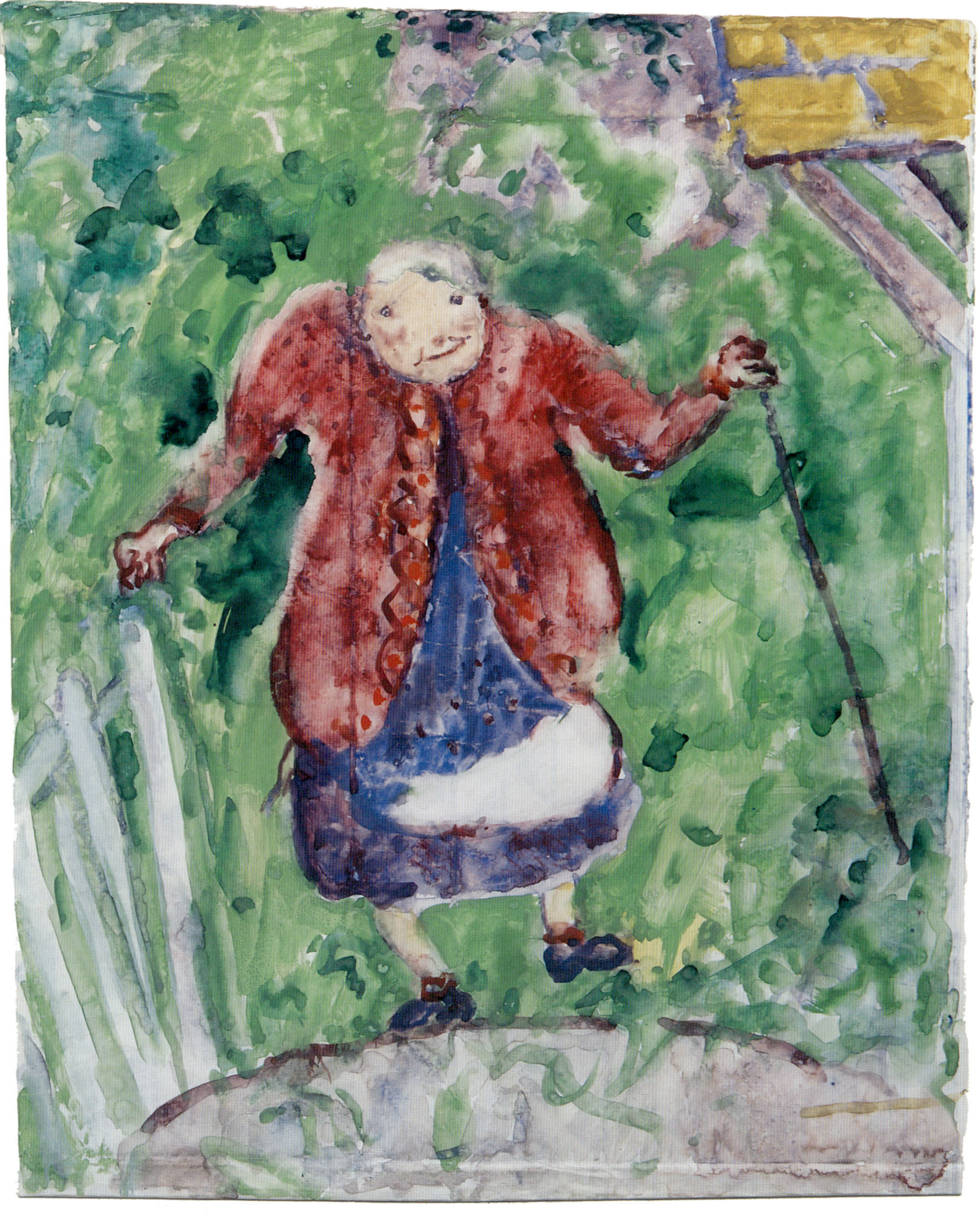

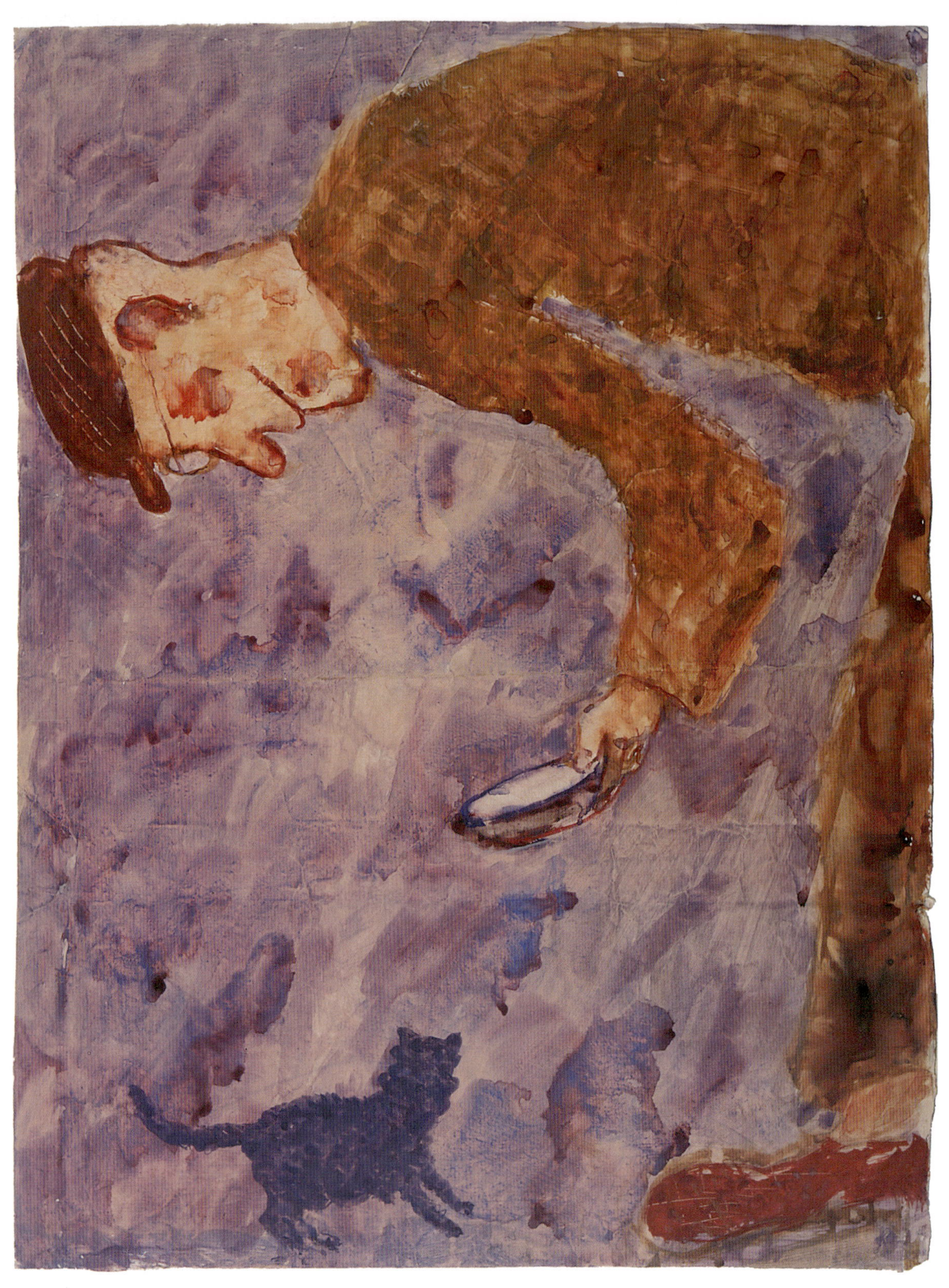

57. Milk Time*
70 × 53 cm
Bequest Collection

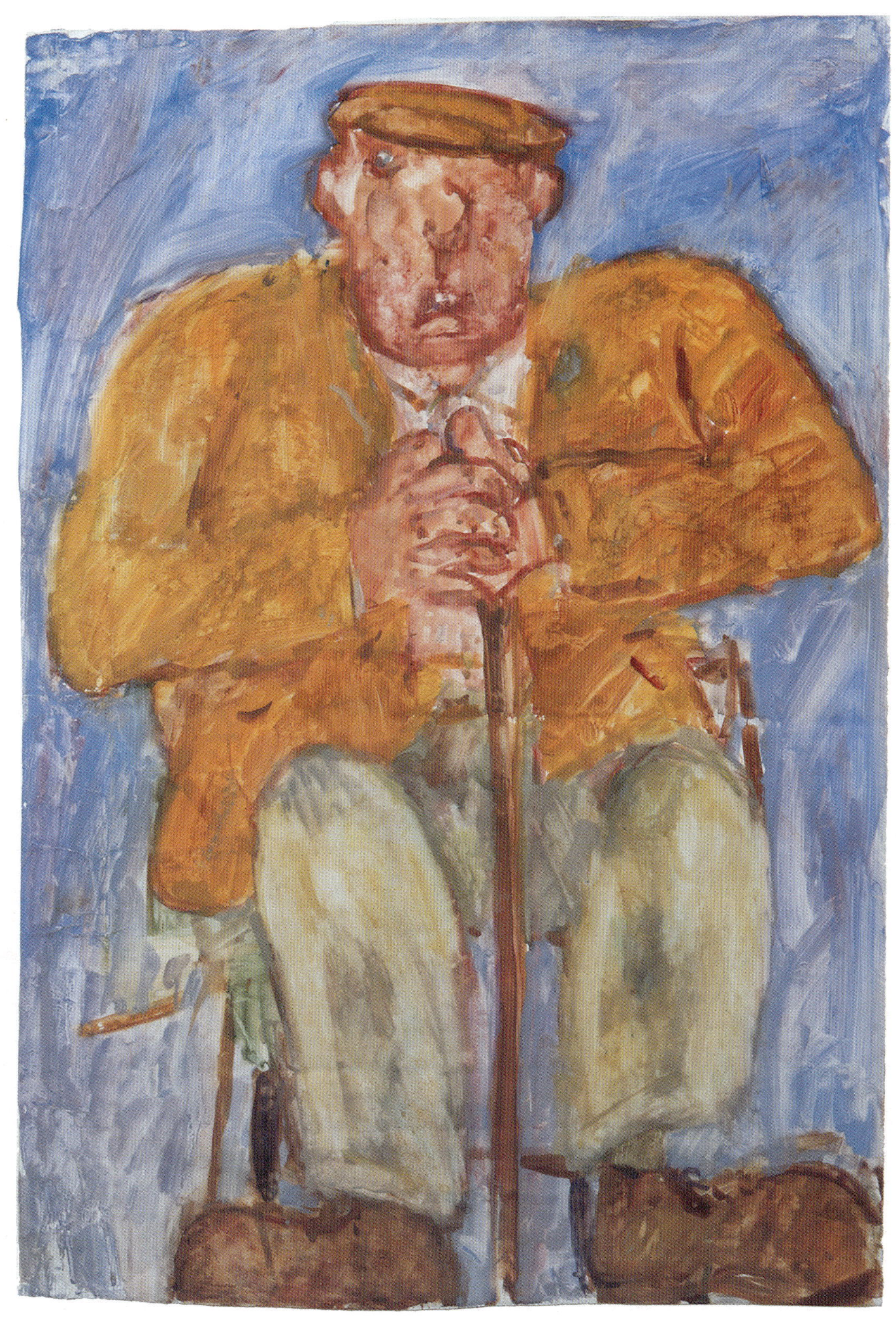

58. Snug Resident*

62.5 × 44 cm
Bequest Collection

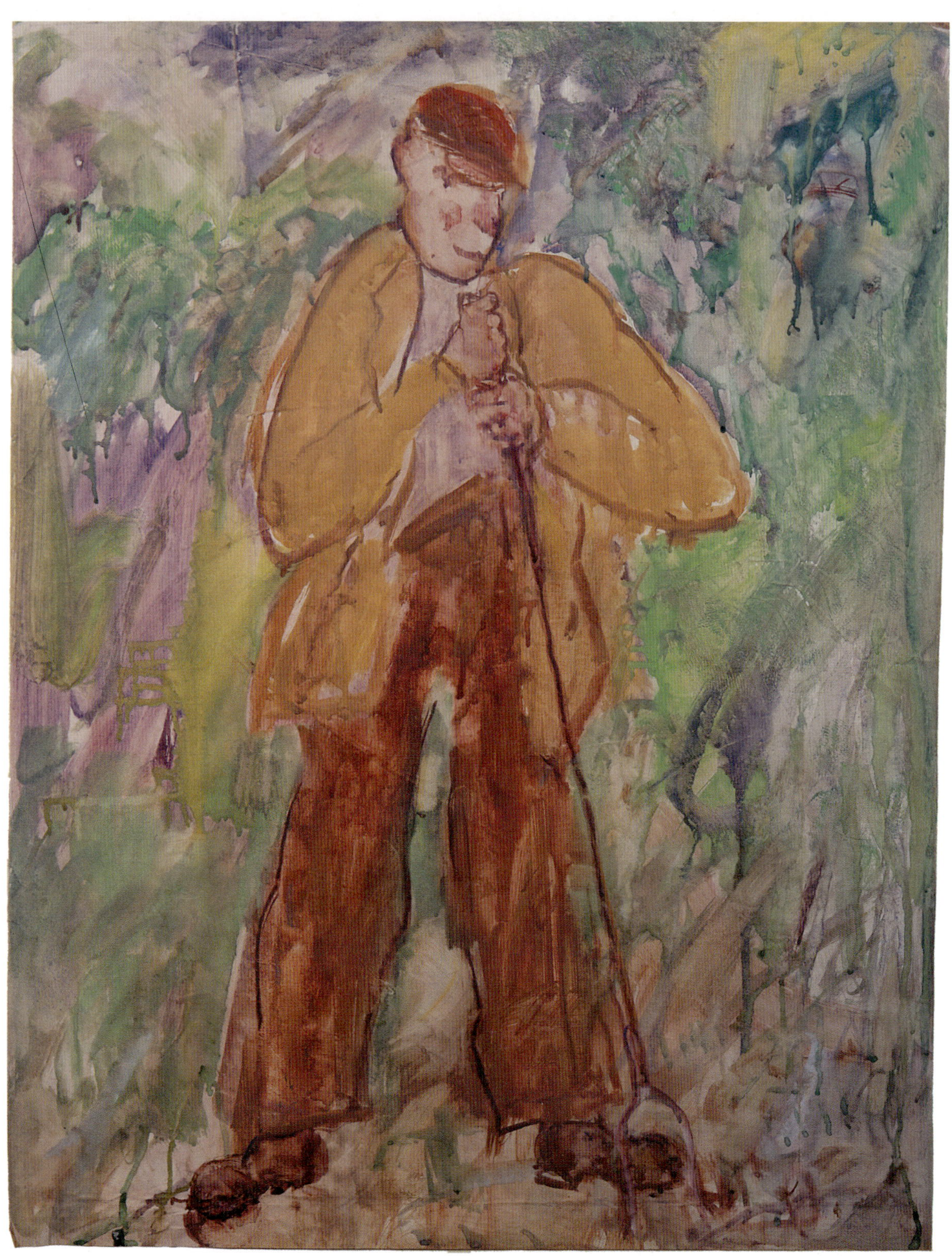

59. Jarge

64.5 × 50 cm
Bequest collection

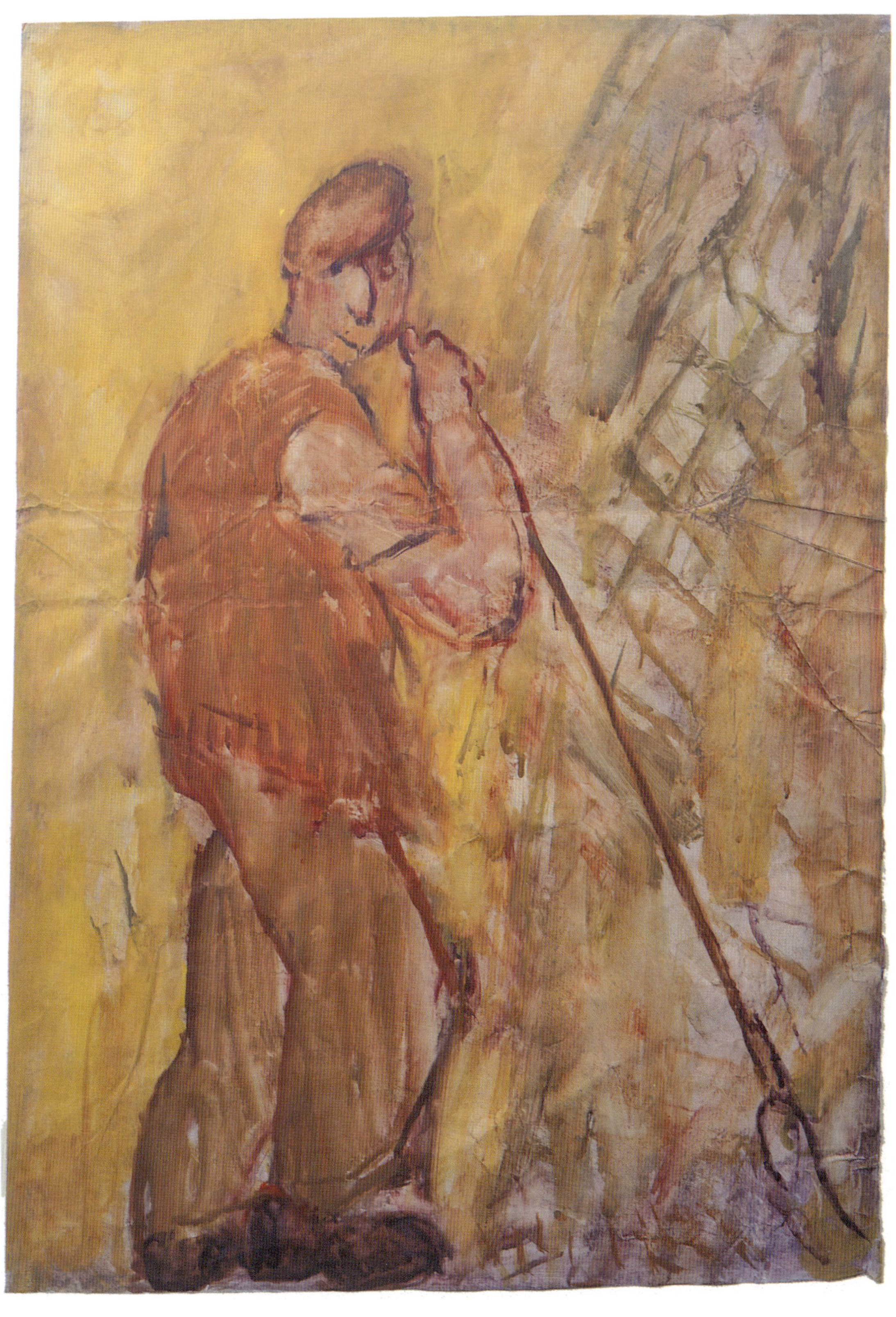

60. Smiler

64 × 47 cm
Bequest Collection

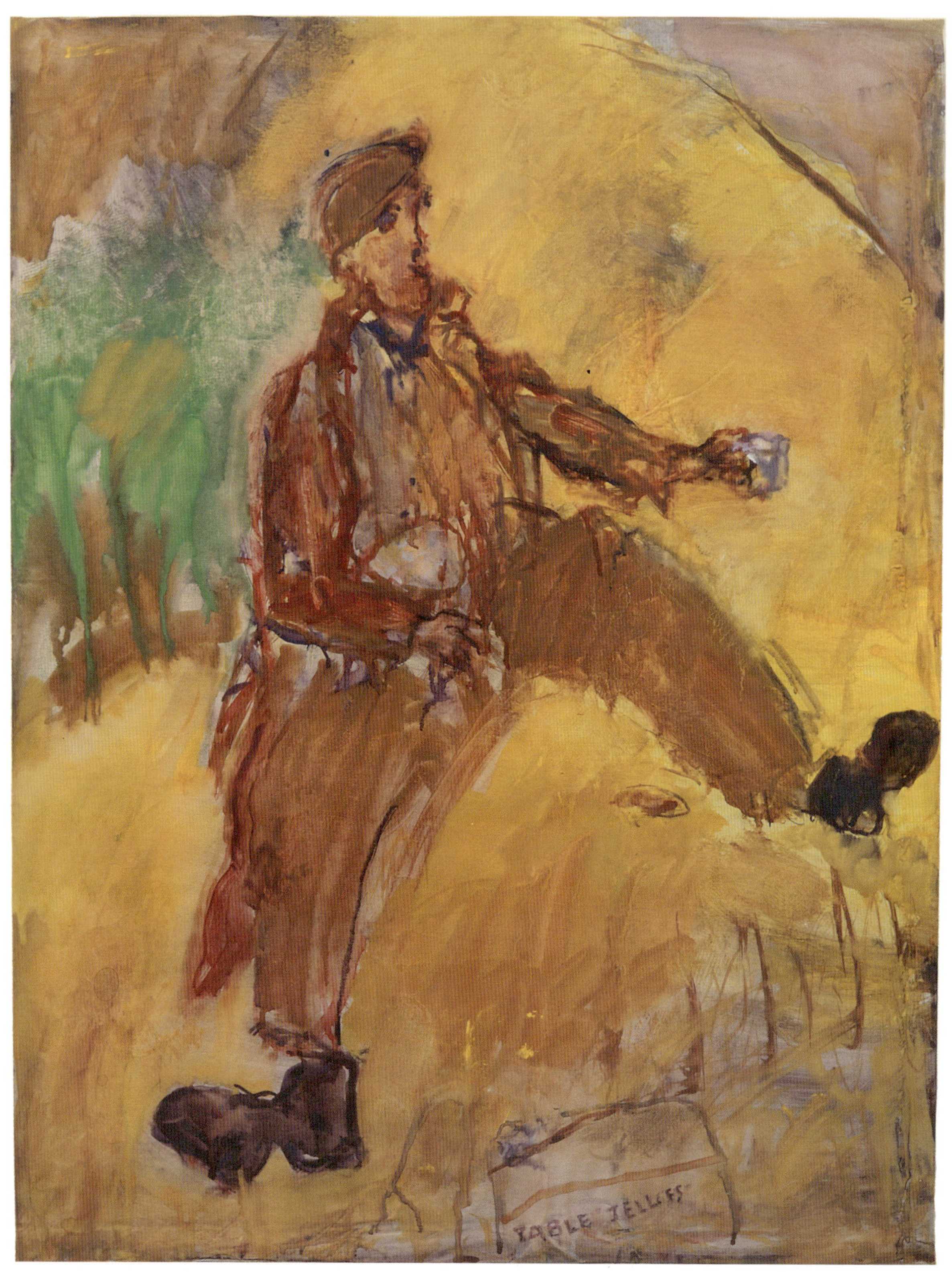

61. Cheers

61 × 47 cm
Bequest Collection

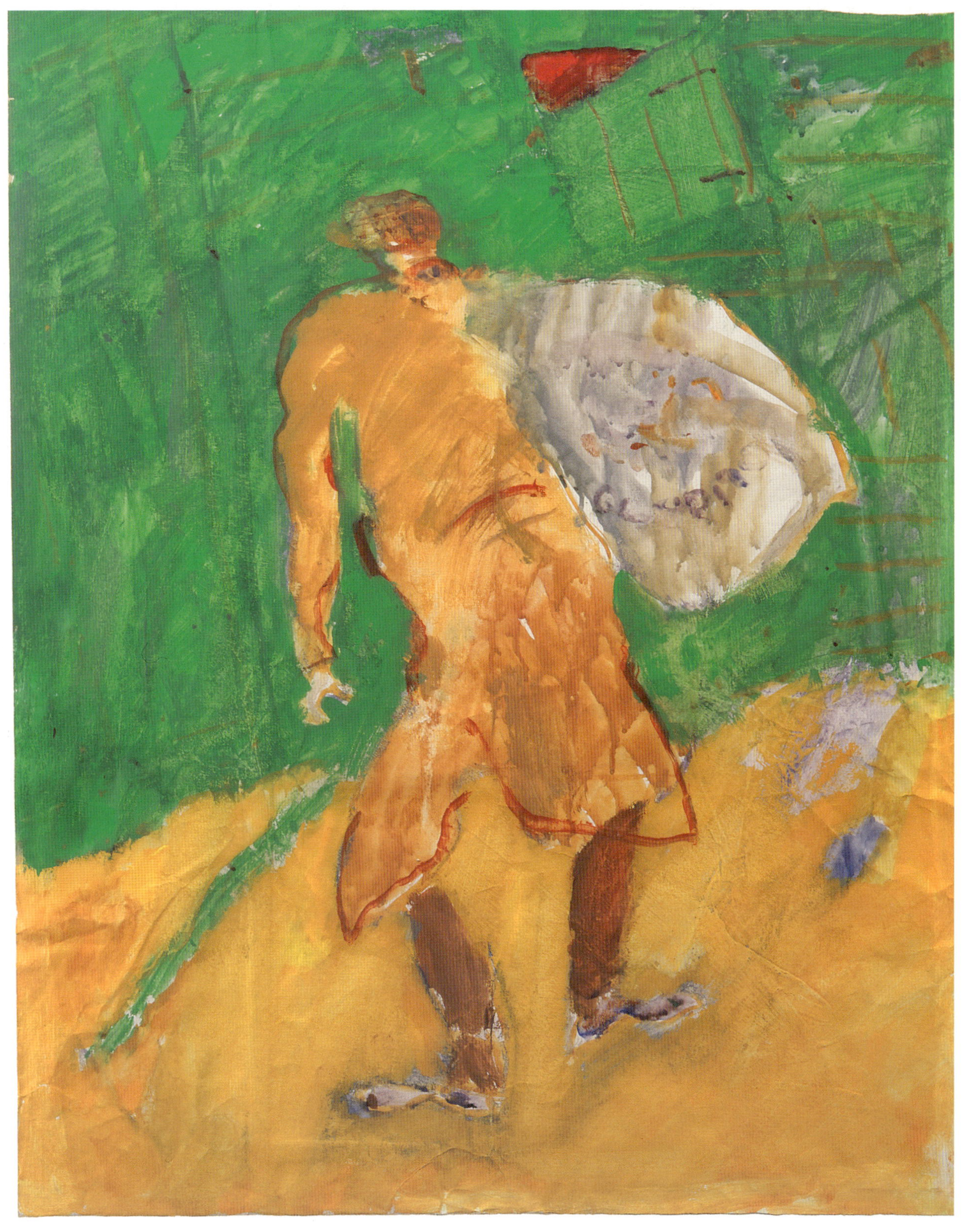

62. Holbetonwards

67 × 55 cm
Bequest Collection

Ben Hartley

Biography

1933 born November. The family lives in Mellor in Derbyshire. Maternal grandparents farm in Mellor. His father a tailor with a business in Manchester
1945 – 50 Manchester Grammar School
1950 – 52 Stockport Art School
1952 – 54 Manchester Regional Art School
1954 – 57 Royal College of Art (Printmaking Department)
1958 – 60 Part-time lecturer, Manchester Regional Art School
1958 first visit to Herefordshire and the Border Country
1960 moves to Plymouth as part-time lecturer at Plymouth College of Art
1963 first of four trips to Ireland
1965 spends four months (September to December) in Norfolk with the Church Art Community in North Repps, near Cromer
1968 converts to Roman Catholicism
1969 final visit to Ireland
1979 end of part-time teaching in Plymouth
1983 moves to live in Presteigne in Wales
1996 dies March. His work is bequeathed to Bernard Samuels

Exhibitions

One-man shows

1977 Plymouth Arts Centre
1979 Plymouth Arts Centre
1979 – 80 Plymouth Arts Centre touring exhibition: Festival Gallery, Bath; Ikon Gallery, Birmingham; The Plough, Torrington; Otterton Mill; John Hansard Gallery, Southampton
1983 Beaux Arts Gallery, Bath
1983 – 84 Plymouth Arts Centre touring exhibition: Newlyn Gallery; Dartington Hall; Beaford Centre; Spacex, Exeter; Lyric Theatre, Hammersmith
1984 Restaurant at the Arnolfini Gallery, Bristol; Andrew Knight Gallery, Cardiff
1985 Beaux Arts Gallery, Bath; Coombe Studios, Dittisham
1987 Beaux Arts Gallery, Bath; Wolf at the Door, Penzance; Otterton Mill
1989 Beaux Arts Gallery, Bath; New Street Gallery, Plymouth
1991 Beaux Arts Gallery, Bath; White Lane Gallery, Plymouth; Chapel Gallery, Saltram House, Plymouth
1992 – 93 Plymouth Arts Centre touring exhibition: Glyn Vivian Gallery, Swansea; Oriel 31, Welshpool; Llantaram Grange
1993 Seymour Gallery, Totnes
1996 Seymour Gallery, Totnes
1997 Memorial exhibition Assembly Rooms, Presteigne, organized by Mid-Border Arts
1998 Otterton Mill; Alpha House Gallery, Sherborne
1999 The King of Hearts, Norwich Festival

Group shows

1957 Royal Academy Summer Exhibition
1984 TSWA National Open Painting Competition: Animals in Art, Cirencester Workshops
1991 Carel Weight's Friends Eightieth Birthday Exhibition, The Arts Club, London

Public Collections

Dartington Hall
Arts Council
Plymouth City Art Gallery
NatWest Art Collection

Publications

'Eight Little Pictures' from *Ben Somewhen* 1983
Ben Somewhen Complete Ink Drawings, limited edition of 150, 2000

Articles and catalogue essays

'Beyond the Rainbow' catalogue essay by John Lane, 1983
Essay for exhibition Alpha House Gallery, Sherborne, by Tony Birks-Hay 1998
'Always a Beginner' by Bernard Samuels *Resurgence*, May/June 1998
'Ben Hartley' by Bernard Samuels *London Magazine* August/September 1998
Catalogue essay by Bernard Samuels, Otterton Mill 1998
Catalogue essay by Bernard Samuels, King of Hearts/Norwich Festival 1999
Article by Bernard Samuels for *The Countryman* December 2000

List of Plates